ADVANCED STATISTICAL METHODS WITH PYTHON

for Quantitative Finance

Hayden Van Der Post

Reactive Publishing

CONTENTS

Reactive Publishing

First Printing, 2025

Library of Congress Cataloging-in-Publication Data [Data Information] ```

This optimized copyright notice provides a comprehensive and protective statement for the book "Mastering Advanced Statistical Methods with Python for Quantitative Finance" published by Reactive Publishing, covering the necessary legal and rights information without specific details about the author.

PREFACE

Welcome to Mastering Advanced Statistical Methods with Python for Quantitative Finance. This book is designed to ignite your passion, stimulate your intellect, and equip you with the strategic and technical prowess necessary to excel in the intertwining realms of quantitative finance and advanced statistical analysis.

A Journey into the Financial Frontier

In today's data-driven world, the ability to distill actionable insights from complex statistical methods and harness the computational power of Python is more than an asset—it's a necessity. Whether you are a seasoned finance professional seeking to deepen your technical skillset, a data scientist aspiring to venture into the financial sector, or an academic aiming to bridge theory and practice, this book is your gateway to mastering the sophisticated tools and methodologies that drive modern finance.

Emotional Commitment to Mastery

Mastering Advanced Statistical Methods with Python for Quantitative Finance is more than a textbook; it's a catalyst for transformation. Imagine the satisfaction of decoding the enigmatic tapestries of financial markets, the thrill of accurately forecasting stock prices, or the immense pride in constructing a robust, risk-optimized portfolio that withstands market tumult. With each page, you are not just learning; you are evolving into a formidable force in quantitative analysis—capable of crafting strategies that are both brilliant and impactful.

Structure of the Book

Ready to Transform?

The journey you are about to embark on with this book is transformative. As you turn each page, engage with every case study, and apply each method, remember—you are not just learning a skill; you are sculpting a new, empowered version of yourself. One that is ready to master the intricate dance of numbers, code, and markets.

Unlock your potential, and let's master advanced statistical methods with Python for quantitative finance together.

Happy reading and learning,

Hayden Van Der Post

CHAPTER 1: INTRODUCTION TO QUANTITATIVE FINANCE AND PYTHON

Picture yourself amidst the heartbeat of a thriving financial district, where soaring skyscrapers reflect not just sunlight but a complex interplay of data, algorithms, and market dynamics. This is the realm of quantitative finance, where rigorous mathematics coalesces with the art of finance, forging strategies that empower investors to predict and optimize returns with uncanny precision.

quantitative finance—often lovingly dubbed 'quant finance'—is a discipline that leverages mathematical models and cutting-edge computational techniques to navigate the intricate landscape of financial markets and securities. This field has transformed into an indispensable component of modern finance, equipping firms to manage risks, evaluate portfolio performance, and refine trading tactics. Stepping into this arena allows analysts to bridge the gap between abstract financial theories and actionable insights, converting raw numbers into compelling narratives that inform investment strategies.

The Birth of Quantitative Finance

The narrative of quantitative finance finds its roots in pioneering research, most notably by Louis Bachelier in the early 20th century. His seminal dissertation introduced revolutionary concepts such as Brownian motion to describe stock price movements, laying the groundwork for future explorations. Fast forward to the transformative 1970s; the arrival of the Black-Scholes model not only revolutionized options pricing but also catalyzed a richer comprehension of derivatives, offering a robust framework that traders still rely on today.

Over the decades, quantitative finance has harnessed advances from diverse fields, notably statistics, computer science, and econometrics. In our data-rich era, analysts have access to extensive datasets—from historical price movements to real-time economic indicators—enabling them to employ sophisticated methodologies to unravel patterns and correlations. With the surge of technology and computational capabilities, quantitative finance has matured significantly, facilitating high-frequency trading, intricate risk management strategies, and innovative hedge-fund tactics. At the heart of this evolution lies programming languages like Python, which serve as powerful tools for implementing complex financial models.

The Components of Quantitative Finance

Quantitative finance is built on crucial components, each one indispensable for crafting resilient financial models. Key elements include:

- **Statistical Analysis**: Fundamental techniques such

as regression analysis, hypothesis testing, and time series forecasting serve as the backbone of predictive modeling. Financial analysts employ these tools to sift through historical data, uncover trends, and establish relationships among various financial variables.

- **Financial Derivatives**: A deep understanding of financial derivatives—options, futures, and swaps—is essential for effective risk management and strategic speculation. The mathematical formulations developed over the decades guide traders in hedging against potential losses and making informed market plays.
- **Portfolio Theory**: At the heart of quantitative finance lies Modern Portfolio Theory (MPT), offering a blueprint for optimizing investment returns while balancing risk and diversification. Concepts like asset allocation, risk-return analysis, and the construction of efficient frontiers are critical focal points for professionals navigating this domain.

These components illustrate that quantitative finance transcends mere computations; it embodies an intricate ecosystem intertwining mathematics, finance, and technology.

Practical Applications of Quantitative Finance

The practical implications of quantitative finance are vividly illustrated in the world of algorithmic trading, where firms increasingly adopt algorithms to execute trades at lightning speed, far beyond human capability. These sophisticated systems analyze real-time market data and news sentiments, enabling them to make rapid decisions based on well-defined rules and statistical models. For example, an algorithm might trigger a buy order for a stock when its moving average surpasses that of a specified threshold, simultaneously adjusting the portfolio's exposure based on continual risk assessments.

Moreover, quantitative finance sparks innovation in investment strategies, particularly in the realm of statistical arbitrage and factor investing. Consider a quantitative fund utilizing machine learning algorithms to pinpoint undervalued securities.

The Role of Technology in Quantitative Finance

In this landscape, Python has emerged as the language of choice for quant professionals, celebrated for its versatility and the extensive libraries it offers for analytical tasks. With powerful tools like NumPy, pandas, and SciPy at their disposal, analysts can manipulate and interpret vast datasets with impressive ease. To illustrate this, let's examine a practical example of how Python can be employed to calculate the moving average of a stock's closing price, a common technique in quantitative trading strategies:

```python
import numpy as np import pandas as pd

\# Sample stock price data
data = {'Date': ['2023-01-01', '2023-01-02', '2023-01-03',
'2023-01-04', '2023-01-05'],
    'Close': [150, 152, 153, 155, 154]}

df = pd.DataFrame(data)
df['Date'] = pd.to_datetime(df['Date'])
df.set_index('Date', inplace=True)

\# Calculate the moving average
df['Moving_Average'] = df['Close'].rolling(window=3).mean()

print(df)
```

Running this code calculates the moving average of closing prices over a three-day rolling window, exemplifying a fundamental technique quant analysts employ to smooth out price fluctuations and derive trends.

Standing at the nexus of finance, statistics, and technology opens a world filled with promise and potential. As the industry continues to evolve, the fusion of big data analytics, machine learning, and artificial intelligence with quantitative finance heralds an era of even greater sophistication in investment strategies. To navigate this unfolding landscape, aspiring financial analysts must not only master theoretical principles but also cultivate practical skills in programming and data analysis.

The financial analysts of tomorrow will thrive in their ability to merge complex quantitative techniques with the latest technological advancements, charting innovative pathways that drive growth and transformation in the markets.

In the forthcoming sections, we will delve deeper into the statistical foundations fundamental to quantitative finance, equipping you with essential tools to master this dynamic and exciting field.

The Vital Role of Statistical Methods in Finance

In the intricate world of modern finance, the significance of statistical methods cannot be overstated. These techniques serve not just as ancillary tools, but as essential pillars that support effective decision-making and strategic development. The financial environment is characterized by uncertainty and complexity, necessitating rigorous statistical analysis to translate chaotic market data into actionable insights. For those aiming to excel in areas such as risk management, portfolio optimization, or quantitative trading, a profound comprehension of statistical principles is vital.

The Analytical Perspective Provided by Statistics

Picture yourself walking into a dynamic brokerage office in New York City, where traders and quantitative analysts cluster around an array of screens illuminated by fluctuating stock prices. In this fast-paced setting, statistical methods become the beacons of clarity, guiding analysts through vast seas of data. From traditional statistical approaches to advanced machine learning techniques, each offers a unique perspective on market dynamics and investor behavior.

At the heart of applying statistics in finance lies the ability to discern patterns, evaluate risks, and forecast future trends. Methods such as regression analysis empower analysts to quantitatively explore relationships between diverse financial variables, while probability distributions provide a framework for understanding asset price behavior. As we explore these techniques further, we reveal their crucial roles in guiding sound investment decisions.

Comprehensive Risk Assessment and Management

In the finance sector, risk is a constant companion, manifesting in various forms including market risk, credit risk, operational risk, and liquidity risk. Effective risk assessment relies heavily on statistical methods that quantify uncertainty and support robust risk mitigation strategies.

Take, for instance, Value at Risk (VaR), one of the most widely utilized risk measures in financial institutions. VaR estimates the potential loss a portfolio could incur over a specified timeframe under normal market conditions. This powerful statistical tool leverages historical price data to determine downside risk. Imagine an analyst, armed with a 95% confidence interval, concluding that a portfolio worth (1 million could realistically face a maximum loss of)100,000 on any given trading day based on historical market fluctuations. The following Python code snippet provides a basic illustration of how an analyst can calculate daily VaR using historical returns:

```python import numpy as np import pandas as pd

\# Sample daily returns data
returns = np.random.normal(0, 0.02, 1000) \# Simulated daily
```

```
returns
portfolio_value = 1000000 \# Portfolio value of \(1 million

\# Calculate the VaR at the 95% confidence level
VaR_95 = np.percentile(returns, 5) * portfolio_value
print(f"Value at Risk (95%): \){-VaR_95:.2f}")
```

While this example introduces the fundamental calculation of VaR, financial institutions often deploy sophisticated techniques such as Monte Carlo simulations to account for an expansive range of potential market scenarios, enhancing their risk management framework.

Strategic Portfolio Optimization

At the heart of portfolio management lies the pursuit of a delicate equilibrium between risk and return. Here, statistical methods emerge as critical allies, enabling investors to construct optimal portfolios that align with their unique investment goals.

The principles of Modern Portfolio Theory (MPT), pioneered by Harry Markowitz, play a significant role in this domain. Understanding covariance and correlation matrices is crucial for analyzing how different assets interact within the portfolio.

For example, envision an analyst tasked with optimizing a two-asset portfolio, comprised of assets A and B, with known expected returns and risks. Through calculations of expected returns and standard deviations for various weight combinations of assets A and B, the analyst is able to plot the efficient frontier—an informative representation demonstrating optimal risk-return profiles:

```python
import numpy as np import matplotlib.pyplot as plt

\# Asset return and standard deviation
```

```
returns = [0.1, 0.2] \# Expected returns
risks = [0.15, 0.25] \# Standard deviation

\# Portfolio weights
weights = np.linspace(0, 1, 100)
portfolio_returns = [r * w + returns[1] * (1 - w) for w in weights]
portfolio_risks = [np.sqrt((r**2 * w**2) + (risks[1]**2 * (1 - w)**2) + (2 *
w * (1 - w) * np.cov(returns)[0][1]))
        for w in weights]

\# Plotting the efficient frontier
plt.plot(portfolio_risks, portfolio_returns, label='Efficient Frontier')
plt.xlabel('Risk (Standard Deviation)')
plt.ylabel('Return')
plt.title('Optimal Risk-Return Portfolio')
plt.legend()
plt.show()
```

This graphical representation aids stakeholders in making informed decisions about their desired risk levels, ultimately guiding asset allocation strategies in a coherent manner.

The Power of Forecasting and Predictive Analytics

Statistical methods extend their reach far beyond merely fitting historical data; their predictive capabilities are essential for successful financial forecasting. Time series analysis, in particular, has become indispensable for understanding trends and cycles in financial data. Techniques like ARIMA (AutoRegressive Integrated Moving Average) modeling allow analysts to dissect temporal data, capturing trends, seasonality, and cycles—components crucial for formulating informed future projections.

Imagine you are analyzing a stock's historical price data to predict its performance over the next quarter. Utilizing an ARIMA model allows you to forecast price movements grounded in past behaviors. The following example demonstrates how accessible and efficient it is to construct and implement such a model using Python's statsmodels library:

```python
import pandas as pd from
statsmodels.tsa.arima.model import ARIMA

\# Sample time series data
data = pd.Series([150, 152, 151, 155, 154, 158, 157, 159, 160])
model = ARIMA(data, order=(2, 1, 2)) \# ARIMA(p, d, q) model

\# Fit the model
model_fit = model.fit()

\# Forecast future values
forecast = model_fit.forecast(steps=3)
print(f"Forecasted values: {forecast}")
```

This ability to anticipate market trajectories becomes an invaluable asset for analysts striving to maintain a competitive edge.

Statistical methods form the cornerstone upon which financial strategies are constructed, guiding analysts through the volatile waters of market dynamics.

Introduction to Python for Financial Analysis

In today's fast-paced world of quantitative finance, the adoption of sophisticated programming tools has transformed the way analysts and researchers approach their work. Among these tools, Python has emerged as a standout player, hailed for its versatility and efficiency. With its extensive collection of libraries, intuitive syntax, and an active community, Python streamlines complex calculations and data processing, making it an essential asset for anyone eager to extract meaningful insights from financial data.

The Allure of Python in Finance

Why is Python becoming the go-to programming language for finance professionals? Picture a bustling financial hub where seasoned analysts exchange insights and strategies. One common thread in their discussions is the allure of Python—not just for its powerful capabilities, but for its adaptability to various tasks, including data manipulation, statistical analysis, machine learning, and data visualization. Far more than a mere coding language, Python serves as a multifaceted toolkit, empowering analysts to tackle a wide range of projects with ease.

Imagine a financial analyst in London, sifting through vast datasets spanning multiple markets while striving to maximize efficiency. Instead of wrestling with complicated syntax, the analyst utilizes Python's approachable nature to extract pertinent information, perform analyses, and generate visualizations—all within a unified platform. This ease of use not only fosters efficiency but also accelerates informed decision-making, resulting in a significant advantage in a competitive environment.

Key Features of Python for Financial Analysis

1. Extensive Libraries for Data Handling

One of Python's most compelling strengths is its rich library ecosystem. Libraries like Pandas are indispensable for data manipulation and analysis. For instance, analysts can easily integrate and manage time series data, making transactions with financial datasets a breeze. Let's consider an example where stock price data is imported from a CSV file:

```python
import pandas as pd

\# Load stock data
stock_data = pd.read_csv('stock_prices.csv', parse_dates=['Date'], index_col='Date')

\# Display the first few rows of the dataset
print(stock_data.head())
```

```

This simple command allows analysts to swiftly access and examine their data, creating a solid foundation for deeper analyses without the burden of excessive boilerplate code.

**2. Statistical and Machine Learning Libraries**

In finance, where data-driven decisions hinge on rigorous statistical calculations, Python's libraries like NumPy and SciPy play a crucial role. They equip analysts with the tools necessary to execute a myriad of statistical analyses with confidence. For instance, using NumPy, analysts can calculate moving averages, a staple technique for smoothing out price volatility:

```python # Calculate a simple moving average
stock_data['SMA_30'] =
stock_data['Close'].rolling(window=30).mean()
print(stock_data[['Close', 'SMA_30']].tail())
```

When it comes to predictive analytics, Scikit-learn is vital for constructing machine learning models. Picture an analyst who is modeling stock price movements based on historical data—Scikit-learn simplifies the implementation of regression models and classification algorithms:

```python from sklearn.model_selection import
train_test_split from sklearn.linear_model import
LinearRegression

\# Prepare data for regression
X = stock_data[['Open', 'High', 'Low', 'Volume']]
y = stock_data['Close']

\# Split the data
X_train, X_test, y_train, y_test = train_test_split(X, y, test_size=0.2,
random_state=42)

```
\# Train a linear regression model
model = LinearRegression()
model.fit(X_train, y_train)

\# Predictions
predictions = model.predict(X_test)
```

With such concise syntax, analysts can focus on the essence of financial modeling rather than getting overwhelmed by complex language constructs.

3. Powerful Data Visualization Tools

In an industry where decisions must be data-driven and transparent, effective data visualization is critical. Python libraries like Matplotlib and Seaborn empower analysts to create compelling visualizations that clearly communicate their findings. For example, consider a scenario where an analyst wishes to visualize stock price trends alongside the Simple Moving Average (SMA):

```python
import matplotlib.pyplot as plt

plt.figure(figsize=(14, 7))
plt.plot(stock_data['Close'], label='Stock Price', color='blue')
plt.plot(stock_data['SMA_30'], label='30-Day SMA', color='orange')
plt.title('Stock Price and 30-Day Moving Average')
plt.xlabel('Date')
plt.ylabel('Price')
plt.legend()
plt.grid()
plt.show()
```

These visual representations are instrumental in helping stakeholders understand market dynamics, facilitating informed discussions about potential strategic adjustments in investment portfolios.

Applications of Python in Financial Analysis

The potential applications of Python in finance are extensive and varied. From risk assessment and portfolio management to algorithmic trading and predictive analytics, Python forms the backbone of modern financial analysis practices.

In risk management, Python's capabilities can be harnessed to calculate vital metrics like Value at Risk (VaR), which contribute to comprehensive analysis frameworks that underlie crucial financial decisions. In the domain of trading strategies, analysts can utilize Python scripts for backtesting, significantly enhancing efficiency by minimizing the time required to evaluate strategies.

A practical illustration of this is in feedback trading strategies. Here, algorithms can analyze massive datasets to uncover patterns and execute trades based on established criteria:

```python
# Pseudo code for a simple trading strategy if market_signal == 'buy': execute_buy_trade() # Trigger a buying action elif market_signal == 'sell': execute_sell_trade() # Trigger a selling action
```

This predictive capability, bolstered by Python's extensive libraries, enables financial analysts to navigate the trading landscape with agility and precision.

As we navigate the intricate web of quantitative finance, it's evident that Python is more than just a programming tool; it's a catalyst for innovation and efficiency.

With these capabilities at hand, analysts and finance professionals are encouraged to venture beyond basic analytical tasks, exploring integrations and methodologies that define a data-driven approach to finance. The journey into Python not only promises to deepen analytical expertise but also to enrich decision-making prowess as you tackle the multifaceted challenges of the financial realm.

Setting Up Your Python Environment for Financial Analysis

Embarking on the journey of financial analysis with Python can be both exciting and rewarding. However, to fully leverage Python's capabilities, establishing a well-organized development environment is essential. A properly configured setup not only boosts your productivity but also empowers you to conduct advanced analysis, visualize complex data, and uncover vital insights. In this guide, we will walk you through the process of setting up a Python environment specifically designed for quantitative finance.

Selecting the Right Python Distribution

The first step in this journey is choosing an appropriate Python distribution. For finance professionals, **Anaconda** stands out as a popular choice. This robust distribution comes pre-packaged with numerous libraries that are essential for data analysis, including **Pandas**, **NumPy**, **Scikit-learn**, and **Matplotlib**. Beyond simply providing these tools, Anaconda simplifies package management and enhances your ability to create and manage multiple environments.

Installation Steps: 1. **Download Anaconda**: Head over to the Anaconda website and choose the version that matches your operating system—be it Windows, macOS, or Linux. 2. **Install Anaconda**: Follow the installation instructions, ensuring you select the option to add Anaconda to your system's PATH. This enables access to Anaconda via the command line. 3. **Verify the Installation**: Open your terminal or Anaconda Prompt and run the command: ` ` `bash conda --version

` ` ` If installed correctly, you should see the version number of Conda displayed, confirming a successful setup.

Creating an Isolated Environment

One of the remarkable features of Anaconda is its ability to create isolated environments. This is particularly beneficial in financial analysis, allowing you to keep different projects and their dependencies organized, preventing any conflicts that may arise from varying requirements.

Creating a New Environment: 1. **Open Anaconda Prompt**: Launch the Anaconda Prompt on your machine. 2. **Generate the Environment**: Input the following command to create an environment named quant_finance: ```bash conda create --name quant_finance python=3.9

``` Here, we specify Python 3.9, a stable and well-supported version as of this writing.

1. **Activate the Environment**: Once the environment is successfully created, activate it by running: ```bash conda activate quant_finance

```

Installing Essential Libraries

With your environment activated, it's time to equip it with the key libraries necessary for in-depth financial analysis.

Installing Libraries: - **Pandas and NumPy**: These libraries are the backbone of data manipulation and numerical computations. - **Matplotlib and Seaborn**: These tools are vital for creating engaging visualizations and making your data come to life. - **Scikit-learn**: This library is indispensable for building and deploying machine learning models.

To install these libraries, execute the following command within your activated environment: ```bash conda install pandas numpy matplotlib seaborn scikit-learn

``` This command fetches and installs the libraries directly from Anaconda's repositories.

*Embracing Jupyter Notebook*

For many financial analysts, **Jupyter Notebook** is the go-to platform. It offers an interactive interface that allows you to write and run Python code seamlessly while documenting
```

your process. Jupyter's capability to visualize outputs and handle code snippets in real-time makes it an invaluable tool in your analytical toolkit.

Installing Jupyter Notebook: To set up Jupyter, simply run: ```bash conda install jupyter

```

**Launching Jupyter Notebook**: Initialize Jupyter with the command: ```bash jupyter notebook

``` This command opens a new browser tab featuring a dashboard where you can create and manage notebooks.

1. **Creating a New Notebook**: Click on "New" and select Python [conda env:quant_finance] to launch a new notebook within your dedicated environment.
2. **Executing Code Cells**: Type your Python code into the cells, and run it by pressing Shift + Enter. You will see outputs—including charts and data tables—immediately below your code.

*Customizing Your Workspace*

To enhance your productivity, consider customizing your Jupyter Notebook environment. Extensions, such as Jupyter Notebook extensions, can greatly improve your user experience, offering features that help you work more efficiently, like variable inspectors and code folding.

**Installing Jupyter Extensions**: 1. **Install the Jupyter Nbextensions Configurator**: ```bash conda install -c conda-forge jupyter_contrib_nbextensions

``` 2. **Enable Extensions**: After installation, access the configurator from the Jupyter dashboard, where you can tailor the interface to fit your personal workflow.

Setting up your Python environment is a vital first step in unlocking the vast potential offered by quantitative finance. A well-structured environment not only facilitates streamlined
```

analyses but also lays the groundwork for rigorous statistical assessments and compelling visualizations.

With your environment primed for operation, you're now positioned to explore everything from basic statistical analyses to complex machine learning models, enhancing your financial decision-making strategies. As you continue on this analytical journey, remember that the ability to adapt and refine your setup will significantly impact your efficiency and effectiveness in the world of quantitative finance.

Essential Libraries for Financial Data Analysis in Python

At the core of financial data analysis in Python is **Pandas**, an incredibly versatile library specifically designed for data manipulation and analysis. Its powerful data structures, such as Series and DataFrame, allow users to handle structured data in an intuitive manner, making it easier to perform complex operations without getting bogged down in code.

Installation:

To incorporate Pandas into your environment, simply execute:

```bash
conda install pandas
```

Key Features:

- **DataFrames**: Analogous to spreadsheets, DataFrames enable the storage and manipulation of tabular data with labeled axes, fostering an organized way to work with datasets.
- **Data Cleaning**: Pandas excels at cleaning data, offering straightforward methods for handling missing values, transforming data, and filtering datasets.
- **Time Series Capabilities**: Given that financial data is often time-sensitive, Pandas includes robust tools for

time series analysis, allowing seamless manipulation of datetime objects, resampling, and more.

Example: Loading and Analyzing Financial Data

Imagine you have a CSV file containing historical stock prices. Here's how to load and analyze daily returns using Pandas:

```python
import pandas as pd

# Load the historical stock prices dataset
data = pd.read_csv('historical_stock_prices.csv', parse_dates=['Date'], index_col='Date')

# Calculate the daily returns
data['Daily Return'] = data['Close'].pct_change()

# Display summary statistics to glean insights
print(data.describe())
```

In this example, you'll see how Pandas can effortlessly manage stock price data, calculate returns, and generate summary statistics, all with minimal code.

*2. **NumPy: Fueling Numerical Operations and Linear Algebra***

NumPy is a fundamental library for performing numerical computations, geared towards multi-dimensional array and matrix manipulation. Its efficiency is vital for scientific computing in Python, especially in finance.

Installation:

You can install NumPy as follows:

```bash
conda install numpy
```

Key Features:

- **Array Manipulations**: NumPy arrays allow for much faster computations than traditional Python lists, particularly with large datasets.
- **Mathematical Functions**: This library provides a

comprehensive suite of mathematical functions that operate on arrays elements, paving the way for sophisticated analysis.

- **Linear Algebra Functionality**: Financial analysts often rely on concepts such as covariance and correlation matrices, where NumPy shines, providing essential tools for risk assessment.

Example: Calculating a Covariance Matrix

Here's a simple way to calculate the covariance matrix for a set of stock returns using NumPy:

```python
import numpy as np

\# Example daily returns for a few stocks
returns = np.array([[0.001, 0.002, -0.003],
          [0.004, -0.002, 0.001],
          [0.002, 0.003, 0.002]])

\# Compute the covariance matrix
covariance_matrix = np.cov(returns.T)
print(covariance_matrix)
```

This example demonstrates NumPy's strengths in executing advanced calculations essential for understanding risk and returns.

3. Matplotlib and Seaborn: Crafting Visual Narratives

The ability to visualize data is crucial in finance, enabling analysts to uncover trends and patterns that numerical analyses alone may overlook. **Matplotlib** and **Seaborn** are two powerful libraries that excel in this domain.

Installation:

To install both libraries at once, run:

```bash
conda install matplotlib seaborn
```

Key Features:

- **Matplotlib**: Renowned for its versatility, Matplotlib can create a wide range of visual outputs, from line graphs to bar charts and histograms, making it a go-to for detailed plotting.
- **Seaborn**: Built on top of Matplotlib, Seaborn simplifies the creation of aesthetically pleasing statistical graphics and works seamlessly with Pandas DataFrames, ideal for visualizing complex datasets.

Example: Visualizing Stock Prices

Here's how you can visualize historical stock price movements using these libraries:

```python
import matplotlib.pyplot as plt
import seaborn as sns

# Set the aesthetic style for the plots
sns.set(style='whitegrid')

# Create the plot for stock prices
plt.figure(figsize=(12, 6))
plt.plot(data.index, data['Close'], label='Close Price', color='b')
plt.title('Historical Stock Prices')
plt.xlabel('Date')
plt.ylabel('Price')
plt.legend()
plt.show()
```

This code generates a visually appealing line graph, showcasing how Seaborn and Matplotlib collaborate to produce insightful and informative data visualizations.

*4. **SciPy: Unlocking Advanced Analytical Techniques***

While not limited to finance, **SciPy** enhances the capabilities of NumPy by providing a variety of advanced mathematical functions, including optimization, integration, and interpolation techniques.

Installation:

To add SciPy to your toolkit, simply run:
```bash
conda install scipy
```

Example: Portfolio Optimization

Let's say you're tasked with finding the optimal asset weights for a portfolio aimed at minimizing risk. SciPy's optimization functionalities make this process straightforward:

```python
from scipy.optimize import minimize

\# Define the portfolio volatility function
def portfolio_volatility(weights):
    return np.sqrt(np.dot(weights, np.dot(covariance_matrix, weights)))

\# Set constraints and bounds for the optimization problem
constraints = ({'type': 'eq', 'fun': lambda x: np.sum(x) - 1}) \# Weights must sum to 1
bounds = tuple((0, 1) for asset in range(num_assets)) \# No short selling

\# Initial guess for weights
initial_weights = num_assets * [1. / num_assets]

\# Perform optimization
optimized = minimize(portfolio_volatility, initial_weights, method='SLSQP', bounds=bounds, constraints=constraints)
print(optimized.x)
```

This example highlights how easily SciPy facilitates sophisticated analyses such as portfolio optimization, empowering analysts to make informed decisions.

Navigating the complex landscape of quantitative finance demands proficiency in Python's essential libraries. Each of these tools—Pandas for data manipulation, NumPy for numerical analysis, Matplotlib and Seaborn for visualization, and SciPy for advanced analytics—offers unique functionalities that, when integrated, provide a formidable toolkit for financial analysts. Mastering these libraries not only optimizes your workflow but also deepens the quality of your insights, enabling you to analyze complex financial datasets with confidence.

As you continue your financial journey, leveraging these libraries will empower you to address a spectrum of challenges, from fundamental data tasks to intricate analytical projects.

Python Syntax Essentials for Financial Analysts

Python's syntax is designed to be straightforward, allowing for a seamless learning experience. Code typically executes linearly, but more complicated operations can be encapsulated in functions, enhancing modularity and promoting the reuse of code. Here are a few foundational concepts:

- **Variables**: These are used to store data values. In Python, there's no need to explicitly declare a variable's type; the interpreter automatically infers it based on the assigned value.

```python # Example of variable assignment stock_price = 150.25
```

- **Data Types**: Python supports a variety of data types, ensuring flexibility in your analyses:
- **Integers (int)**: Whole numbers (e.g., 42).
- **Floats (float)**: Numbers containing decimals (e.g., 3.14).
- **Strings (str)**: Sequences of characters (e.g., "Hello, World!").
- **Booleans (bool)**: Represents truth values (True or False).

```python # Sample data types in use interest_rate = 0.05 # float company_name = "Tech Innovations" # string is_profitable = True # boolean
```

2. Control Flow: Decision Making and Looping

- **Conditional Statements**: Utilize if, elif, and else to execute blocks of code depending on certain criteria.

```python # Assessing an investment based on expected return expected_return = 0.07 if expected_return > 0.05: print("This investment is considered profitable.") elif expected_return == 0.05: print("This investment breaks even.") else: print("This investment is not profitable.")
```

- **Loops**: Use for and while loops to iterate through collections or perform repetitive tasks efficiently.

```python # Calculating daily returns for a series of stock prices daily_prices = [150.25, 152.00, 151.50, 153.75] daily_returns = []

for i in range(1, len(daily_prices)):
  daily_return = (daily_prices[i] - daily_prices[i-1]) / daily_prices[i-1]
  daily_returns.append(daily_return)

print(daily_returns)
```

3. Functions: Enhancing Code Organization

Functions in Python facilitate the encapsulation of code into reusable segments, which greatly enhances the organization and maintainability of your analyses. Here's how you can define and utilize a function:

```python def calculate_returns(prices): returns = [] for i in range(1, len(prices)): return_value = (prices[i] - prices[i-1]) / prices[i-1] returns.append(return_value) return returns
```

```
\# Invoke function to compute daily returns for stock prices
daily_stock_prices = [150.25, 152.00, 151.50, 153.75]
returns = calculate_returns(daily_stock_prices)
print(returns)
```

4. Essential Data Structures: Lists, Tuples, and Dictionaries

Python offers a variety of data structures, each uniquely suited to managing financial data effectively.

- **Lists**: Ordered and mutable collections that can accommodate varied data types.

```python
# Managing a list of asset prices asset_prices = [150.25, 152.00, 151.50] asset_prices.append(153.75) # Adding a new price to the list print(asset_prices)
```

- **Tuples**: Immutable sequences ideal for collections of items that should not be changed post-creation.

```python
# Tuple to represent stock symbols stock_symbols = ("AAPL", "GOOGL", "MSFT") print(stock_symbols[1]) # Accessing the second element
```

- **Dictionaries**: Key-value pairs that provide efficient data indexing, particularly useful for handling detailed financial records.

```python
# Dictionary containing stock price information stock_data = { "AAPL": 150.25, "GOOGL": 2800.50, "MSFT": 299.80 } print("Apple Stock Price: ", stock_data["AAPL"]) # Accessing value via key
```

5. String Formatting: Communicating Insights Effectively

As analysts, your ability to present findings in a clear and engaging manner is crucial. Python offers multiple methods for string formatting, enhancing the readability of your reports.

- **F-Strings (Python 3.6+)**: This modern method allows the inclusion of variables or expressions directly within strings.

```python stock_name = "AAPL" stock_price = 150.25 print(f"The current price of {stock_name} is ({stock_price:.2f}.")
```

6. Commenting Code: Promoting Clarity

Integrating meaningful comments into your code is vital for ensuring clarity, especially when revisiting your work after some time or when collaborating with others.

```python # Function to calculate daily returns based on stock prices def calculate_returns(prices): returns = [] for i in range(1, len(prices)): return_value = (prices[i] - prices[i-1]) / prices[i-1] returns.append(return_value) return returns
```

As you navigate the intricate world of financial data, remember: a solid grounding in Python syntax not only enhances your coding proficiency but also equips you to craft compelling narratives that drive meaningful financial insights. Let's embark on this exciting journey into the realm of financial analysis with Python!

Data Structures and Types in Python

Python's rich assortment of data types is crucial for effective data manipulation:

- **Integers (int)**: These represent whole numbers without decimal accuracy, playing a vital role in scenarios like counting occurrences, evaluating asset quantities, or tallying transactions.

```python
total_shares = 1000 # Number of shares owned
```

- **Floats (float)**: Given the nature of financial calculations—stock prices, returns, and interest rates—floats are indispensable for incorporating decimal precision into analytical models.

```python
stock_price = 150.75 # Current price of the stock
```

- **Strings (str)**: As sequences of characters, strings can represent identifiers such as company names, stock tickers, or other pertinent textual data within financial datasets.

```python
company_name = "Tech Innovations Inc."
```

- **Booleans (bool)**: These data types represent binary states, such as determining whether a stock is considered underpriced or overpriced, which can greatly enhance decision-making processes in algorithmic trading strategies.

```python
is_profitable = True # Indicates a profitable investment
```

2. Complex Data Structures

While basic types are vital, complex data structures allow for more sophisticated management of financial data:

- **Lists**: Python lists are ordered and mutable, capable of containing varied data types. This flexibility makes them ideal for managing collections of financial figures, such as daily closing prices or transaction amounts.

```python prices = [150.25, 152.00, 151.50] # Daily closing prices
```

Lists enable easy addition of new elements, iterative analysis of trends, and targeted subsetting.

```python prices.append(153.75) # Adding another day's price to the list
```

- **Tuples**: In contrast to lists, tuples are immutable, making them suitable for representing collections that should not change, such as stock symbols throughout the life of an analysis.

```python stock_symbols = ("AAPL", "GOOGL", "MSFT") # Immutable set of stock symbols
```

Accessing tuple elements is straightforward and efficient.

```python print(stock_symbols[0]) # Output: AAPL
```

- **Dictionaries**: This data structure utilizes key-value pairs, excelling in managing structured data effectively. In financial contexts, dictionaries can encapsulate a multitude of metrics for each asset.

```python stock_data = { "AAPL": {"price": 150.25, "volume": 100000}, "GOOGL": {"price": 2800.50, "volume": 50000}, "MSFT": {"price": 299.80, "volume": 200000} }
```

Accessing stock-specific information is both efficient and intuitive.

```python print("AAPL Price: ", stock_data["AAPL"]["price"]) # Pulling a value using a key
```

```

### *3. Advanced Data Types and Their Applications*

Python additionally offers a range of advanced data types that further enhance financial analyses:

- **Sets**: Sets are unordered collections that inherently filter duplicates, ideal for situations requiring distinctive transactions or stock identifications.

```python unique_stocks = set(["AAPL", "GOOGL", "MSFT", "AAPL"]) # Result: Only distinct stocks
```

Sets support mathematical operations like unions and intersections, useful for assessing risk across portfolios.

```python other_stocks = set(["AMZN", "MSFT"]) common_stocks = unique_stocks.intersection(other_stocks) # Identifying stocks present in both sets
```

- **DataFrames with Pandas**: One of Python's most potent tools for financial data analysis is the Pandas library, introduced with the DataFrame structure. This two-dimensional, size-mutable format is invaluable for handling tabular data, such as historical price records.

```python import pandas as pd

 data = {
  "Date": ["2023-01-01", "2023-01-02", "2023-01-03"],
  "AAPL": [150.25, 152.00, 151.50],
  "GOOGL": [2800.50, 2795.00, 2810.00]
}

 df = pd.DataFrame(data)
print(df)

```

The versatility of Pandas allows for seamless filtering, sorting, and aggregating of financial data, making it a staple in any analyst's toolkit.

4. String Operations for Financial Insights

Strings can be manipulated in various ways to extract and convey insights from textual financial data. Python provides a diverse selection of string methods suitable for reporting metrics and generating valuable insights.

- **String Formatting**: Python's f-strings (available in version 3.6 and later) allow for dynamic insertion of variables, making outputs more readable and informative.

```python symbol = "AAPL" price = 150.25 print(f"The current price of {symbol} is ){price:.2f}.")
```

5. Tools for Data Analysis and Visualization

Data structures in Python not only serve to store information but also enhance visualization capabilities. The following library complements your analytical endeavors, facilitating the interpretation of financial data.

- **Matplotlib**: Frequently used for visualizing financial trends, Matplotlib empowers analysts to create informative plots.

```python import matplotlib.pyplot as plt

plt.plot(df["Date"], df["AAPL"], label="AAPL Prices")
plt.title("AAPL Stock Prices Over Time")
plt.xlabel("Date")
plt.ylabel("Price")
plt.legend()
plt.show()

```
```

In conclusion, an understanding of data structures and types in Python is foundational for effective financial analysis. These elements streamline data management and fundamentally enhance your analytical prowess. As you advance in quantitative finance, mastery of these concepts will empower you to make informed financial decisions, automate analyses, and communicate insights clearly and engagingly.

Importing Financial Data

Before we plunge into the intricacies of data importing, it's essential to familiarize ourselves with the various types of financial data available and the sources from which they can be obtained. Financial data typically falls into several distinct categories:

- **Market Data**: This includes prices, trading volumes, and other metrics relevant to securities.
- **Fundamental Data**: These are key performance indicators such as earnings, revenue, and asset figures that reflect a company's economic health.
- **Macro Data**: This encompasses broader economic indicators like GDP, inflation rates, and employment statistics.

You can source financial data from a variety of platforms, including:

- **APIs**: Numerous financial service providers offer application programming interfaces (APIs) that allow for real-time and historical data access.
- **CSV Files**: Many datasets can be downloaded in CSV (Comma-Separated Values) format, which can be easily manipulated within Python.
- **Databases**: For larger datasets, it may be necessary to utilize databases such as SQL or MongoDB for

efficient storage and retrieval.

Importing Data Using Pandas

Pandas is widely regarded as the definitive library for data manipulation in Python, particularly well-suited for financial data analysis. Let's explore how to seamlessly import data from various sources.

A. Importing Data from CSV Files

CSV files remain one of the most prevalent formats for financial data. They can be generated easily through spreadsheet software or downloaded from numerous online platforms. Importing CSV data into your Python environment is a straightforward process:

```python
import pandas as pd

\# Importing a CSV file containing historical stock prices
file_path = 'path/to/historical_stock_data.csv'
stock_data = pd.read_csv(file_path)

print(stock_data.head()) \# Display the first few rows of the dataset
```

This brief command loads your CSV data directly into a Pandas DataFrame—a powerful data structure essential for analysis. The head() function allows you to preview the first five rows of the dataset, giving you a glimpse into the imported information.

B. Fetching Data from APIs

For real-time data collection, many financial services provide accessible APIs. One notable library for retrieving historical market data is yfinance, which interfaces seamlessly with Yahoo Finance. Here's how to fetch data using it:

```python
import yfinance as yf

\# Fetching historical data for a specific stock
ticker = "AAPL"
```

```
stock_data = yf.download(ticker, start="2022-01-01", end="2023-01-01")

print(stock_data.head()) \# Display the first few entries
```

In this example, the download() function retrieves Apple Inc.'s stock price data for the specified date range, illustrating Python's capability to access timely financial information effortlessly.

C. Using SQL Databases

As financial datasets expand, utilizing databases often becomes indispensable for effective data management. Python's sqlite3 module enables you to connect to SQLite databases and execute SQL queries directly from your programs:

```python
import sqlite3

\# Establishing a connection to the SQLite database
connection = sqlite3.connect('financial_data.db')
query = "SELECT * FROM stock_prices WHERE ticker = 'AAPL'"

\# Importing SQL data directly into a DataFrame
stock_data = pd.read_sql_query(query, connection)

print(stock_data.head()) \# Show the fetched data
```

Employing this method allows you to tailor your queries to specific datasets, ensuring you obtain precisely the information you need for your financial analyses.

D. Web Scraping for Financial Data

When APIs or downloadable files are unavailable, web scraping can be a powerful alternative to gather data directly from websites. The BeautifulSoup library is an excellent tool for this purpose. Here's a basic example of how to scrape stock price data:

```python
import requests from bs4 import BeautifulSoup

\# URL of the webpage with stock price data
url = 'https://example.com/stock/AAPL'
response = requests.get(url)
soup = BeautifulSoup(response.text, 'html.parser')

\# Extracting specific data
stock_price = soup.find('div', class_='price').text
print(f'Current AAPL Price: {stock_price}')
```

Though effective, remember to use web scraping responsibly and in compliance with the website's terms of service, as it empowers you to acquire data that may not otherwise be readily accessible.

Data Preprocessing After Importing

Once you have successfully imported your data, it's imperative to preprocess it before delving into analysis. Financial datasets can often come with missing values, inconsistencies, or unnecessary columns. Here are some basic preprocessing steps to clean your data:

```python
# Dropping rows with missing values stock_data.dropna(inplace=True)

\# Converting date strings to Python datetime objects
stock_data['Date'] = pd.to_datetime(stock_data['Date'])

\# Checking the data types
print(stock_data.dtypes)
```

These operations are crucial for refining your dataset, ensuring that your analyses produce reliable and actionable insights.

Importing financial data serves as a pivotal gateway to

uncovering valuable insights and formulating informed strategies within quantitative finance. Mastering diverse import techniques—whether it's through CSV files, APIs, databases, or web scraping—empowers you to gather and prepare relevant data for analysis effectively.

As we progress through this book, you will continuously apply these data management techniques alongside advanced statistical methods and analytical models. This foundational skill will not only enhance your analytical capabilities but also position you at the cutting edge of financial data analysis using Python. Remember, the quality of your analysis is intrinsically linked to the integrity and relevance of the data you collect.

Data Cleaning and Preprocessing: The Cornerstones of Financial Analysis

Imagine you are a stock analyst charged with evaluating a company's stock performance. You begin with a dataset promising valuable insights: stock prices spanning the last five years. However, as you dive deeper, you discover a multitude of missing values, outliers, and inaccurate entries. Such flawed data could lead to misguided predictions, a situation as undesirable as executing a poorly timed trade. Therefore, adopting a robust data cleaning strategy is imperative.

2. Common Data Cleaning Tasks

As you embark on the data cleaning process, several essential tasks typically arise. These can be grouped into key categories:

- **Managing Missing Values**: Missing data can distort analyses significantly. Techniques for addressing these gaps include deletion, imputation, or interpolation.
- **Eliminating Duplicates**: Duplicate entries can artificially inflate the dataset, leading to misleading interpretations regarding stock prices or trading

volumes.

- **Correcting Data Types**: Financial data often requires strict adherence to specific data types. For instance, ensuring date fields are treated as datetime objects and numerical values are properly formatted is critical.
- **Addressing Outliers**: Outliers can disproportionately sway statistical measures. Identifying and managing these anomalies ensures the analytical process remains reliable.
- **Normalization and Standardization**: When dealing with diverse data types, standardization is essential to ensure that all entries conform to a uniform scale, allowing for more precise analysis.

3. A Step-by-Step Guide to Data Cleaning Using Pandas

For data manipulation in Python, Pandas is an invaluable ally. It provides a comprehensive suite of tools to facilitate the tasks outlined above. Here's a detailed walkthrough of how to clean a sample financial dataset:

A. Importing Libraries and Data

Begin by importing the necessary libraries and loading your dataset into a Pandas DataFrame:

```python
import pandas as pd

\# Load the dataset
file_path = 'path/to/financial_data.csv'
data = pd.read_csv(file_path)

print(data.head()) \# Preview the data
```

B. Handling Missing Values

Start by assessing the extent of missing values in your dataset:

```python
# Check for missing values
print(data.isnull().sum())
```

If you discover significant gaps in crucial columns, such as dates or prices, consider dropping those rows or filling in the gaps:

```python
# Dropping rows with missing values
data.dropna(inplace=True)

\# Alternatively, filling missing values
data['Price'].fillna(method='ffill', inplace=True) \# Forward-fill method
```

Forward-filling replaces missing entries with the last valid observation, which is particularly useful in time series data.

C. Removing Duplicates

Next, check for and eliminate duplicate records to ensure your analysis is based on unique observations:

```python
# Remove duplicate entries
data.drop_duplicates(inplace=True)
```

This command solidifies the foundation of your analysis by relying on distinct records.

D. Correcting Data Types

Next, confirm that all data types are correct. For instance, if the date column is misclassified, convert it as follows:

```python
# Convert the 'Date' column to datetime
data['Date'] = pd.to_datetime(data['Date'])

\# Verify the changes
print(data.dtypes)
```

E. Identifying and Handling Outliers

Outliers can significantly distort your analysis, so it's important to examine and address them. While data visualization tools like box plots offer insight, you can also apply statistical methods, such as the z-score approach:

```python
# Identify outliers based on z-score (threshold of 3) data['z_score'] = (data['Price'] - data['Price'].mean()) / data['Price'].std() outliers = data[abs(data['z_score']) > 3]

\# Remove outliers
data = data[abs(data['z_score']) <= 3]
```

This code efficiently filters out extreme values, thereby enhancing the dataset's accuracy.

F. Normalization and Standardization

In many analyses, especially those involving multiple variables, normalizing or standardizing your data is crucial. Here's an example of standardization:

```python
# Standardize the 'Price' feature data['Price'] = (data['Price'] - data['Price'].mean()) / data['Price'].std()
```

Such normalization ensures that all features contribute equally during the analysis.

4. Final Steps of Data Preparation

Having completed the primary cleaning tasks, consider additional preprocessing techniques:

- **Creating Dummy Variables**: If your dataset contains categorical variables, transforming these into dummy/indicator variables is vital for certain analytical models.

```python
data = pd.get_dummies(data,
```

columns=['Category'], drop_first=True)
```

- **Feature Scaling**: Adjusting feature values into a specified range (e.g., 0 to 1) is essential for models sensitive to input data scaling.

A final check of your dataset might appear like this:

```python
# Final inspection before analysis
print(data.info()) print(data.describe())
```

Data cleaning and preprocessing transcend mere procedural steps; they are foundational practices that refine the clarity of your dataset while shaping your analytical pursuits. This careful groundwork enables you to draw meaningful conclusions about market behaviors and trends.

Case Study: Transforming Financial Analysis Through Python

Nestled within the dynamic financial heart of London, we meet Amelia, an ambitious young financial analyst eager to carve her niche in the competitive world of finance. Like many of her peers, Amelia confronts the daunting task of navigating vast seas of data in search of insights that can influence investment strategies. With a steadfast belief in the power of data-driven decision-making, she resolves to leverage Python, a programming language renowned for its analytical capabilities, to elevate her financial analysis skills.

Setting the Scene

Amelia's mission is both simple and bold: to scrutinize the historical stock price data of a leading technology company —Tech Innovations Inc. Equipped with a treasure trove of historical data, she envisions using Python not only to identify market trends and calculate returns but also to create compelling visualizations that bring the data to life.
```

She begins her quest by querying various financial databases, successfully acquiring three years' worth of monthly and daily price data. This dataset comprises critical information such as date, opening price, closing price, daily highs and lows, and trading volumes. Yet, the true challenge lies not merely in gathering the data but meticulously cleaning and analyzing it for meaningful insights.

Step 1: Setting Up the Python Environment

The journey begins with Amelia configuring her Python environment, incorporating several essential libraries. She selects Pandas for data manipulation, Matplotlib for visualizations, and NumPy for numerical analysis. Here's a glimpse of her initial setup:

```python
import pandas as pd import matplotlib.pyplot as plt import numpy as np
```

Step 2: Importing the Data

Next, Amelia loads her carefully curated dataset into a Pandas DataFrame, allowing her to manipulate the data efficiently. This structured format is crucial for the analytical tasks ahead.

```python
# Load the historical stock data data = pd.read_csv('tech_innovations_inc.csv')
```

Once the data is loaded, she inspects its structure to verify the integrity of her initial import:

```python
print(data.head())
```

Step 3: Cleaning and Preprocessing the Data

Real-world financial data is rarely pristine. Amelia encounters missing values and format inconsistencies. Determined to rectify these issues, she devises a comprehensive cleaning strategy that includes converting the 'Date' column to datetime format, dropping any rows containing missing information, and ensuring type consistency across her dataset.

```python
# Convert date to datetime format data['Date'] = pd.to_datetime(data['Date'])

\# Drop missing values
data.dropna(inplace=True)

\# Ensure proper data types
data['Volume'] = data['Volume'].astype(int)
```

Step 4: Conducting Basic Financial Analysis

With a clean dataset in hand, Amelia begins her analytical journey. A key component of her analysis involves calculating daily returns—an essential indicator for investment decisions.

```python
# Calculate daily returns data['Returns'] = data['Close'].pct_change()
```

Using the pct_change() function, she determines the percentage change between successive closing prices. To further enrich her analysis, she calculates cumulative returns over the entire dataset's lifespan.

```python
data['Cumulative Returns'] = (1 + data['Returns']).cumprod() - 1
```

Step 5: Visualizing Essential Insights

After completing her calculations, Amelia turns her attention to visual storytelling. She crafts two pivotal visualizations: one charting daily closing prices and another tracking cumulative returns, providing a clear visual representation of her findings.

```python
# Plotting the closing prices plt.figure(figsize=(14, 7)) plt.plot(data['Date'], data['Close'], label='Closing Price', color='blue') plt.title('Daily Closing Prices of Tech Innovations Inc.') plt.xlabel('Date') plt.ylabel('Price (in ()') plt.legend() plt.grid() plt.show()

\# Plotting the cumulative returns
plt.figure(figsize=(14, 7))
plt.plot(data['Date'], data['Cumulative Returns'], label='Cumulative Returns', color='green')
plt.title('Cumulative Returns of Tech Innovations Inc.')
plt.xlabel('Date')
plt.ylabel('Cumulative Returns')
plt.legend()
plt.grid()
plt.show()
```

Insights Uncovered

From her rigorous analysis, Amelia gains crucial insights into the stock behavior of Tech Innovations Inc. The daily price trend reveals periods of notable volatility, often coinciding with significant company announcements. The cumulative return chart further illustrates a generally upward trajectory, suggesting a promising investment landscape over the analyzed timeframe.

However, Amelia understands this is merely the beginning. She is motivated to delve deeper, examining correlations with industry indices, conducting volatility assessments, and optimizing her portfolio strategies—fuelled by the insights gleaned from her initial explorations with Python.

Amelia's journey encapsulates more than just a technical exercise in coding or numerical crunching. It embodies the transformation of complex data into actionable narratives, significantly influencing investment decisions. This case study showcases Python as a formidable ally in financial analysis, equipped with methodologies and tools that unravel the nuances of market data.

As we conclude Amelia's narrative for now, we embrace the potential for expanding into sophisticated statistical approaches and machine learning techniques. This paves the way for deeper and more insightful analyses as we journey forward through the financial landscape together.

CHAPTER 2: STATISTICAL FOUNDATIONS FOR FINANCE

As we embark on this enlightening journey through the world of descriptive statistics in finance, imagine the vibrant hustle of a bustling market in New York City—where every tick of the stock price pulses like the rhythm of traders moving in and out of the exchanges. In the realm of quantitative finance, descriptive statistics form the bedrock of analysis. They provide the crucial insights that inform investment strategies and guide decision-making processes, unlocking stories hidden within mere numbers.

The Essence of Descriptive Statistics

Descriptive statistics serve as powerful tools that distill vast amounts of data into clear, digestible insights. They simplify complex datasets, enabling analysts to grasp underlying patterns and trends. Fundamental measures within descriptive statistics include the mean, median, mode, variance, standard deviation, and more, each illuminating different aspects of the data.

To illustrate their application, let's revisit Amelia's analysis of Tech Innovations Inc., examining the monthly closing prices of the company's stock over the past three years.

Key Measures in Descriptive Statistics

1. **Mean**: Commonly recognized as the average, the mean signifies a central value within a dataset.

[\text{Mean} = \frac{\sum_{i=1}^{n} x_{i}}{n}]

When calculating the average closing price, for instance, Amelia will apply this formula to derive insights from historical price data.

```python
average_price = data['Close'].mean()
print("Average Closing Price:", average_price)
```

1. **Median**: The median reveals the middle value, offering insight into the dataset's central tendency, particularly valuable in finance where outliers may skew results.

For example, analyzing ordered monthly closing prices, the median may reflect a more realistic central value than the mean.

```python
median_price = data['Close'].median()
print("Median Closing Price:", median_price)
```

1. **Mode**: The mode identifies the most frequently occurring price, spotlighting common trading levels or transaction volumes that might inform trading strategies.

```python
mode_price = data['Close'].mode()[0] # .mode() returns a series; we take the first mode.
print("Mode Closing Price:", mode_price)
```

1. **Variance and Standard Deviation**: Variance quantifies the degree of spread or dispersion in the dataset, while the standard deviation provides a measure in the same units as the data. High values of either indicate increased volatility—critical for traders assessing market risk.

```python
variance_price = data['Close'].var()
std_deviation_price = data['Close'].std()
print("Variance of Closing Prices:", variance_price)
print("Standard Deviation of Closing Prices:", std_deviation_price)
```

1. **Range**: The range offers a snapshot of data spread, calculated as the difference between the maximum and minimum values.

```python
price_range = data['Close'].max() - data['Close'].min()
print("Range of Closing Prices:", price_range)
```

1. **Quartiles and Interquartile Range (IQR)**: Quartiles categorize data into four equal parts. The IQR, measuring the variability of data, indicates the spread within the middle 50% of values, paramount for identifying outliers.

```python
Q1 = data['Close'].quantile(0.25)
Q3 = data['Close'].quantile(0.75)
IQR = Q3 - Q1
print("IQR of Closing Prices:", IQR)
```

The Power of Visualization in Data Interpretation

While raw numbers communicate essential insights, visualization transforms them into a compelling narrative. Recognizing this, Amelia would leverage Python's Matplotlib library to craft engaging histograms and box plots, turning sophisticated datasets into visual stories.

For instance, a histogram of closing prices can vividly display price distribution, potentially revealing correlations to market dynamics or investor sentiment.

```python plt.figure(figsize=(10, 6)) plt.hist(data['Close'], bins=30, edgecolor='k', alpha=0.7) plt.title('Histogram of Closing Prices') plt.xlabel('Price ())') plt.ylabel('Frequency') plt.grid() plt.show()
```

Similarly, a box plot delineates the presence of outliers while reflecting the overall distribution and spread of the dataset.

```python plt.figure(figsize=(10, 6)) plt.boxplot(data['Close']) plt.title('Box Plot of Closing Prices') plt.ylabel('Price (()') plt.grid() plt.show()
```

Insights and Strategic Applications of Descriptive Statistics

Descriptive statistics empower analysts like Amelia to extract actionable insights that influence trading and investment decisions. A higher variance and standard deviation may signal greater risk, prompting her to explore hedging strategies or diversification options.

This analytical exploration of descriptive statistics serves not merely as an exercise in number crunching; it lays the groundwork for sophisticated inferential statistics and machine learning practices. These foundational insights act as a springboard for deeper analyses and more advanced decision-making techniques. From calculating averages to crafting compelling visualizations, these techniques weave an engaging narrative from raw data. As we traverse the intersecting pathways of finance and advanced analytical methods, the insights derived from descriptive statistics will enhance our understanding and guide our strategic maneuvers in the intricate landscape of quantitative finance.

As Amelia prepares to delve into more advanced analyses, she carries forward the empowerment drawn from her understanding of descriptive statistics—a testament to the profound influence of recognizing data's intrinsic patterns before navigating the complexities that await.

Understanding Probability Distributions in Finance

Navigating the intricate landscape of finance often feels like standing at the helm of a ship, steering through the unpredictable waters of market dynamics. A critical beacon in this voyage is the concept of probability distributions. Far from being mere abstractions of mathematical theory, these distributions serve as essential instruments for risk assessment and informed decision-making within the financial realm. Just as seasoned explorers rely on maps to chart their course, financial analysts harness probability distributions to traverse uncertainty, illuminating the pathways to potential market outcomes.

The Role of Probability Distributions

In the world of finance, probability distributions offer a structured way to comprehend the range of possible outcomes, whether relating to investment returns or stock price fluctuations. When analyzing the rhythmic ebb and flow of stock returns, certain patterns emerge—much like characters in a compelling narrative.

Consider Alex, a dedicated portfolio manager at a leading hedge fund. Each day, he delves into the intricacies of various investment strategies, assessing their likelihood of success based on past performance. Utilizing probability distributions enables Alex to spotlight risks and uncover opportunities that might otherwise remain obscured in the murky depths of market data.

Common Probability Distributions in Finance

1. **Normal Distribution**

The normal distribution, often depicted as the bell curve, is foundational in statistical analysis. It characterizes scenarios in finance where asset returns cluster around a central mean. Defined by its mean (μ) and standard deviation (σ), the normal distribution allows analysts to gauge the dispersion of returns.

For instance, if Alex reviews the daily stock returns of a particular asset over the last year, he might find an average return of 0.1% with a standard deviation of 1%.

```python
import numpy as np import matplotlib.pyplot as plt from scipy.stats import norm

mu, sigma = 0.001, 0.01 \# mean and standard deviation
x = np.linspace(mu - 3*sigma, mu + 3*sigma, 100)
plt.plot(x, norm.pdf(x, mu, sigma))
plt.title('Normal Distribution of Stock Returns')
plt.xlabel('Return')
plt.ylabel('Probability Density')
plt.grid()
plt.show()
```

1. **Log-Normal Distribution**

Unlike the normal distribution, the log-normal distribution applies to variables that cannot take negative values, making it particularly useful for modeling stock prices. When a variable follows a log-normal distribution, it signifies that the logarithm of that variable adheres to a normal distribution. This characteristic is especially pertinent in finance, where asset prices tend to grow over time while remaining above zero.

For example, suppose Alex examines the stock price of a tech company that has consistently appreciated over recent years.

```python
from scipy.stats import lognorm

s = 0.954 \# shape parameter
x = np.linspace(0, 3, 100)
plt.plot(x, lognorm.pdf(x, s, scale=np.exp(0.2)))
plt.title('Log-Normal Distribution of Stock Prices')
plt.xlabel('Price')
plt.ylabel('Probability Density')
plt.grid()
plt.show()
```

1. **Binomial Distribution**

The binomial distribution is pivotal for modeling scenarios with two distinct outcomes—success or failure—across a fixed number of trials. In finance, it can illustrate the odds of a stock price rising or falling within a specified timeframe. The classic binomial model underpins option pricing, providing a comprehensive understanding of various potential market conditions.

Imagine Alex, who is keenly tracking the price movements of a particular stock with a 60% probability of an upward shift and a 40% chance of a decline each day for ten days. The binomial distribution equips him with the necessary framework to calculate the likelihood of an array of outcomes.

```python
from scipy.stats import binom

n = 10 \# number of trials
p = 0.6 \# probability of success
k = np.arange(0, n + 1)
plt.bar(k, binom.pmf(k, n, p))
plt.title('Binomial Distribution of Stock Movements')
plt.xlabel('Number of Upward Movements')
plt.ylabel('Probability')
plt.grid()
plt.show()
```

```
```

1. **Exponential Distribution**

The exponential distribution delineates the time until a specific event occurs, making it relevant for modeling market waiting times, such as the intervals until trades are executed. This distribution is crucial in risk management, particularly when assessing time-to-failure for financial instruments like bonds or options.

If Alex analyzes the time intervals between successive trades for a volatile stock, he might discover that these intervals exhibit an exponential distribution. This insight aids him in understanding the stock's trading dynamics and potential liquidity issues.

```python
from scipy.stats import expon

scale = 1.0 \# mean
x = np.linspace(0, 5, 100)
plt.plot(x, expon.pdf(x, scale=scale))
plt.title('Exponential Distribution of Trade Intervals')
plt.xlabel('Time (days)')
plt.ylabel('Probability Density')
plt.grid()
plt.show()
```

Implications of Probability Distributions

Grasping and implementing probability distributions empower financial analysts like Alex to quantify uncertainty and adeptly manage risk. These statistical constructs form the backbone of advanced forecasting models that project asset price movements, calculate expected returns, and assess the ramifications of varying market scenarios.

As financial markets grow increasingly complex and diverse, analysts rely on these principles to glean nuanced insights—an endeavor that marries skill with intuition. For Alex, mastering the intricacies of probability distributions translates into enhanced analytical capabilities, thereby facilitating the development of successful investment strategies that stand resilient against market fluctuations.

Equipped with a profound understanding of probability distributions, financial professionals illuminate the path through the complexities of market behavior. As they navigate the diverse landscapes of stock returns, market movements, and investment strategies, knowledge of how to apply these distributions becomes an indispensable tool. With each exploration of new distributions—from the familiar domains of the normal distribution to the intricate contours of binomial and log-normal frameworks—the insightful narratives within data unfold, guiding the pursuit of financial stability and growth. As Alex continues his analytical journey, he recognizes that adeptly utilizing probability distributions is more than just a statistical pursuit; it is a vital element of his professional toolkit, significantly influencing each investment decision he makes.

Hypothesis Testing Overview

In the intricate landscape of finance, characterized by volatility and uncertainty, analysts and investors are continually challenged to make informed decisions. Hypothesis testing serves as a strategic tool in this endeavor, offering a systematic approach to decipher complex data.

Understanding the Basics of Hypothesis Testing

hypothesis testing is a methodical way to evaluate assertions about a population parameter using sample data. This process involves two primary competing hypotheses: the null hypothesis (H_0) and the alternative hypothesis (H_1). The null hypothesis asserts that any observed effect or difference is due to chance, while the alternative hypothesis contends that there is indeed a significant effect or difference.

Consider the case of Sarah, a dedicated financial analyst at a rapidly growing fintech startup. Eager to innovate, she aims to determine whether a new investment strategy provides significantly greater returns than the traditional approach her firm has relied on. Here's how she formulates her hypotheses:

- **Null Hypothesis (H_0):** The new investment strategy does not yield higher returns than the existing strategy.
- **Alternative Hypothesis (H_1):** The new investment strategy does yield higher returns than the existing strategy.

The Hypothesis Testing Process: Step by Step

To test her hypotheses, Sarah embarks on a structured hypothesis testing journey, encompassing several essential steps:

1. **Selecting a Significance Level (α):**

Setting a significance level is crucial for making informed decisions. This threshold, commonly established at 0.05 or 0.01, represents the probability of incorrectly rejecting the null hypothesis when it is true—a Type I error.05, Sarah acknowledges a 5% risk of drawing the wrong conclusion.

1. **Data Collection and Analysis:**

In the realm of quantitative finance, robust data is invaluable. Sarah diligently gathers historical return data for both investment strategies. Utilizing statistical software and programming languages such as Python, she analyzes this data to derive meaningful insights.

```python import pandas as pd from scipy import stats

\# Example returns for the existing and new investment strategies
existing_strategy_returns = [0.02, 0.01, 0.03, 0.015, 0.017]
new_strategy_returns = [0.03, 0.025, 0.035, 0.04, 0.045]
```

\# Performing a t-test to compare the means
t_stat, p_value = stats.ttest_ind(new_strategy_returns, existing_strategy_returns)
```

1. **Calculating the Test Statistic:**

Next, Sarah computes the test statistic based on her sample data. The t-test, which identifies differences between the means of two groups, sheds light on the significance of the observed disparities.

1. **Comparing Against the Critical Value:**

After determining the test statistic, Sarah compares it against a critical value derived from statistical tables. If her test statistic exceeds the critical value, she possesses sufficient evidence to reject the null hypothesis.

1. **Interpreting the p-value:**

The p-value is a foundational element of hypothesis testing. It quantifies the likelihood of observing the test statistic, or something more extreme, given that the null hypothesis is true. If the p-value falls below the predetermined significance level (α), Sarah can confidently reject the null hypothesis.

Continuing her analysis: ```python print(f"T-statistic: {t_stat}, P-value: {p_value}") if p_value &lt; 0.05: print("Reject the null hypothesis: the new strategy likely offers higher returns.") else: print("Fail to reject the null hypothesis: insufficient evidence to claim improved returns.")
```

Diverse Types of Hypothesis Tests in Finance

The financial domain encompasses various hypothesis tests, each tailored to specific scenarios and types of data:

1. **t-Test for Means:**

This test evaluates whether there is a statistically significant difference between the means of two groups. Sarah applied this test in her evaluation of the two investment strategies.

1. **Chi-Square Test:**

This test investigates relationships between categorical variables. It can be instrumental in analyzing whether the performance of a portfolio's various strategies is independent of prevailing market conditions.

1. **ANOVA (Analysis of Variance):**

ANOVA expands upon the t-test, facilitating comparisons of means among three or more groups. Had Sarah needed to assess multiple investment strategies simultaneously, ANOVA would have been her go-to method.

1. **Non-parametric Tests:**

In scenarios where data does not meet the assumptions of normality, non-parametric tests like the Mann-Whitney U test provide alternative avenues for hypothesis testing, without relying on strict normality constraints.

Common Pitfalls in Hypothesis Testing

While hypothesis testing offers a structured approach to financial analysis, several pitfalls could lead to misleading interpretations:

- **Misunderstanding p-values:** Analysts may mistakenly prioritize p-values in isolation, disregarding the broader context, which can result in incorrect conclusions.
- **Overlooking assumptions:** Each hypothesis test is predicated on certain assumptions regarding the data; failing to acknowledge these can significantly compromise results.
- **Dismissing effect sizes:** A statistically significant finding does not inherently imply practical relevance. Analysts should always consider the effect size—the

magnitude of difference—to fully assess real-world implications. With a well-rounded understanding of the hypothesis testing process—from formulation to statistical analytics—they can make informed decisions that lead to favorable financial outcomes. As Sarah continues her analytical journey, the principles of hypothesis testing illuminate the nuances of market behavior, equipping her with the confidence and precision required to steer through volatile financial environments. Through this lens, readers are encouraged to delve deeper into statistical analysis, enhancing their understanding and improving their financial decision-making capabilities.

Confidence Intervals and Estimation: Navigating Financial Uncertainty

In the realm of finance, where uncertainty is ubiquitous and decision-making can feel daunting, the concept of confidence intervals emerges as a beacon of clarity. These statistical tools serve as essential navigational aids, allowing financial analysts to glean insights about a population parameter based on sample statistics.

What Are Confidence Intervals?

a confidence interval quantifies the uncertainty that accompanies estimating a population parameter from a finite sample. It provides a range of plausible values, which is typically accompanied by a confidence level—commonly set at either 90% or 95%. For instance, when a financial analyst states, “We are 95% confident that the average annual return of our investment portfolio lies between 3% and 5%,” they imply a rigorous analysis has been conducted, lending a calculated assurance about where the true average return likely falls within that interval.

To construct a confidence interval, analysts rely on the

sample mean ((\bar{x})), applying the following foundational formula:

[\text{Confidence Interval} = \bar{x} \pm \left(Z \cdot \frac{s}{\sqrt{n}}\right)]

Where: - (\bar{x}): Sample mean - (Z): Z-score corresponding to the desired confidence level - (s): Standard deviation of the sample - (n): Sample size

This straightforward yet powerful approach equips analysts with the capacity to assess their confidence in estimates —whether they are projecting returns, evaluating risks, or analyzing performance metrics.

Constructing a Confidence Interval: A Step-by-Step Example

Let's delve into a practical scenario involving James, an investment analyst tasked with estimating the average return of a new financial product. He gathers annual return data from a sample of 30 clients over the past five years, resulting in the following returns (expressed as percentages):

(4.8, 5.1, 4.7, 6.0, 5.4, 4.3, 5.6, 5.7, 5.9, 4.5, 5.2, 5.8, 6.1, 4.0, 5.3, 4.6, 5.0, 4.9, 5.5, 6.2, 5.8, 4.4, 4.7, 5.1, 5.3, 5.5, 5.2, 4.8, 5.0, 6.0, 5.6).

1. Calculate the Sample Mean and Standard Deviation:

Using Python, James can effortlessly compute the mean and standard deviation of his collected data:

```python
import numpy as np from scipy import stats

returns = [4.8, 5.1, 4.7, 6.0, 5.4, 4.3, 5.6, 5.7, 5.9, 4.5,
    5.2, 5.8, 6.1, 4.0, 5.3, 4.6, 5.0, 4.9, 5.5, 6.2,
    5.8, 4.4, 4.7, 5.1, 5.3, 5.5, 5.2, 4.8, 5.0, 6.0, 5.6]

sample_mean = np.mean(returns)
sample_std = np.std(returns, ddof=1) \# Sample standard deviation
sample_size = len(returns)
```

2. Determine the Z-score:

For a 95% confidence level, the associated Z-score—indicating the point that leaves just 5% of the data beyond it—is approximately (1.96). This value can be sourced from Z-tables or derived through statistical libraries.

3. Construct the Confidence Interval:

With these calculations in hand, James can now apply the confidence interval formula:

```python
Z = 1.96 # For 95% confidence level
margin_of_error = Z * (sample_std / np.sqrt(sample_size))
confidence_interval = (sample_mean - margin_of_error, sample_mean + margin_of_error)
```

In this step, James determines the margin of error and erects the confidence interval, outlining the bounds that indicate where the true population parameter may reside.

4. Interpreting the Results:

Finally, James compiles his findings into a coherent narrative:

```python
print(f"Sample Mean: {sample_mean:.2f}%, Confidence Interval: ({confidence_interval[0]:.2f}%, {confidence_interval[1]:.2f}%)")
```

If his calculations reveal that the confidence interval extends from 4.80% to 5.40%, he can assert with confidence that he anticipates the true average return of the financial product to lie within those confines, based on comprehensive analysis of his sample data.

Exploring Variations in Confidence Intervals

While the Z-distribution is prevalent in situations where the population standard deviation is known or when the sample size is substantial, other methodologies may be appropriate:

1. **t-Distribution:** In cases involving smaller samples (typically (n < 30)), the t-distribution is more apt. It accommodates the increased variability associated with a smaller dataset. The approach remains largely similar, but James would apply the t-score in place of the Z-score.
2. **Proportion Confidence Intervals:** In financial contexts where binary outcomes are assessed—such as determining if an investment will achieve a designated return—analysts might leverage confidence intervals to estimate proportions. Though the underlying principles are similar, the specific formulas differ to reflect the nature of the data.

Common Pitfalls to Avoid

- **Overlooking Sample Size Effects:** Analysts must recognize that larger sample sizes usually culminate in narrower confidence intervals, reflecting greater precision in estimates.
- **Misconstruing Confidence Levels:** A 95% confidence level does not imply a 95% probability that the true parameter lies within the interval. Instead, it suggests that if the sampling were repeated infinitely, 95% of those intervals would contain the true parameter.
- **Neglecting Data Distribution:** Analysts should remain vigilant about the distribution of their data. For non-normally distributed data, alternative techniques such as bootstrapping may offer more reliable intervals.

In the fast-paced landscape of quantitative finance, confidence intervals provide a robust framework for statistical estimation. As they navigate the intricate dance of risk and reward, mastering confidence intervals and the accompanying estimation processes becomes key to fostering sustainable financial success. This knowledge not only helps analysts ground their insights in quantifiable metrics but also empowers them to approach uncertainty with greater confidence and clarity.

Correlation and Covariance: Unraveling Financial Interrelationships

Demystifying Covariance

Covariance serves as a measure of the degree to which two random variables co-move. When the values of two assets tend to rise and fall together, the covariance is positive. Conversely, if one asset's value increases while the other's decreases, the covariance reflects this with a negative value. While covariance provides valuable insights into the relationship between assets, it lacks a standardized measure, which can complicate its interpretation.

The formula for calculating the covariance between two variables (X) and (Y) is expressed as:

[\text{Cov}(X, Y) = \frac{1}{n-1} \sum_{i=1}^{n} (X_i - \bar{X}) (Y_i - \bar{Y})]

Where: - (X) and (Y) are the random variables. - (\bar{X}) and (\bar{Y}) denote the means of (X) and (Y), respectively. - (n) represents the total number of data points.

To illustrate this concept more clearly, let's consider a hypothetical analysis of monthly returns for two stocks, Stock A and Stock B, over a six-month period:

To calculate the covariance using Python, you could use the following code snippet:

```python import numpy as np

\# Monthly returns
stock_a = np.array([3, 2, -1, 4, 2, 5])
stock_b = np.array([4, 3, 1, 5, 3, 6])
```

```
\# Calculate covariance
covariance = np.cov(stock_a, stock_b)[0][1]
print(f"Covariance between Stock A and Stock B: {covariance:.2f}")
```

If the computed covariance is positive, this suggests a tendency for Stock A and Stock B to move together, pointing to a potential correlation.

Correlation: A Standardized Insight

While covariance provides a useful initial view of how two variables might relate, correlation takes this a step further. It offers a standardized measure that simplifies interpretation, with values ranging from -1 to 1. A correlation of 1 represents a perfect positive correlation, indicating that as one variable increases, the other follows suit. Conversely, a correlation of -1 signifies a perfect negative correlation, where one variable increases as the other decreases. A correlation close to 0 implies no discernible relationship.

To calculate the correlation coefficient (r), the formula used is:

[r = \frac{\text{Cov}(X, Y)}{s_X s_Y}]

Where: - (s_X) and (s_Y) are the standard deviations of variables (X) and (Y), respectively.

Let's apply this understanding to compute the correlation between Stock A and Stock B:

```python
# Calculate correlation correlation = np.corrcoef(stock_a, stock_b)[0][1] print(f"Correlation between Stock A and Stock B: {correlation:.2f}")
```

A solid grasp of correlation enables investors to make astute decisions regarding portfolio diversification.

Real-World Scenarios: Examining Positive and Negative Correlation

Consider an investment manager evaluating both technology stocks and utility stocks for their portfolio. Historically, technology stocks often exhibit positive correlation, moving in tandem during bullish market phases. In contrast, utility stocks may display negative correlation with technology stocks, gaining attractiveness during market downturns when investors prioritize stability and dividends.

Let's paint a clearer picture through fictional scenarios:

1. **Positive Correlation Example:**
2. In a vibrant tech boom, the returns for Tech Stock A and Tech Stock B might soar from 5% to 10% as market optimism drives strong earnings reports, resulting in a correlation of approximately 0.85.
3. **Negative Correlation Example:**
4. During an economic downturn, Tech Stock A could plunge by 15%, whereas Utility Stock B remains stable or even appreciates due to its defensive characteristics. This scenario might yield a correlation near -0.75 between the two asset classes.

Common Misunderstandings

It's crucial to remember that correlation does not imply causation. A strong correlation between two stocks does not mean that one is directly influencing the movements of the other. Additionally, investors should be wary of "spurious correlation," where two unrelated variables seem correlated due to coincidental relationships driven by external factors.

In summary, mastering the concepts of correlation and covariance empowers finance professionals to navigate the intricate web of asset relationships with greater acumen. While covariance lays the groundwork for understanding these relationships, correlation enhances insights that can aid in diversification and risk management. As financial markets evolve, leveraging these statistical tools becomes essential for making sound investment decisions.

Linear Regression Basics: Uncovering Financial Insights Through Data Analysis

In the fast-paced world of finance, where data-driven decisions can spell triumph or disaster, linear regression stands out as one of the most valuable analytical techniques. This statistical approach empowers investors and analysts to unravel the connections between variables, predict trends, and gain strategic insights into asset performance. In this exploration of linear regression, we will delve into its foundational principles, showcase its practical applications within finance, and provide actionable steps for implementation using Python.

Understanding Linear Regression: Laying the Groundwork

linear regression is a statistical method used to model the relationship between a dependent variable and one or more independent variables through a linear equation. The core structure of this equation can be expressed as:

[Y = \beta_0 + \beta_1X + \epsilon]

Where: - (Y) represents the dependent variable (often indicating a financial metric like stock returns). - (X) denotes the independent variable(s), which could include market indicators, economic indicators, or rival company performances. - (\beta_0) is the y-intercept of the regression line, representing the expected value of (Y) when (X) is zero. - (\beta_1) captures the slope of the regression line, illustrating how much (Y) changes for a one-unit change in (X). - (\epsilon) signifies the error term, accounting for variations in (Y) not explained by (X).

Each of these components aligns with a visual representation of a regression line on a scatter plot, where individual data points reflect distinct observations.

The Methodology: Constructing a Linear Regression Model

To effectively utilize linear regression, analysts typically adopt a structured approach encompassing data collection, model fitting, and thorough evaluation of results. Let's walk through this process with a hypothetical example analyzing stock returns in relation to a pertinent market index.

Imagine we have gathered monthly return data for a specific stock alongside the corresponding market index over a one-year period:

The first step involves employing Python to conduct the linear regression analysis. Below is a code snippet that demonstrates how to leverage the statsmodels library—a robust tool for statistical analysis in Python.

```python
import pandas as pd import statsmodels.api as sm

\# Creating a DataFrame with the data
data = {
  'Stock Returns': [2.5, 1.5, 3.0, 0.5, 4.0, -1.0, 2.8, 3.5, -0.5, 1.0, 3.2, 4.0],
  'Market Index Returns': [3.0, 1.8, 2.5, 0.8, 4.2, -0.8, 2.3, 3.9, -1.5, 1.7, 3.1, 4.5]
}
df = pd.DataFrame(data)

\# Defining the dependent and independent variables
X = df['Market Index Returns']
y = df['Stock Returns']

\# Adding a constant to the independent variable for the intercept
X = sm.add_constant(X)

\# Fitting the linear regression model
model = sm.OLS(y, X).fit()

\# Viewing the model summary
print(model.summary())
```

Once executed, this code yields a comprehensive model summary that highlights critical statistics, including coefficients for both the intercept and slope, R-squared values, p-values, and more. Each of these parameters is instrumental in assessing the model's efficacy.

Interpreting Results: Decoding the Regression Output

Upon reviewing the model summary, several key insights emerge. The coefficient associated with the market index return demonstrates the anticipated change in stock returns corresponding to a one-percentage point increase in market returns. For instance, if the slope coefficient is 0.6, this indicates that a 1% rise in the market index is associated with an approximate 0.6% increase in the stock's return.

Furthermore, the R-squared value, ranging from 0 to 1, quantifies how much variance in stock returns can be explained by changes in market index returns. An R-squared of 0.85 would indicate that a substantial 85% of the variability in stock returns can be attributed to market movements, thus underscoring the model's strong explanatory capability.

Practical Application: Leveraging Predictions for Strategic Decisions

The true power of linear regression lies not only in elucidating past relationships but also in facilitating forecasts of future outcomes. Once a reliable regression model is established, it becomes an essential tool for predicting future stock returns based on anticipated market fluctuations.

Consider the scenario of predicting a market upswing, characterized by an expected 3% increase in the market index. Utilizing our earlier example, the forecasted stock return could be computed as follows:

[\text{Predicted Stock Return} = \beta_0 + (3 \times \beta_1)]

Ultimately, financial analysts can apply these forecasts to a myriad of applications, including the development of investment strategies, risk assessment, and dynamic asset allocation.

Considerations and Limitations

While linear regression furnishes invaluable insights, it is crucial to recognize its inherent limitations. A fundamental assumption of this model is the linearity of the relationship between the dependent and independent variables. However, in the complex landscape of financial markets, relationships can frequently exhibit nonlinearity, warranting further scrutiny and potentially the use of more sophisticated modeling techniques.

Moreover, the presence of outliers can significantly distort results, leading to potential misinterpretations. Therefore, meticulous data assessment and preprocessing are paramount before fitting a linear regression model.

Another critical consideration is multicollinearity—the scenario where independent variables are highly correlated—which can obscure the interpretability and reliability of the regression coefficients.

In summary, linear regression is not just an analytical tool but a vital asset for those navigating the intricate world of finance. As we delve deeper into advanced statistical methods, linear regression serves as a foundational stepping stone, enabling individuals to harness data effectively in pursuit of financial success. This exploration empowers readers to adeptly navigate market complexities with enhanced confidence and insight.

Limitations of Basic Statistical Methods: Understanding the Constraints in Financial Analysis

In today's financial landscape, data is often referred to as the "new oil." However, deriving meaningful insights from this abundant resource requires far more than straightforward collection; it demands sophisticated analytical techniques. While basic statistical methods, such as linear regression and descriptive statistics, provide a solid foundation for analyzing financial data, they come with considerable limitations. Understanding these constraints is essential for analysts and investors, as it directly impacts the effectiveness of their decision-making processes.

A cornerstone of many statistical methods is the assumption that underlying data follows a normal distribution. This is particularly relevant in linear regression analysis. Yet, in the volatile world of financial markets, the reality often diverges sharply from this assumption. For instance, the phenomenon of fat tails in return distributions indicates that extreme market events—like crashes or booms—occur far more frequently than predicted by a normal distribution. The 2008 financial crisis serves as a poignant illustration of how market behaviors can stray significantly from the Gaussian bell curve.

When analysts rely on methods that presuppose normality for datasets that clearly do not meet this criterion, they risk drawing misguided conclusions. For example, the calculation of Value at Risk (VaR), which often hinges on the assumption of normally distributed returns, may underestimate the likelihood of significant losses, thereby compromising effective risk management strategies.

2. The Limitation of Linear Relationships

Basic statistical tools often operate under the premise that relationships between variables are linear. Yet, many financial interactions unfold in complex, nonlinear ways, influenced by various interrelated factors. Take, for example, the connection between interest rates and stock prices—it is rarely a straight line and instead reflects a curvature that responds to fluctuating macroeconomic conditions.

Sticking rigidly to linear models can gloss over critical dynamics inherent in the data. This highlights the increasing necessity for analysts to explore more sophisticated nonlinear models, including polynomial regression and machine learning techniques, which excel at capturing such complexities. A notable case is the application of Autoregressive Integrated Moving Average (ARIMA) models, which integrate time dynamics to yield more nuanced forecasts, providing deeper insights into market trends.

3. Overfitting and Underfitting

In the realm of statistical modeling, analysts face the delicate challenge of balancing between underfitting (too simplistic a model) and overfitting (too complex a model). A model that oversimplifies relationships might overlook significant patterns, while one that is overly complex may merely pick up on noise rather than reveal underlying trends. For instance, consider a regression analysis incorporating too many predictors to explain stock price movements; while it may achieve an excellent fit with past data, it often falters in its ability to generalize to future outcomes.

This misalignment can lead to erroneous forecasts that misguide financial decision-making. A practical example is found in algorithmic trading, where models that are overfitted can falter dramatically when faced with real-time data that behave differently from historical trends.

4. The Impact of External Factors

Basic statistical methods frequently operate under the assumption that all relevant variables are included in the model. In the intricate realm of finance, this is rarely the case, as external factors—ranging from economic changes and geopolitical events to regulatory shifts—can drastically alter market dynamics. For example, a simplistic predictive model might focus solely on a company's earnings, neglecting broader macroeconomic signals such as shifts in consumer sentiment or fiscal policies. Such oversights can lead to predictions falling woefully short of actual market outcomes.

To combat this limitation, analysts are increasingly employing multivariable analyses and regression techniques that account for more complex interdependencies and interactions. This broader approach minimizes the risk of omitted variable bias, enabling a deeper understanding of market behavior.

5. Susceptibility to Outliers

The presence of outliers can significantly skew the results of basic statistical analyses. In financial datasets, outliers can appear frequently, often triggered by extreme market fluctuations, such as major drops in stock prices or surges in trading volumes. A striking example occurred during the GameStop short squeeze in early 2021, when the stock price catapulted from)20 to (483 in mere days, generating an outlier that could warp traditional analyses based on historical averages.

Basic statistical models may misinterpret such outliers, leading to flawed conclusions that can result in poor financial decisions. To mitigate this issue, analysts should consider employing robust statistical techniques, including trimmed means and data transformations, which reduce the influence of outliers and facilitate sound analytical conclusions.

6. Neglecting Temporal Dynamics

Fundamental statistical models often fall short in accounting for the temporal dimension of financial data. Time series analysis is vital in finance given the critical reliance on historical data for making informed projections. Static models can neglect the sequence of events and miss valuable trends embedded in time-driven data. For instance, asset price movements today can significantly impact tomorrow's forecasts, a dynamic best captured through advanced time series methodologies like ARIMA or GARCH models.

To enhance their analysis, financial analysts must integrate temporal dynamics into their models, ensuring that their evaluations reflect the evolving landscape of market conditions. Recognizing time as a core component of predictive analysis is crucial for generating accurate forecasts.

7. Constrained Predictive Power

Finally, while basic statistical methods can effectively illustrate correlations, they often lack the predictive power necessary for anticipating future events accurately. The inherently unpredictable nature of financial markets, influenced by various elements beyond simple models, presents considerable challenges. For example, relying solely on historical performance to predict stock returns can lead to erroneous forecasts, as past performance is not a reliable predictor of future outcomes amidst shifting market conditions and investor behaviors.

To bolster predictive accuracy, analysts should marry basic statistical methods with advanced machine learning techniques, ensemble methods, or artificial intelligence. These modern approaches excel at discerning intricate patterns and relationships within complex datasets that traditional methods may overlook.

Recognizing the limitations of basic statistical methods is vital for anyone engaged in quantitative finance. While these techniques are invaluable starting points for data analysis, a nuanced understanding of their constraints allows for enhanced analytical precision and more informed decision-making.

In an ever-evolving financial landscape, integrating advanced methodologies and a wider array of analytical tools empowers professionals to refine their insights and adapt their strategies effectively. As we further explore advanced statistical methods, the journey toward data-driven financial success becomes increasingly attainable, equipping analysts and investors with the confidence and acuity to navigate the complexities of today's markets.

Common Statistical Mistakes: Navigating Pitfalls in Financial Analysis

One of the most prevalent errors is conflating correlation with causation. When two variables seem to move in tandem, it can be tempting to assume that one influences the other. A classic illustration is the correlation observed between ice cream sales and shark attacks; both tend to spike in the summer months, but it is misleading to conclude that higher ice cream sales cause an increase in shark encounters. In reality, both phenomena are linked to the warmer weather.

In the realm of finance, misinterpretations can be particularly dire. For instance, if analysts notice a strong correlation between a company's advertising expenditures and its stock price, they might wrongfully conclude that increased ad spending directly leads to higher stock valuations. Such a perspective neglects other crucial factors, like overall market conditions or consumer sentiment. To navigate this risk, analysts must dig deeper into causal relationships, utilizing controlled experiments or sophisticated statistical models to reach sound conclusions.

2. Overlooking Sample Size and Statistical Significance

The size of a sample is critical to the accuracy of statistical analyses. A common pitfall is relying on a small sample that may not capture the full breadth of the data's variability. In finance, where trends can be volatile, small datasets can lead to misleading conclusions. For example, an analyst examining a portfolio's performance over just a few quarters might claim a particular investment strategy is successful based on only five data points, which lacks statistical significance.

To enhance the reliability of analyses, methods such as p-value assessments should be used to evaluate statistical significance. A standard threshold of 0.05 is often employed; if the p-value is below this level, it provides strong evidence against the null hypothesis. Understanding and utilizing appropriate sample sizes ensures that insights derived from analyses are both robust and trustworthy.

3. Ignoring Multiple Comparisons

Conducting multiple statistical tests increases the probability of Type I errors, which occur when a true null hypothesis is incorrectly rejected. This concern is particularly relevant in finance, where analysts may test numerous hypotheses in search of a viable investment strategy. For instance, if an analyst evaluates ten different stock screening criteria using a 5% significance level, the likelihood of mistakenly identifying a "significant" result purely by chance escalates.

To mitigate this risk, it is prudent to apply corrections for multiple comparisons, like the Bonferroni correction. This adjustment modifies the significance threshold based on the number of tests conducted, assuring that findings are less likely to stem from random fluctuations.

4. Disregarding Confounding Variables

Confounding variables can obscure the true relationships between the variables being analyzed, leading to erroneous conclusions. For example, a financial analyst correlating GDP growth and rising stock prices might fail to consider critical confounding factors such as interest rates or inflation, which can significantly influence their findings. The interplay among various economic indicators can introduce biases that mislead investment decisions based solely on GDP figures.

Using multiple regression analysis is one effective strategy to account for these confounding variables. This approach allows analysts to control for the effects of outside variables, enabling them to isolate the specific relationship they wish to examine.

5. Neglecting Non-stationarity in Time Series Data

Time series data, such as stock prices and interest rates, often exhibit non-stationarity, whereby their statistical properties evolve over time. Ignoring this characteristic can lead to misleading results in statistical tests. For example, applying a linear regression model to non-stationary data may yield spurious correlations—relationships that seem valid but are mere artifacts of fluctuating data.

To avoid falling into this trap, analysts should utilize tests like the Augmented Dickey-Fuller test to assess stationarity. If non-stationarity is detected, techniques such as differencing or detrending should be employed to stabilize the mean or variance before applying traditional statistical models.

6. Succumbing to Confirmation Bias

Analysts frequently encounter confirmation bias, wherein they favor information that supports their preconceived notions while disregarding contrary evidence. This cognitive distortion can significantly skew analyses. For instance, a trader convinced of a stock's bullish potential may ignore negative forecasts or adverse price trends, compromising their overall trading strategy.

To mitigate confirmation bias, a systematic analytical approach is essential. Engaging in peer reviews, implementing controls, and actively seeking constructive criticism can enhance objectivity, equipping analysts to maintain a comprehensive viewpoint rather than one clouded by personal biases.

7. Overlooking Data Cleaning and Validation

The adage "garbage in, garbage out" aptly captures the essence of quality data in analysis. Analysts who rush into their work without adequately cleaning and validating their datasets run the risk of producing skewed results. Outliers, inaccuracies, and gaps in data can distort findings. For example, erroneous entries in a stock's historical pricing data may yield flawed conclusions about its performance.

Establishing a thorough data cleaning process is critical.

Techniques such as outlier detection, imputation for missing values, and rigorous verification of data sources are essential for ensuring that analyses rest on a solid empirical foundation.

Awareness of these common statistical mistakes is paramount for anyone navigating the intricate landscape of quantitative finance. A diligent and methodical approach to statistical analysis not only bolsters the credibility of insights but also empowers investors to make informed, data-driven decisions. As we delve deeper into the realm of statistical methods, the lessons learned from past missteps can guide practitioners toward more reliable analytical practices, ultimately enhancing their success in financial endeavors.

Descriptive Statistics: The Cornerstone of Data Understanding

Descriptive statistics act as an essential lens through which we can view and comprehend data sets. The most important measures include:

- **Mean**: Often referred to as the average, the mean provides a central tendency of a data set. It is calculated by summing all observations and dividing by the total number of data points. For instance, consider stock prices of)25, (30, and)35 over three days. The mean price can be determined as follows:

  [\text{Mean} = \frac{25 + 30 + 35}{3} = 30]

- **Median**: The median identifies the middle value in a sorted data set, effectively dividing it into two equal halves. In our previous example, with stock prices arranged as 25, 30, and 35, the median is also (30.

- **Mode**: This measure represents the most frequently occurring value within a data set. Suppose we observe stock prices of)25, (30,)30, and (35; here, the mode would be)30, as it appears twice.

- **Standard Deviation**: This metric quantifies the extent to which the values in a data set deviate from the mean, providing insights into volatility. A higher standard deviation signals greater variability in stock prices, while a lower standard deviation indicates more stable behavior. Returning to our example of stock prices, the standard deviation can be calculated as follows:

  [\sigma = \sqrt{\frac{(25 - 30)^2 + (30 - 30)^2 + (35 - 30)^2}{3}} = \sqrt{\frac{(25)^2 + (0)^2 + (5)^2}{3}} = \sqrt{\frac{25 + 0 + 25}{3}} = \sqrt{\frac{50}{3}} \approx 4.08]

Probability Distributions: Mapping Uncertainty

Probability distributions are central to financial analysis, illustrating the likelihood of various outcomes within a dataset. Familiarity with common distributions enhances risk modeling and return estimation:

- **Normal Distribution**: This distribution plays a critical role in finance due to the Central Limit Theorem, which asserts that the means of large samples of independent random variables tend to follow a normal distribution, regardless of the underlying distribution. Typically depicted as a bell-shaped curve, in this distribution, the mean, median, and mode are all equal.
- **Log-normal Distribution**: Particularly useful in finance, this distribution is applied to stock prices, where the logarithm of the variable adheres to a normal distribution. Since prices cannot be negative, this results in a positively skewed distribution, reflecting realistic market conditions.

Hypothesis Testing: A Structured

Approach to Validation

Hypothesis testing provides a systematic framework for inferential statistics, enabling analysts to assess the validity of assumptions about populations based on sampled data. Key concepts within this approach include:

- **Null Hypothesis (H0)**: Serving as the baseline assumption, the null hypothesis posits that no significant effect or difference exists. For example, we might propose that a new trading strategy does not outperform a benchmark (e.g., H0: $\mu_{new} = \mu_{benchmark}$).
- **Alternative Hypothesis (H1)**: This hypothesis represents the researcher's assertion that an effect or difference does exist (e.g., H1: $\mu_{new} > \mu_{benchmark}$).
- **p-Value**: The p-value indicates the significance of the results; a low value (typically below 0.05) suggests that the null hypothesis can be rejected. For instance, a p-value of 0.03 implies a statistically significant difference at the 5% level when testing whether the new strategy outperforms the benchmark.

Confidence Intervals: Embracing Uncertainty in Estimates

A confidence interval provides a range within which we expect the true population parameter to lie, based on sample statistics. This concept accounts for uncertainty in estimations.

For example, if an analyst determines the average return of a stock to be 10% with a standard deviation of 2%, from a sample of 100 observations, the 95% confidence interval can be calculated as follows:

[\text{Confidence Interval} = \text{Mean} \pm Z

\left(\frac{\sigma}{\sqrt{n}} \right)] Where (Z) is the Z-score corresponding to the desired confidence level (1.96 for 95%).

Determining the interval:

[\text{Confidence Interval} = 10\% \pm 1.96 \left(\frac{2\%}{\sqrt{100}} \right) = 10\% \pm 0.392\% = (9.608\%, 10.392\%)]

This calculation indicates that we can be 95% confident that the true average return lies between approximately 9.61% and 10.39%.

Correlation and Covariance: Understanding Relationships Between Assets

Assessing the relationships between various financial assets necessitates a grasp of correlation and covariance:

- **Covariance**: This measure captures the directional relationship between two variables. A positive covariance indicates that as one variable increases, the other tends to increase as well, while a negative covariance suggests an inverse relationship.
- **Correlation Coefficient**: Standardizing covariance, this coefficient ranges from -1 to +1, reflecting the strength and direction of a linear relationship. A correlation of 0 indicates no relationship at all. For example, a correlation coefficient of 0.85 between two asset prices suggests a strong tendency for them to move in the same direction—information that is valuable when considering diversification strategies in portfolio management.

Linear Regression: Predicting Outcomes with Precision

Linear regression is a fundamental statistical technique used to forecast the value of one variable based on another.

It enables analysts to quantify the relationships between dependent and independent variables.

In its simplest form, a linear regression model can be expressed mathematically as:

[y = a + bx] Where: - (y) is the predicted value, - (a) is the y-intercept, - (b) is the slope, - (x) represents the independent variable.

This method proves particularly essential in finance for predicting stock prices based on economic indicators and other relevant variables.

Familiarity with these key statistical terms lays the groundwork for a deeper understanding of quantitative finance. As you navigate the complexities of financial modeling and analysis, this clarity in terminology will not only empower you in tackling sophisticated financial models but also facilitate effective communication of your findings. to extract impactful financial insights with confidence.

Case Study: Unleashing the Power of Statistics in Market Analysis

In the dynamic realm of quantitative finance, effectively interpreting market data is not just a skill—it's a critical asset. This case study explores a practical application of statistics, focusing on the analysis of historical stock prices for a well-known tech company, which we'll refer to as TechCorp to maintain confidentiality.

Understanding the Dataset

Our analysis begins with a robust dataset comprised of daily closing prices of TechCorp's stock over a five-year period, yielding approximately 1,260 data points. This wealth of information provides a fertile ground for employing various statistical techniques, including descriptive statistics, probability distributions, and regression analysis.

To facilitate our exploration, we will harness the power of Python libraries: Pandas, NumPy, and Matplotlib. Below is the roadmap for our analysis:

1. **Importing Necessary Libraries** ```python import pandas as pd import numpy as np import matplotlib.pyplot as plt

```

1. **Loading the Data** After importing the essential libraries, we load the dataset into a Pandas DataFrame, which paves the way for smooth data manipulation and analysis. ```python data = pd.read_csv('techcorp_stock_data.csv', parse_dates=['Date'], index_col='Date')

```

1. **Exploring Key Descriptive Statistics** Our first analytical step is to summarize the dataset's essential features.

```python summary_statistics = data['Close'].describe() print(summary_statistics)
```

This will yield a comprehensive summary, highlighting the count, mean, standard deviation, minimum and maximum values, and quartiles—essential context for assessing the stock's performance.

Visualizing Historical Performance

Visual representation of data is crucial for uncovering insights that raw numbers may overlook.

```python plt.figure(figsize=(12, 6)) plt.plot(data['Close'], label='TechCorp Closing Prices', color='blue') plt.title('Historical Closing Prices of TechCorp') plt.xlabel('Date') plt.ylabel('Closing Price (()') plt.legend()
```

```
plt.grid() plt.show()
```

This visualization vividly illustrates how TechCorp's stock has fluctuated, allowing us to pinpoint periods of significant growth and decline. Especially during major market events—such as product launches or economic downturns—this visual tool allows for a closer examination of how the stock price reacts.

Applying Probability Distributions

To gain a clearer understanding of stock performance, examining the distribution of stock returns is insightful. We calculate daily returns with the following formula:

$$Return_t = \frac{Price_t - Price_{t-1}}{Price_{t-1}}$$

We can then visualize this distribution using a histogram, which reveals the spread and shape of daily returns:

```python
data['Returns'] = data['Close'].pct_change() returns = data['Returns'].dropna()

plt.figure(figsize=(10, 5))
returns.hist(bins=50, color='green', alpha=0.75)
plt.title('Distribution of Daily Returns for TechCorp')
plt.xlabel('Return')
plt.ylabel('Frequency')
plt.grid()
plt.show()
```

The resulting histogram aids in assessing the risk and volatility of TechCorp stocks. Understanding the return distribution is critical as it informs our financial models, particularly regarding the common assumption of normality in stock returns.

Conducting Hypothesis Testing

Next, we might aim to evaluate the question: Is TechCorp's average daily return statistically significantly greater than zero? To investigate this, we formulate our hypotheses:

- **Null Hypothesis (H0)**: The average daily return equals zero ((\mu = 0)).
- **Alternative Hypothesis (H1)**: The average daily return is greater than zero ((\mu > 0)).

To test this hypothesis, we will conduct a one-sample t-test using SciPy's statistical tools:

```python
from scipy import stats

t_statistic, p_value = stats.ttest_1samp(returns, 0)
print(f"T-statistic: {t_statistic}, P-value: {p_value}")
```

Assuming a significance level of (\alpha = 0.05), if our computed (p)-value falls below this threshold, we can confidently reject the null hypothesis, establishing that TechCorp has a statistically significant positive average daily return.

Regression Analysis for Predictive Insights

To enhance our analysis further, we can use regression techniques to explore the relationship between TechCorp's stock performance and external economic indicators, such as the S&P 500 index. This involves aligning our TechCorp data with S&P 500 data to perform a robust analysis.

Utilizing the statsmodels library, we can conduct linear regression to quantify the relationship between TechCorp's returns and the S&P 500's performance:

```python
import statsmodels.api as sm

\# Assuming S&P 500 returns are in a DataFrame called sp500_data
merged_data = pd.concat([returns, sp500_data['Returns']], axis=1, keys=['TechCorp Returns', 'SP500 Returns']).dropna()
```

```
X = merged_data['SP500 Returns']
y = merged_data['TechCorp Returns']

X = sm.add_constant(X)  \# Adding an intercept
model = sm.OLS(y, X).fit()
print(model.summary())
```

This regression analysis yields critical insights, illustrating how fluctuations in the S&P 500 correlate with TechCorp's returns. Such information is invaluable, aiding in the formulation of intelligent investment strategies.

This case study underscores the transformative power of statistical methods in fostering a profound understanding of market dynamics through quantitative analysis.

As we progress through this book, we will delve deeper into sophisticated techniques and tools, weaving them into a cohesive framework for quantitative finance. We will leverage Python as our analytical backbone, enhancing your capacity to generate insights and navigate the complexities of financial data, paving the way for strategic opportunities in an increasingly competitive landscape.

CHAPTER 3: TIME SERIES ANALYSIS

Time series data serves as a pivotal foundation in quantitative finance, enabling analysts and investors to analyze and forecast the behavior of financial assets over time. Unlike conventional datasets where each observation stands alone, time series data comprises sequences of observations collected at consistent intervals—be it daily stock prices, quarterly earnings, or annual interest rates.

The Nature of Time Series Data

time series data captures the evolution of a variable over time, often illustrating trends, cycles, and seasonal variations. Consider, for instance, the daily closing prices of Tesla, Inc. (referred to as TSLA for convenience) across multiple years. Each price point is more than just a number; it is connected to surrounding price points, weaving a narrative that analysts seek to interpret.

This interdependence distinguishes time series analysis from other forms of statistical examination. To visualize this, imagine standing at the edge of a serene lake, where your reflection vividly mirrors the landscape surrounding it. Similarly, time series data provides a reflective view of past financial behaviors, offering insights into potential future movements.

Key Characteristics of Time Series Data

A comprehensive understanding of the key characteristics of time series data is essential for effective analysis. Here are the four primary components to recognize:

1. **Trend**: This refers to the overarching direction in which the data moves over a long period. For example, if TSLA's stock price shows a steady increase over five years, we identify this trajectory as a positive trend, signaling potential growth.
2. **Seasonality**: Many financial datasets display recurring patterns over specific intervals. Retail stocks, for instance, may exhibit increased sales during holiday seasons.
3. **Cyclical Patterns**: In contrast to seasonality, cyclical patterns emerge over irregular timeframes, often tied to broader economic cycles. A recession can affect various sectors differently, leading to unpredictable fluctuations in stock prices. Identifying these patterns requires advanced analytical skills and a deep understanding of the underlying economic environment.
4. **Irregularity (Noise)**: Time series data often contains noise—unexpected anomalies that diverge from established trends. Sudden market crashes, corporate scandals, or geopolitical events can significantly impact stock prices, making it crucial for analysts to distinguish between authentic trends and random noise.

Analyzing Time Series Data

A cornerstone of time series analysis is effective data

visualization. Let's explore how to visualize TSLA's stock prices using Python, leveraging its powerful libraries for clarity and insight.

```python
import pandas as pd import matplotlib.pyplot as plt

\# Load the time series data
tsla_data = pd.read_csv('TSLA_stock_data.csv', parse_dates=['Date'], index_col='Date')

\# Plotting the closing price over time
plt.figure(figsize=(14, 7))
plt.plot(tsla_data['Close'], label='TSLA Closing Price', color='orange')
plt.title('Tesla Inc. Closing Price Over Time')
plt.xlabel('Date')
plt.ylabel('Price (\))')
plt.legend()
plt.grid()
plt.show()
```

This visual representation not only illustrates the historical trajectory of closing prices but also facilitates the identification of trends, seasonal variations, and other temporal patterns worthy of further investigation.

Stationarity in Time Series

Before delving into more sophisticated analyses and modeling techniques, it is imperative to grasp the concept of stationarity. A stationary time series is defined by consistent statistical properties, such as mean and variance, over time. Many statistical models, including AutoRegressive Integrated Moving Average (ARIMA), necessitate stationary data. Consequently, testing for stationarity becomes a critical step in time series analysis.

Methods like the Augmented Dickey-Fuller (ADF) test are instrumental in this evaluation. If our data proves non-stationary, we can employ methods such as differencing—subtracting the previous observation from the current one—to transform it into a stationary series:

```python
from statsmodels.tsa.stattools import adfuller

\# Perform the ADF test
result = adfuller(tsla_data['Close'])
print('ADF Statistic: %f' % result[0])
print('p-value: %f' % result[1])
```

If the p-value resides below a designated significance threshold (commonly 0.05 or 0.01), we can confidently reject the null hypothesis indicating that the time series has a unit root, thus suggesting stationarity.

Engaging with time series data is crucial for building dynamic models capable of forecasting future behaviors based on historical patterns. The principles of time series analysis not only lay the groundwork for the advanced discussions awaiting readers in this book, but they also arm financial practitioners with essential skills to navigate the complexities of market behaviors.

As we progress, we will explore more advanced techniques for modeling and forecasting, utilizing the power of Python to distill actionable insights from these datasets. With a solid understanding of time series data and its characteristics, subsequent sections will take us deeper into the thrilling realms of quantitative finance. Every methodology and model we examine will circle back to the time series data at hand, equipping you to excel in an ever-evolving financial landscape.

Understanding Stationarity and Differencing in Time Series Analysis

A deep understanding of stationarity is essential for effective time series analysis in the realm of quantitative finance. a stationary time series is one where statistical properties—

such as mean, variance, and autocovariance—remain constant over time. This inherent stability is crucial because many statistical forecasting models, particularly the renowned ARIMA (AutoRegressive Integrated Moving Average) model, require the input series to be stationary for accurate predictions.

The Significance of Stationarity

Imagine a financial analyst working tirelessly at a vibrant investment firm in London, eager to forecast the future prices of a volatile stock. If this analyst compiles historical data without first establishing whether the time series is stationary, they risk drawing misguided conclusions. Non-stationary time series can obscure genuine relationships, making variables seem correlated when they are not; these deceptive patterns vanish upon proper differencing or transformation. Thus, recognizing and ensuring stationarity empowers analysts to construct robust predictive models and enhances the credibility of their forecasting endeavors.

How to Identify Stationarity

To ascertain whether a time series exhibits stationarity, analysts can employ a variety of statistical tests. One of the most widely used is the Augmented Dickey-Fuller (ADF) test, which assesses the presence of a unit root in an autoregressive model of the data. In this test, the null hypothesis posits that a unit root exists, indicating non-stationarity, while the alternative hypothesis argues for stationarity.

Here's a concise guide to conducting the ADF test using Python:

```python
import pandas as pd from statsmodels.tsa.stattools import adfuller

\# Load the time series data
tsla_data = pd.read_csv('TSLA_stock_data.csv', parse_dates=['Date'], index_col='Date')
```

```
\# Perform the ADF test
result = adfuller(tsla_data['Close'])

\# Print the results
print('ADF Statistic: %f' % result[0])
print('p-value: %f' % result[1])
```

If the resulting p-value is less than a chosen significance level (typically 0.05), we reject the null hypothesis, indicating that the series is stationary. Conversely, failing to reject the null hypothesis suggests that the time series is non-stationary, and corrective steps are needed.

Differencing: A Pathway to Achieve Stationarity

When confronted with a non-stationary series, one of the most effective methods to convert it into a stationary series is the process of differencing. This technique involves calculating the differences between consecutive observations, effectively eliminating trends and seasonal patterns from the data.

For example, let's visualize differencing using a hypothetical dataset representing daily closing prices. The following Python code demonstrates how to calculate the first differences:

```python
# Calculate first differences tsla_data['Differenced'] = tsla_data['Close'].diff().dropna()

\# Plot the original and differenced series
import matplotlib.pyplot as plt

plt.figure(figsize=(14, 7))
plt.subplot(2, 1, 1)
plt.plot(tsla_data['Close'], label='Original Series', color='blue')
plt.title('Original TSLA Closing Prices')
plt.xlabel('Date')
```

```
plt.ylabel('Price (\()')
plt.legend()

plt.subplot(2, 1, 2)
plt.plot(tsla_data['Differenced'], label='Differenced Series', color='green')
plt.title('First Differencing of TSLA Closing Prices')
plt.xlabel('Date')
plt.ylabel('Difference (\))')
plt.legend()

plt.tight_layout()
plt.show()
```

The above plots provide a clear visual contrast between the original series and the differenced version, illustrating how differencing can effectively stabilize the mean and remove underlying trends.

In scenarios where the differenced series still demonstrates non-stationary characteristics, analysts can consider higher-order differencing—applying the differencing technique multiple times. However, caution is warranted, as excessive differencing might strip away valuable information from the data, resulting in overly complex models.

Testing for Stationarity After Differencing

After implementing differencing, it is vital to re-evaluate the time series for stationarity using the ADF test. This step ensures that the applied transformations have sufficiently purged the series of any non-stationary elements.

```python
# Perform ADF test on the differenced data
result_diff = adfuller(tsla_data['Differenced'].dropna())
print('ADF Statistic after Differencing: %f' % result_diff[0])
print('p-value after Differencing: %f' % result_diff[1])
```

If the differenced series yields a p-value below the specified threshold, we can conclude with confidence that the data is now stationary, thus paving the way for more sophisticated analysis and modeling.

Differencing transcends mere mathematical manipulation; it serves as a fundamental preparatory step in the analysis of time series data. Recognizing the importance of achieving stationarity equips analysts with the essential tools needed to build effective models that accurately reflect market dynamics. As we progress towards more intricate analytical techniques, a solid grasp of these foundational concepts will facilitate our exploration of the complex world of quantitative finance, ultimately enhancing our ability to make informed, data-driven financial decisions.

With a clear understanding of stationarity and the differencing technique now established, we are primed to uncover the deeper intricacies of time series data, including autocorrelation and advanced modeling approaches. This foundational knowledge dismantles the conventional tools typically relied upon by analysts, setting the stage for impactful decision-making grounded in robust statistical principles.

Autocorrelation and Partial Autocorrelation in Time Series Analysis

The Concept of Autocorrelation

Autocorrelation, the correlation of a time series with a delayed version of itself, serves as a foundational element in time series analysis. Essentially, it measures the extent to which the current value of a series is related to its past values. For financial analysts, such insights can be instrumental in pinpointing recurring cycles or trends, ultimately aiding the creation of more robust predictive models.

Consider the journey of Sarah, a quantitative analyst

immersed in a historical dataset of a well-known cryptocurrency. As she navigates through the fluctuating price points, she poses a pivotal question: **Are these price movements predictable? Is there a correlation between today's prices and those from yesterday or even earlier?** This curiosity is where the power of autocorrelation comes into play.

Calculation of Autocorrelation

The autocorrelation function (ACF) quantifies how values in a time series correlate at varying lags. A high autocorrelation at lag (k) indicates that understanding the value from (k) steps earlier can provide critical insights into the current value. The mathematical representation of autocorrelation for a time series (X) with mean (\mu) and variance (\sigma^2) is expressed as:

[\rho(k) = \frac{E[(X_t - \mu)(X_{t-k} - \mu)]}{\sigma^2}]

Where: - (\rho(k)) denotes the autocorrelation at lag (k) - (E) stands for the expected value - (X_t) represents the observation at time (t)

To illustrate the practical application of autocorrelation using Python's statsmodels library, let's compute and plot the ACF for a stock's closing prices.

```python
import pandas as pd import matplotlib.pyplot as plt from statsmodels.graphics.tsaplots import plot_acf

\# Load the stock price data
stock_data = pd.read_csv('AAPL_stock_data.csv', parse_dates=['Date'], index_col='Date')

\# Plot the ACF
plt.figure(figsize=(12, 6))
plot_acf(stock_data['Close'], lags=30)
plt.title('Autocorrelation Function of AAPL Closing Prices')
plt.xlabel('Lags')
plt.ylabel('Autocorrelation')
```

```
plt.show()
```

In examining this plot, we observe the autocorrelation values across various lags. For instance, a notable autocorrelation at lag (1) may indicate a strong connection between today's closing price and that of the previous day, potentially suggesting a momentum effect in the stock price.

Understanding Partial Autocorrelation

While autocorrelation offers a broad view of temporal influences, it often leaves out the nuances of how much each individual lag contributes uniquely to the overall correlation. This is where partial autocorrelation steps in. The partial autocorrelation function (PACF) provides a way to measure the correlation between observations separated by (k) time units, isolating the effects of all previous observations.

Following Sarah's analytical path, she contemplates: **Which portion of the correlation at lag (k) is independent of shorter lags?** This distinction is crucial for determining the appropriate order of autoregressive models.

Calculation of Partial Autocorrelation

Mathematically, the partial autocorrelation at lag (k) can be computed by estimating the regression of (X_t) on its past (k) values while accounting for all earlier values:

$$\phi(k) = E[X_t | X_{t-1}, X_{t-2}, \ldots, X_{t-k}]$$

To visualize the PACF, we can plot it for a given time series, as demonstrated in the following example:

```python
from statsmodels.graphics.tsaplots import plot_pacf

# Plot the PACF
plt.figure(figsize=(12, 6))
plot_pacf(stock_data['Close'], lags=30)
```

```
plt.title('Partial Autocorrelation Function of AAPL Closing Prices')
plt.xlabel('Lags')
plt.ylabel('Partial Autocorrelation')
plt.show()
```

This visual representation allows us to identify which lags are significantly contributing to the autocorrelation, guiding our model selection if we intend to use autoregressive integrated moving average (ARIMA) models.

Application in Model Selection

The insights garnered from ACF and PACF plots are instrumental in pinpointing the appropriate orders for ARIMA models:

- The **ACF** is key in identifying the **Moving Average (MA)** component of the model. A noticeable cutoff after a certain lag in the ACF indicates the order of the MA component.
- Conversely, the **PACF** assists in determining the **Autoregressive (AR)** component. A sharp decline in the PACF after a certain lag suggests the order of the AR term.

With our foundation in autocorrelation and partial autocorrelation established, we are well-prepared to explore more sophisticated aspects of time series analysis, including the implementation of ARIMA models in Python. This exploration is a critical step for any financial analyst aiming to thrive in today's fast-paced market environments.

ARIMA Models: Fundamentals and Practical Applications

Demystifying ARIMA: Key Components and Framework

An ARIMA model is built on three integral components, represented as ARIMA(p, d, q):

- **AR (Autoregressive)**: This component focuses on understanding the relationship between an observation and a series of prior observations (or "lags"). It helps identify patterns based on historical data points.
- **I (Integrated)**: Here, the aim is to make the time series stationary—a critical step for effective modeling. This involves differencing the data to remove trends or seasonality.
- **MA (Moving Average)**: This part models the relationship between an observation and the error term derived from lagged observations, allowing for the error's influence over time to be quantified.

The Significance of Stationarity

Before embarking on ARIMA modeling, it's crucial to understand the concept of stationarity. A stationary time series maintains consistent statistical properties—mean, variance, and autocorrelation—over time. If your data is non-stationary, it can lead to skewed results and unreliable forecasts. Therefore, the integrated part of ARIMA is essential for achieving stationarity through differencing techniques.

For example, let's examine a series of daily closing prices for a well-established blue-chip stock. If we observe increasing volatility, analysts might take first differences of the series to mitigate trends:

[Y_t = X_t - X_{t-1}]

This differenced series will showcase fluctuations without the influence of long-term trends, providing a clearer picture of underlying price movements.

Constructing an ARIMA Model

The journey to building an effective ARIMA model begins with parameter identification: (p), (d), and (q). This process can be facilitated through Autocorrelation Function (ACF) and Partial Autocorrelation Function (PACF) plots:

1. **Determining (d)**: The integer (d) indicates how many times the original data must be differenced to achieve stationarity. Techniques like the Augmented Dickey-Fuller test can assist in determining this value.
2. **Selecting (p) and (q)**: After establishing stationarity, analysts analyze ACF and PACF plots:
3. A sudden drop in the ACF plot suggests the MA order (q).
4. A sharp decline in the PACF plot points to the AR order (p).

Example: Building an ARIMA Model with Python

Let's walk through the process of creating an ARIMA model using Python, focusing on a dataset of monthly retail sales. We will first set up our environment and import the necessary libraries.

```python
import pandas as pd import numpy as np import matplotlib.pyplot as plt from statsmodels.tsa.stattools import adfuller from statsmodels.tsa.arima.model import ARIMA

\# Load the sample dataset
data = pd.read_csv('retail_sales.csv', parse_dates=['Date'], index_col='Date')
sales = data['Sales']

\# Visualizing the original data
plt.figure(figsize=(12, 6))
plt.plot(sales)
plt.title('Monthly Retail Sales')
plt.xlabel('Date')
plt.ylabel('Sales')
plt.show()
```

Assessing Stationarity with the Dickey-Fuller Test

Next, we conduct the Dickey-Fuller test to ascertain whether our time series is stationary:

```python def test_stationarity(timeseries): result = adfuller(timeseries) print('ADF Statistic:', result[0]) print('p-value:', result[1]) print('Critical Values:') for key, value in result[4].items(): print(f' {key}: {value:.3f}')

test_stationarity(sales)

```

A low p-value (typically < 0.05) indicates that the series is stationary. If the results suggest non-stationarity, we proceed with differencing:

```python sales_diff = sales.diff().dropna() test_stationarity(sales_diff)

```

Fitting the ARIMA Model

Once we confirm the stationarity of our differenced data, we can fit the ARIMA model. Let's assume our analysis leads us to select (p=1), (d=1), and (q=1).

```python model = ARIMA(sales, order=(1, 1, 1)) model_fit = model.fit()

\# Model summary
print(model_fit.summary())

```

The model summary provides valuable insights, including coefficient estimates, significance levels, and overall model fit statistics.

Generating Forecasts

The final step involves creating forecasts based on our fitted model:

```python
forecast = model_fit.forecast(steps=12) # Forecasting the next 12 months
plt.figure(figsize=(12, 6))
plt.plot(sales, label='Historical Sales')
plt.plot(forecast.index, forecast, label='Forecast', color='red')
plt.title('Forecasted Retail Sales')
plt.xlabel('Date')
plt.ylabel('Sales')
plt.legend()
plt.show()
```

Practical Applications of ARIMA in Finance

The utility of ARIMA models in quantitative finance is extensive, with a range of applications including:

- **Stock Price Forecasting**: Investors utilize ARIMA to estimate future stock prices based on historical trends, thereby crafting informed trading strategies.
- **Economic Indicator Prediction**: Economic analysts leverage ARIMA to project key metrics such as GDP and unemployment rates, supporting policymakers in their decision-making processes.
- **Risk Management**: Financial institutions employ ARIMA to model fluctuations in financial assets, aiding in the assessment of metrics like Value at Risk (VaR) to inform hedging strategies.

Grasping the concepts and implementation of ARIMA models is foundational for anyone venturing into the domain of quantitative finance. From discerning historical trends to forecasting future movements, ARIMA equips analysts with indispensable tools to navigate the complexities of financial data. As we explore the depths of quantitative methodologies, the principles outlined here will serve as a sturdy foundation for further exploration into advanced analytical techniques, empowering finance professionals to unearth actionable data-driven insights.

Demystifying Time Series Components

Time series decomposition entails breaking down a sequence of data points into its essential elements:

1. **Trend Component**: This segment reveals the overarching direction of the data over time, highlighting whether it is generally increasing, decreasing, or remaining stable.
2. **Seasonal Component**: Representing recurring patterns that manifest at regular intervals—be it daily, monthly, or quarterly—this component captures the cyclical dynamics of the data. A typical example is the increase in retail sales during December, driven by holiday shopping.
3. **Residual Component (or Irregular Component)**: This part accounts for the noise or randomness remaining after the trend and seasonal components have been extracted. It encompasses irregular fluctuations that are not tied to predictable seasonal changes or long-term trends.

The Importance of Seasonal Decomposition

In financial markets, neglecting seasonality can lead to misguided interpretations of data, potentially skewing investment decisions. For instance, if a financial analyst observes a surge in quarterly sales without considering seasonal effects, they might mistakenly conclude that a company's growth trajectory is consistently upward. Through seasonal decomposition, analysts can discern whether such spikes are typical seasonal patterns or indicative of more profound shifts in market dynamics.

Approaching Classical Decomposition

There are two primary models that define the classical method of seasonal decomposition:

1. **Additive Model**: This model is appropriate when the

changes in the trend and seasonal components are relatively constant over time. It is mathematically expressed as:

$$Y(t) = T(t) + S(t) + R(t)$$

Where: - ($Y(t)$) is the observed value, - ($T(t)$) represents the trend, - ($S(t)$) denotes the seasonal component, - ($R(t)$) is the residual.

1. **Multiplicative Model**: Ideal for situations in which seasonal variations are proportional to the magnitude of the data series. This model is defined as:

$$Y(t) = T(t) \times S(t) \times R(t)$$

By selecting the appropriate model, analysts can more accurately capture the underlying dynamics of the time series.

Implementing Seasonal Decomposition in Python

To exemplify the process of seasonal decomposition, let's work with a hypothetical dataset representing monthly sales figures for a retail store. Below, we outline the steps involved in this analysis using Python, harnessing the capabilities of libraries like pandas and statsmodels.

Step 1: Preparing the Environment

First, we need to set up our Python environment and load the relevant data:

```python
import pandas as pd import matplotlib.pyplot as plt from statsmodels.tsa.seasonal import seasonal_decompose

\# Load sample dataset containing monthly retail sales data
data = pd.read_csv('monthly_retail_sales.csv', parse_dates=['Date'], index_col='Date')

\# Confirm our data is structured as a time series
sales = data['Sales']
```

Step 2: Visualizing the Raw Data

Visual representation of the sales data enables us to discern any visible trends or seasonal patterns:

```python
plt.figure(figsize=(12, 6)) plt.plot(sales, label='Monthly Sales', color='blue') plt.title('Monthly Retail Sales Over Time') plt.xlabel('Date') plt.ylabel('Sales') plt.legend() plt.show()
```

Such a plot might reveal a discernible upward trend punctuated by seasonal spikes, especially around key retail periods.

Step 3: Conducting Seasonal Decomposition

Now, we can apply seasonal decomposition using the seasonal_decompose() function from statsmodels. To keep it straightforward, we will start with the additive model:

```python
result = seasonal_decompose(sales, model='additive') result.plot() plt.show()
```

The resulting visualizations typically delineate the trend, seasonal, and residual components, offering insights into the dynamics affecting the observed series:

- **Trend**: A smoothed curve illustrating long-term movement.
- **Seasonal**: Peaks and valleys corresponding to seasonal influences.
- **Residual**: Variability that remains after accounting for trends and seasonality.

Interpreting the Results

Imagine our decomposition reveals a conspicuous increase in sales every December alongside a gradual upward trajectory. Analysts can interpret this as evidence that holiday demand significantly boosts retail performance, while the overarching trend remains positive. Such detailed analysis can inform strategic decisions regarding inventory management or hiring practices, particularly as the holiday season approaches.

Practical Applications in Financial Analysis

The benefits of seasonal decomposition extend far beyond mere analysis, offering practical applications such as:

- **Forecasting Revenues**: Organizations can leverage identified seasonal patterns to formulate precise revenue forecasts for better financial planning.
- **Identifying Anomalies**: Deviations from expected seasonal trends can signal operational challenges, shifts in consumer behavior, or broader economic impacts that warrant immediate scrutiny.
- **Investment Timing**: Investors can analyze seasonal trends within industries like retail or tourism to optimize their market entries and maximize potential returns.

Seasonal decomposition serves as a vital tool for financial analysts eager to navigate the complexities of time series data. As we further explore the intricate relationships within quantitative finance, the methodologies discussed here lay a solid foundation for advanced analytical strategies that are poised to shape the future of financial analysis.

GARCH Models for Volatility Forecasting

Understanding Volatility in Finance

Volatility represents the degree of variation in the returns of a financial instrument over a specific time frame. It serves as an indicator of risk—high volatility signals greater uncertainty, while low volatility typically indicates a more stable investment environment. A common misconception is that volatility remains constant; however, financial markets often display heightened uncertainty during periods of economic distress, leading to patterns of volatility clustering. GARCH models adeptly capture these fluctuations, enabling analysts to forge more accurate risk assessments and formulate effective trading strategies.

The Framework of GARCH Models

GARCH models were originally developed by Robert Engle and later expanded by Tim Bollerslev, building on the foundations of autoregressive integrated moving average (ARIMA) models. What sets GARCH apart is its ability to integrate prior variances into the modeling process. Specifically, GARCH posits that future volatility is influenced not only by recent observations but also by past volatility itself. The fundamental structure of a GARCH(p,q) model is articulated through the equation:

$$\sigma_t^2 = \alpha_0 + \sum_{i=1}^{p} \alpha_i \epsilon_{t-i}^2 + \sum_{j=1}^{q} \beta_j \sigma_{t-j}^2$$

Where: - (σ_t^2) denotes the conditional variance (the square of volatility) at time (t), - (α_0) is a constant, - (ϵ_{t-i}) symbolizes previous error terms, and - (α_i) and (β_j) are coefficients that must be estimated.

In this context, (p) stands for the number of lagged error terms, while (q) indicates the number of lagged volatility terms.

Implementing GARCH Models in Python

To illustrate the practical implementation of GARCH models, we will utilize Python's arch library, a powerful tool crafted for econometric analysis. Below, we outline a step-by-step approach using a hypothetical dataset of daily stock returns.

Step 1: Setting Up Your Environment

Begin by ensuring you have the necessary libraries at your disposal and importing your dataset. You can install the arch library with the following command:

```bash
pip install arch
```

Next, create a script that imports the essential libraries and reads your stock return data:

```python
import pandas as pd
import numpy as np
import matplotlib.pyplot as plt
from arch import arch_model

# Load sample dataset of daily stock returns
data = pd.read_csv('daily_stock_returns.csv', parse_dates=['Date'], index_col='Date')
returns = data['Returns']
```

Step 2: Visualizing the Returns

Before diving into modeling, visualizing the dataset is crucial for identifying trends and anomalies:

```python
plt.figure(figsize=(12, 6))
plt.plot(returns, label='Daily Stock Returns', color='purple')
plt.title('Daily Stock Returns')
plt.xlabel('Date')
plt.ylabel('Returns')
plt.axhline(y=0, color='black', linestyle='--')
plt.legend()
plt.show()
```

This graphical representation establishes a foundation for comprehending the volatility characteristics inherent in the return series.

Step 3: Fitting a GARCH Model

Next, we will fit a GARCH(1,1) model, which has proven effective in capturing volatility clustering due to its straightforward yet potent structure:

```python
# Instantiate the GARCH model
model = arch_model(returns, vol='Garch', p=1, q=1)

# Fit the model
garch_fit = model.fit(disp='off')
print(garch_fit.summary())
```

```

Using the summary() method reveals critical insights, including estimated coefficients for the model parameters, their significance levels, and various goodness-of-fit metrics.

*Step 4: Analyzing the Model Results*

Examining the estimated coefficients is essential:

- **(\alpha_0)**: Represents the baseline level of volatility; a higher value may suggest a more turbulent market.
- **(\alpha_1)**: Reflects the impact of past squared returns (or shocks). A prominent positive value indicates that past shocks can have prolonged effects on current volatility.
- **(\beta_1)**: Illustrates how previous volatility informs current conditions. A significant and elevated (\beta_1) suggests that past volatility has a meaningful influence on future volatility.

These insights are invaluable when evaluating the risk exposure connected to specific trading strategies.

## Forecasting Future Volatility

Once your GARCH model is fitted, it can be employed to generate volatility forecasts. Here's how:

```python
# Generate volatility forecasts for the next 5 days forecast = garch_fit.forecast(horizon=5) predicted_volatility = forecast.variance.values[-1, :] predicted_volatility = np.sqrt(predicted_volatility) # Converting variance to standard deviation

print("Predicted Volatility for the next 5 days:", predicted_volatility)
```

These forecasts provide key input for trading strategies and risk management, allowing market participants to preemptively adjust their positions based on anticipated
```

market dynamics.

Practical Applications of GARCH Models

GARCH models extend far beyond theoretical constructs; they hold significant relevance across various financial applications, including:

1. **Risk Management**: Financial institutions utilize GARCH models to determine Value at Risk (VaR), a critical metric for assessing potential portfolio losses.
2. **Options Pricing**: Precise volatility forecasts serve to enhance the accuracy of options pricing models, where volatility is a pivotal determinant of value.
3. **Portfolio Optimization**: A comprehensive understanding of volatility risk enables better asset allocation strategies tailored to investors' individual risk profiles.
4. **Trading Strategies**: Traders can devise strategies that capitalize on expected volatility, optimizing entry and exit points based on the anticipated market shifts.

GARCH models stand as indispensable tools for navigating the complexities of volatility prediction and management in financial markets. As we delve deeper into the sophisticated realms of quantitative finance, mastering techniques such as GARCH modeling will be vital in harnessing the dynamic nature of markets and achieving financial success. Through the effective application of GARCH models, we position ourselves to adeptly navigate and master the inherent complexities of the financial landscape.

The Importance of Cross-Validation in Time Series

Cross-validation plays a pivotal role in assessing how well a predictive model will generalize to unseen data.

Traditional techniques like k-fold validation can mislead analysts when applied to time series data; random shuffling disrupts the temporal relationships, effectively allowing the model to "look into the future" when making predictions. Such practices lead to overly optimistic performance estimates that don't reflect reality. Thus, time series cross-validation methods are essential for preserving the order of data and providing a more genuine assessment of model performance.

Methods for Time Series Cross-Validation

Rolling Forecast Origin

The rolling forecast is a widely adopted method for validating time series models and closely mirrors real-world forecasting. This approach consists of fitting a model to an expanding dataset as new data becomes available, thus allowing predictions for the next time point. This technique offers a realistic emulation of how financial forecasting operates.

For example, consider daily stock price data: you might use the first year of data as your training set to predict the stock price for the day immediately following that period. Once you've made that prediction, you incorporate the result into your training set, moving forward in time as you predict each subsequent day's stock price.

Implementation Example

We can see how this is practically implemented using Python's pandas and sklearn libraries. Below is a step-by-step guide to executing a rolling forecast validation.

1. **Load the Data**

Start by loading your time series data. In this example, we'll use a hypothetical dataset comprising daily stock prices.

```python
import pandas as pd

# Load daily stock prices
data = pd.read_csv('daily_stock_prices.csv', parse_dates=['Date'], index_col='Date')
prices = data['Close']
```

1. **Define the Rolling Forecast Function**

We'll define a function that generates rolling forecasts and computes performance metrics, such as the Mean Absolute Error (MAE):

```python
from sklearn.metrics import mean_absolute_error

def rolling_forecast(prices, train_size, forecast_size):
    errors = []
    for i in range(train_size, len(prices) - forecast_size + 1):
        train = prices[i - train_size:i]
        test = prices[i:i + forecast_size]

        # Simple predictive model: use the last observed price
        prediction = train.iloc[-1] # Last price as a prediction
        errors.append(mean_absolute_error(test, [prediction] * forecast_size))
    return errors
```

1. **Apply the Rolling Forecast**

Now, let's use our function to generate forecast errors:

```python
train_size = 252 # Roughly equivalent to one trading year
forecast_size = 1 # Predicting one day ahead
forecast_errors = rolling_forecast(prices, train_size, forecast_size)

# Calculate the mean error across all forecasting steps
mean_error = sum(forecast_errors) / len(forecast_errors)
```

```
    print(f'Mean Absolute Error over rolling forecasts: {mean_error:.2f}')
```

By employing this method, we ensure that the model incorporates the most relevant historical data while preserving the natural order of observations.

Expanding Window

The expanding window technique, while similar to the rolling forecast, utilizes all available historical data up to a specific point to make predictions. With every new prediction, all prior observations remain part of the training set. This is particularly advantageous for capturing trends or evolving patterns over time.

Model Selection and Validation

Choosing the right model is crucial when working with time series data. Common contenders include ARIMA (AutoRegressive Integrated Moving Average), Exponential Smoothing State Space Model (ETS), and modern techniques such as Long Short-Term Memory (LSTM) networks. Evaluating these models through the aforementioned time series cross-validation methods is vital for understanding their predictive capabilities.

After identifying a strong candidate model, employing grid search in conjunction with time series cross-validation can help fine-tune its hyperparameters. This systematic approach helps to identify configurations that maximize performance while minimizing the risk of overfitting.

Performance Metrics for Time Series Models

Beyond Mean Absolute Error, various performance metrics provide deeper insights into model efficacy during time series cross-validation:

- **Mean Squared Error (MSE)**: This metric emphasizes

larger errors by squaring deviations, making it particularly valuable in scenarios where significant errors can have profound financial implications.

- **Root Mean Squared Error (RMSE)**: By taking the square root of MSE, RMSE expresses errors in the same units as the predicted values, offering a more intuitive understanding of model performance.
- **Mean Absolute Percentage Error (MAPE)**: This metric allows errors to be expressed as a percentage, making it easier to compare performance across datasets with differing scales.

Proficiently mastering time series cross-validation empowers financial analysts to develop robust predictive models that accurately reflect real-world data dynamics.

Forecasting Techniques

Picture yourself in a lively café in London, the rich scent of freshly brewed coffee filling the air as you navigate through swathes of stock price data on your laptop. Each flicker of your screen communicates more than mere numbers; it signals potential decisions—whether to buy, sell, or hold. Mastering forecasting techniques allows you to transform those raw figures into meaningful insights, guiding you toward intelligent, data-driven choices.

Moving averages stand as one of the most straightforward yet effective forecasting techniques. For instance, if you're interested in forecasting the price of Company X's stock for the upcoming week, a 30-day moving average can be a valuable tool, leveraging the past month's closing prices to help gauge future trends.

Utilizing Python's **Pandas** library, calculating moving averages becomes a seamless task. Here's how you can do it:

```python import pandas as pd import numpy as np import matplotlib.pyplot as plt
```

```
\# Load historical stock data
data = pd.read_csv('company_x_stock_data.csv')
data['Date'] = pd.to_datetime(data['Date'])

\# Calculate the 30-day moving average
data['Moving_Average'] = data['Close'].rolling(window=30).mean()

\# Plotting the results
plt.figure(figsize=(14, 7))
plt.plot(data['Date'], data['Close'], label='Close Price', color='blue')
plt.plot(data['Date'], data['Moving_Average'], label='30-Day Moving
Average', color='orange')
plt.title('Company X Stock Price and 30-Day Moving Average')
plt.xlabel('Date')
plt.ylabel('Price')
plt.legend()
plt.show()
```

With this visualization, the moving average reveals the stock price's trajectory, illuminating potential support and resistance levels essential for crafting your trading strategy.

*2. **Exponential Smoothing: Prioritizing Recent Data***

While moving averages provide valuable insights, they assign equal weight to all past data, which can dilute the significance of recent trends. Enter **Exponential Smoothing**, a method that gives greater emphasis to more recent data through the application of exponentially declining weights. This technique is particularly advantageous when the latest data are more predictive of future price movements.

You can implement exponential smoothing effortlessly in Python using the statsmodels library:

```python
from statsmodels.tsa.holtwinters import ExponentialSmoothing

\# Fit the model
```

```
model = ExponentialSmoothing(data['Close'], trend='add', seasonal='add', seasonal_periods=12)
model_fit = model.fit()
data['ES Forecast'] = model_fit.fittedvalues

\# Visualize the forecast
plt.figure(figsize=(14, 7))
plt.plot(data['Date'], data['Close'], label='Close Price', color='blue')
plt.plot(data['Date'], data['ES Forecast'], label='Exponential Smoothing Forecast', color='green')
plt.title('Exponential Smoothing Forecast for Company X')
plt.xlabel('Date')
plt.ylabel('Price')
plt.legend()
plt.show()
```

This graph illustrates how exponential smoothing provides a dynamic view of anticipated price movements, reinforcing the relevance of recent trends in decision-making.

3. ARIMA Models: Capturing Data Relationships

As we delve deeper into forecasting methodologies, we encounter **ARIMA** (AutoRegressive Integrated Moving Average) models, essential for understanding intricate patterns within time series data. ARIMA allows us to model and predict future values by capturing seasonality and historical dependencies.

Suppose you've been analyzing quarterly sales data for a retail company. An ARIMA model would enable you to effectively forecast future sales by following these critical steps:

1. **Differencing** the data to achieve stationarity.
2. Identifying optimal parameters (p, d, q) for the model.
3. Fitting the ARIMA model and making predictions.

Here's an example utilizing Python's statsmodels library:

```python
from statsmodels.tsa.arima.model import ARIMA

\# Fit an ARIMA model (p=1, d=1, q=1)
model_arima = ARIMA(data['Close'], order=(1, 1, 1))
model_arima_fit = model_arima.fit()

\# Generate forecast
forecast = model_arima_fit.forecast(steps=10)
print(forecast)

\# Visualize the forecast compared to actual data
plt.figure(figsize=(14, 7))
plt.plot(data['Date'], data['Close'], label='Close Price', color='blue')
plt.plot(pd.date_range(start=data['Date'].iloc[-1], periods=11,
freq='D')[1:], forecast, label='ARIMA Forecast', color='red')
plt.title('ARIMA Forecast for Company X')
plt.xlabel('Date')
plt.ylabel('Price')
plt.legend()
plt.show()
```

This visualization not only highlights the actual stock prices but also showcases the ARIMA model's capability to predict future values based on historical trends, providing a robust framework for forecasting.

4. Machine Learning Approaches: Embracing Complexity

With advancements in technology, the incorporation of machine learning into forecasting has become increasingly vital. Techniques such as **Random Forests** and **Neural Networks** allow us to utilize historical data as features, enabling models to capture complex patterns that may elude traditional statistical methods. Libraries like Scikit-Learn and TensorFlow are invaluable in building such predictive models.

For example, consider implementing a Random Forest model to predict stock price movements based on multiple input features:

```python
from sklearn.model_selection import train_test_split
from sklearn.ensemble import RandomForestRegressor
from sklearn.metrics import mean_squared_error

# Create features and label
X = data[['feature1', 'feature2', 'feature3']]
y = data['Close']

# Train-test split
X_train, X_test, y_train, y_test = train_test_split(X, y, test_size=0.2, random_state=42)

# Fit Random Forest model
rf = RandomForestRegressor(n_estimators=100)
rf.fit(X_train, y_train)

# Predictions
predictions = rf.predict(X_test)

# Evaluate the model
mse = mean_squared_error(y_test, predictions)
print(f'Mean Squared Error: {mse}')
```

This example illustrates how machine learning can unveil intricate relationships within data, leading to more precise forecasts and informed trading decisions.

The quest for accurate forecasting transcends mere number crunching; it requires a profound understanding of market dynamics coupled with statistical principles. As we explored techniques ranging from simple moving averages that illuminate trends, to sophisticated ARIMA models and machine learning methods, each approach contributes uniquely to our forecasting toolkit.

At the core of every forecasting endeavor lies the aspiration to mitigate uncertainty and empower strategic decision-making. Through the techniques presented, you'll be equipped to grasp market intricacies, devise well-informed strategies, and pursue your financial goals more effectively. In the upcoming section, we will integrate these forecasting methods into a practical case study, completing our journey into the world of financial forecasting.

Evaluating Forecast Accuracy in Quantitative Finance

Picture yourself in a lively café on Wall Street, immersed in the rhythm of the financial heartbeat. The hushed conversations of traders and the distant chime of stock tickers create an atmosphere ripe with potential. Amid this ambiance, your laptop hums softly as you scrutinize a stock price forecast —a pivotal element in plotting your next trading move. As you ponder your predictions, the vital question arises: "How accurate are these forecasts?" Let's embark on a journey to uncover reliable metrics that unveil the effectiveness of your forecasting methods.

Starting off with one of the most intuitive and widely recognized metrics, Mean Absolute Error (MAE) offers a straightforward approach to understanding forecast accuracy. MAE calculates the average absolute deviation between predicted and actual values, providing a clear snapshot of prediction reliability.

Mathematically, the formula for MAE is expressed as:

[MAE = \frac{1}{n} \sum_{i=1}^{n} |y_i - \hat{y}_i|]

In this equation, (y_i) represents actual values, (\hat{y}_i) denotes predicted values, and (n) is the total number of forecasts.

Let's see how to implement MAE using Python with our stock price predictions:

```python import numpy as np
```

```
\# Actual and predicted stock prices
actual_prices = np.array([100, 102, 101, 105, 104])
predicted_prices = np.array([98, 103, 100, 107, 102])

\# Calculate Mean Absolute Error
mae = np.mean(np.abs(actual_prices - predicted_prices))

print(f'Mean Absolute Error: {mae}')
```

A smaller MAE indicates a closer alignment between predictions and actual results, conveying a high degree of reliability.

2. Mean Squared Error (MSE)

Next, we consider the Mean Squared Error (MSE), which enhances the sensitivity of error measurement. This metric squares the differences between predicted and actual values before averaging, thus assigning greater weight to larger discrepancies.

Mathematically, the formulation for MSE is:

[MSE = \frac{1}{n} \sum_{i=1}^{n} (y_i - \hat{y}_i)^2]

We can compute MSE using Python as follows:

```python # Calculate Mean Squared Error mse = np.mean((actual_prices - predicted_prices) ** 2)

print(f'Mean Squared Error: {mse}')

```

While a lower MSE indicates better forecasting performance, it is essential to keep in mind its dependence on the scale of the data.

3. Root Mean Squared Error (RMSE)

To return MSE to its original measurement scale, we often compute the Root Mean Squared Error (RMSE). This metric is defined as the square root of MSE, offering an interpretable gauge of accuracy in the context of the dependent variable.

The formula for RMSE is:

$$RMSE = \sqrt{MSE}$$

Incorporating RMSE into our Python code could look like this:

```python
# Calculate Root Mean Squared Error
rmse = np.sqrt(mse)
print(f'Root Mean Squared Error: {rmse}')
```

Much like MSE, a lower RMSE suggests a better fit of the forecast to the actual data.

4. Mean Absolute Percentage Error (MAPE)

For those keen on expressing accuracy in percentage terms, the Mean Absolute Percentage Error (MAPE) provides an excellent alternative. MAPE conveys the magnitude of the error as a percentage, facilitating a relative assessment of accuracy against the predicted values.

The calculation for MAPE is given by the formula:

$$MAPE = \frac{100}{n} \sum_{i=1}^{n} \left| \frac{y_i - \hat{y}_i}{y_i} \right|$$

Here's how to implement MAPE in Python:

```python
# Calculate Mean Absolute Percentage Error
mape = np.mean(np.abs((actual_prices - predicted_prices) / actual_prices)) * 100
print(f'Mean Absolute Percentage Error: {mape}%')
```

MAPE allows for intuitive understanding of forecasting performance, though caution is warranted when actual values approach zero, as this can skew the results.

5. Visualizing Errors

Beyond numerical metrics, visualizations can greatly enhance our understanding of forecast accuracy. Residual plots, which plot predicted values on the x-axis against residuals on the y-axis, can reveal patterns or issues related to linearity and constant variance assumptions in time series data.

Here's how you can create a residual plot in Python using Matplotlib:

```python
import matplotlib.pyplot as plt

\# Compute residuals
residuals = actual_prices - predicted_prices

\# Create a residual plot
plt.scatter(predicted_prices, residuals)
plt.axhline(0, color='red', linestyle='--')
plt.title('Residuals vs. Predicted Prices')
plt.xlabel('Predicted Prices')
plt.ylabel('Residuals')
plt.show()
```

A random dispersal of points around the horizontal line at zero suggests a well-fitted model, while identifiable patterns in the residuals may indicate the need for further model refinement.

Navigating the financial landscape demands a robust grasp of forecast accuracy.

As we move forward, we will explore how these forecasting insights can be seamlessly integrated into trading strategies, laying the groundwork for smart, data-driven market participation. With a well-defined evaluation framework in hand, you are now more empowered to navigate the complexities of quantitative finance with renewed confidence.

Case Study: Forecasting Stock Prices

Introduction to Stock Price Forecasting

In today's fast-paced financial landscape, the ability to

accurately forecast stock prices is essential for crafting informed investment strategies. The art of price prediction transcends mere academic interest; it can significantly influence financial outcomes, determining whether an investor reaps rewards or incurs losses. This case study will guide you through the process of using historical data to forecast future stock prices, harnessing statistical techniques and Python programming for deep, insightful analysis.

Before we embark on the forecasting journey, we must first familiarize ourselves with the data landscape. Stock prices are influenced by myriad factors, including market sentiment, economic indicators, breaking news, and company performance. For our analysis, we'll focus on the historical daily closing prices of AAPL over the past five years, enabling us to identify patterns and relationships critical for accurate predictions.

Using Python's yfinance library, we can seamlessly download and visualize AAPL's stock price data. The following code snippet illustrates this process:

```python
import yfinance as yf import matplotlib.pyplot as plt

\# Downloading historical data for Apple Inc.
aapl_data = yf.download("AAPL", start="2018-01-01", end="2023-01-01")

\# Plotting the closing prices
plt.figure(figsize=(14, 7))
plt.plot(aapl_data['Close'], label='AAPL Closing Prices', color='blue')
plt.title('AAPL Stock Prices (2018-2023)')
plt.xlabel('Date')
plt.ylabel('Price (USD)')
plt.legend()
plt.grid()
plt.show()
```

```
```

This visualization provides a vivid depiction of AAPL's price movements, highlighting periods of growth and volatility that will inform our forecasting techniques.

2. Exploratory Data Analysis (EDA)

With our data in hand, we now turn to Exploratory Data Analysis (EDA), a vital step in understanding our dataset's structure and intricacies. This process involves identifying trends, seasonal behaviors, and any irregularities present in the data. For instance, implementing a simple moving average (SMA) offers valuable insights into long-term trends. Here's how to calculate and visualize a 30-day SMA in Python:

```python
# Calculating the 30-day Simple Moving Average aapl_data['SMA_30'] = aapl_data['Close'].rolling(window=30).mean()

\# Plotting the closing prices with SMA
plt.figure(figsize=(14, 7))
plt.plot(aapl_data['Close'], label='AAPL Closing Prices', color='blue')
plt.plot(aapl_data['SMA_30'], label='30-Day SMA', color='orange')
plt.title('AAPL Stock Prices with 30-Day SMA')
plt.xlabel('Date')
plt.ylabel('Price (USD)')
plt.legend()
plt.grid()
plt.show()
```

This chart not only allows us to see AAPL's price behavior but also helps us discern whether the stock is experiencing an upward or downward trend, while contextualizing price fluctuations over time.

3. Choosing the Right Forecasting Model

Selecting an appropriate forecasting model is crucial in our stock price prediction endeavor. While various models exist—ARIMA, Exponential Smoothing, and even advanced machine learning techniques like Linear Regression and LSTM—we will concentrate on the ARIMA (AutoRegressive Integrated Moving Average) model due to its proven efficacy in time series forecasting.

Before proceeding with ARIMA, we need to ensure our data is stationary, meaning its statistical properties remain constant over time. We can accomplish this by conducting the Augmented Dickey-Fuller (ADF) test:

```python
from statsmodels.tsa.stattools import adfuller

\# Performing ADF test
result = adfuller(aapl_data['Close'])
print('ADF Statistic:', result[0])
print('p-value:', result[1])
```

If the p-value is below 0.05, we can confidently reject the null hypothesis, indicating that our data is stationary. If not, we may need to employ differencing or other transformation techniques to achieve stationarity.

4. Fitting the ARIMA Model

Having established that our data is stationary, we can now fit the ARIMA model. Below is a detailed explanation of setting up the ARIMA(1,1,1) model, where the initial 1 denotes the lag order, the second 1 indicates the degree of differencing, and the last 1 reflects the size of the moving average window:

```python
from statsmodels.tsa.arima.model import ARIMA

\# Fitting the ARIMA model
model = ARIMA(aapl_data['Close'], order=(1, 1, 1))
model_fit = model.fit()

\# Summary of the model
print(model_fit.summary())
```

```
```

After fitting the model, we evaluate its performance through diagnostic plots, allowing us to assess the residuals and verify that our model satisfies standard assumptions.

5. Making Predictions

With our model trained, we can shift our focus to making predictions. It's common to forecast future values based on the fitted ARIMA model, achieved through the following command:

```python
# Forecasting the next 10 days
forecast = model_fit.get_forecast(steps=10)
forecast_index = pd.date_range(start=aapl_data.index[-1] + pd.Timedelta(days=1), periods=10, freq='B') # Business days only
forecast_values = forecast.predicted_mean

\# Plotting the results
plt.figure(figsize=(14, 7))
plt.plot(aapl_data['Close'], label='AAPL Closing Prices', color='blue')
plt.plot(forecast_index, forecast_values, label='Forecasted Prices', color='red')
plt.title('Forecasting AAPL Stock Prices')
plt.xlabel('Date')
plt.ylabel('Price (USD)')
plt.legend()
plt.grid()
plt.show()
```

This forecast visually illustrates potential future price trajectories, and including confidence intervals provides insight into the model's uncertainty.

6. Evaluating Forecast Accuracy

It is essential to evaluate our forecasting accuracy by comparing predictions with actual historical prices. Utilizing metrics such as Mean Absolute Error (MAE), Mean Squared Error (MSE), Root Mean Squared Error (RMSE), and Mean Absolute Percentage Error (MAPE) allows us to rigorously assess the model's performance and reliability.

This case study on forecasting AAPL stock prices illustrates a comprehensive approach to financial data analysis, encompassing data collection, exploration, prediction, and evaluation. It highlights the critical nature of forecasting—not as a mere technical skill but as an essential part of navigating market dynamics.

As you advance your skills in quantitative finance, keep in mind that data-driven decision-making is paramount. With Python at your side, your ability to extract meaningful insights from historical data will empower you to engage confidently in the world of finance, transforming the concept of forecasting into a pragmatic tool for success.

CHAPTER 4: MULTI-FACTOR MODELS

The advent of multi-factor models was a response to the limitations inherent in the Capital Asset Pricing Model (CAPM), which fundamentally links expected returns to a lone market risk factor—the market portfolio. While CAPM provides valuable insights, the complexity of real-world financial dynamics necessitated a more comprehensive approach. Imagine a bustling financial institution where analysts vigilantly monitor a spectrum of market sectors impacted by diverse economic variables, such as inflation rates, interest rates, and company-specific developments. In recognizing this complexity, researchers developed multi-factor models to offer a more substantial framework for capturing the realities of market behavior.

Pioneering research by Fama and French introduced the three-factor model, which extended CAPM's framework by incorporating size and value factors alongside market risk. This groundbreaking development revealed that small-cap stocks and value-driven equities often outperformed their larger and growth-oriented counterparts over time. As academic inquiry progressed, models like the Carhart four-factor model emerged, further enriching the toolkit available to finance professionals.

Understanding Factor Exposure

Central to the functionality of multi-factor models is the concept of factor exposure, which refers to an asset's sensitivity to the performance fluctuations of various factors. These factors can be broadly categorized into style factors (value versus growth), sector factors (technology versus healthcare), and macroeconomic factors (interest rates, economic growth). To illustrate, let's delve deeper into the Fama-French model.

In the **Fama-French Three-Factor Model**, the expected return ($E(R_i)$) of an asset (i) can be articulated as follows:

$$E(R_i) = R_f + \beta_{1}(E(R_m) - R_f) + \beta_{2}SMB + \beta_{3}HML$$

Where: - (R_f) signifies the risk-free rate, - (β_{1}) denotes the asset's sensitivity to market risk (the excess return of the market over the risk-free rate), - (SMB) (Small Minus Big) quantifies the historical excess return of small-cap stocks over their large-cap counterparts, - (HML) (High Minus Low) illustrates the performance differential between high and low book-to-market stocks.

This equation exemplifies how an asset's return can be methodically predicted based on its responsiveness to broader market conditions and specific factors.

To bring these concepts to life, envision an investor analyzing the performance of two different mutual funds: one concentrated on small-cap growth stocks, and the other dedicated to large-cap value stocks.

Constructing Factor Models

The foundation of a multi-factor model lies in the identification of relevant factors. This selection process may employ domain expertise, empirical evidence, or established academic theories. Once the factors are identified, historical data is gathered to analyze their relationships with asset returns. This leads to the practical step of developing a regression framework.

Utilizing Python's robust libraries, such as statsmodels, facilitates the execution of multiple regression analyses. Below is a concise example demonstrating how to construct a simple multi-factor model that takes into account market, size, and value factors:

```python
import pandas as pd import statsmodels.api as sm

# Assuming df is a DataFrame containing historical excess returns of a portfolio and our factors
# Columns: 'Excess_Return', 'Market_Excess', 'SMB', 'HML'

# Define dataset
X = df[['Market_Excess', 'SMB', 'HML']]
y = df['Excess_Return']

# Adding a constant for the intercept
X = sm.add_constant(X)

# Fitting the multi-factor model
model = sm.OLS(y, X).fit()

# Model summary
print(model.summary())
```

This code snippet constructs a statistical model that estimates how each factor contributes to the portfolio's excess returns. The output will yield critical statistics, including (R^2) values, indicating the model's goodness of fit and the significance of each factor.

Backtesting Factor Strategies

After a multi-factor model is established, the logical next step is to implement and backtest factor-based investment strategies. This entails simulating how an investment portfolio would have performed over historical periods while employing signals derived from the identified factors.

For instance, consider our investor who wishes to adopt a strategy focused on high book-to-market stocks, representing a value investment approach.

The asset management landscape is constantly evolving, with multi-factor models positioned at the forefront of this transformation. As we navigate the complexities of today's financial markets, leveraging a framework that considers multiple influences allows analysts and investors to strategize with enhanced confidence.

Factor Exposure and Risk Premia

Navigating the intricacies of multi-factor models is much like deciphering the fine print of a complex financial contract. In this context, "factors" refer to the core elements that drive asset returns, while "risk premia" signify the extra returns that investors anticipate for embracing the risks associated with these factors. Join us as we embark on a detailed exploration of these concepts, highlighting their practical relevance in quantitative finance.

Understanding Factor Exposure

Factor exposure gauges the sensitivity of an asset—or an entire portfolio—to various risk factors. Essentially, it quantifies how an asset's returns are likely to respond to fluctuations in underlying economic indicators. These factors can span broad macroeconomic elements—like inflation and interest rates—to particular characteristics tied to individual firms, including growth potential and market valuations.

To illustrate, let's consider a large-cap technology stock. This asset may exhibit positive exposure to the technology sector factor, suggesting that when the sector thrives, the stock's returns are likely to rise. However, it could also show negative exposure to interest rate changes; as rates increase, growth stocks often face pressure due to market shifts favoring value stocks.

Mathematically, factor exposure can be articulated through regression analysis, represented by the following equation:

$$R_i = \alpha_i + \beta_1 F_1 + \beta_2 F_2 + \ldots + \beta_n F_n + \epsilon$$

In this equation: - R_i denotes the return of asset i, - α_i represents the asset's alpha (the excess return beyond the factor model), - β_j signifies the asset's sensitivity to factor j, - F_j denotes the return on factor j, - ϵ encapsulates the error term, accounting for idiosyncratic risk.

Unearthing Risk Premia

Risk premia represent the compensation investors seek for shouldering additional risks linked to specific factors. In simpler terms, they reflect the expected returns that exceed the risk-free rate, compensating investors for the uncertainty connected with asset returns relative to each given factor. Since each factor carries its unique risk profile, the associated premia can vary significantly.

Take, for instance, the value premium, which illustrates the historical trend of value stocks—those priced low relative to their earnings—outperforming their growth counterparts over time. This phenomenon can be interpreted as a market reward for investing in companies that may not have the glamorous appeal of growth stocks but offer potential for substantial returns relative to their risks.

Within the context of the Fama-French model, the expected return for an asset can be summarized as follows:

$$E(R_i) = R_f + \beta_{market}(E(R_m) - R_f) + \beta_{SMB}(E(SMB)) + \beta_{HML}(E(HML))$$

This equation underscores how analysts can quantify the anticipated return of an asset while factoring in the inherent risks associated with each identified factor.

Application in Portfolio Management

Comprehending factor exposure is crucial for investors aiming to construct and manage robust portfolios. For example, if an investor identifies a significant exposure to the value factor in their portfolio, they might anticipate higher average returns. However, they must also brace for heightened volatility, particularly during market conditions that adversely affect value-oriented assets.

To effectively integrate these concepts into investment strategies, strong analytical frameworks are essential. Python serves as an invaluable tool in this regard, allowing for streamlined calculations of factor exposure using historical datasets. Here's a simplified illustration of how this approach can be implemented:

```python
import pandas as pd
import statsmodels.api as sm

\# Sample Data: Imaginary DataFrame containing asset returns and corresponding factor returns
data = {
    'Asset_Returns': [0.02, 0.03, 0.015, 0.06, 0.07, 0.02, 0.04],
    'Market_Returns': [0.01, 0.04, 0.03, 0.05, 0.071, 0.022, 0.038],
    'SMB': [0.005, -0.004, 0.001, 0.002, 0.003, 0.005, 0.006],
    'HML': [-0.001, 0.003, 0.002, 0.001, -0.002, 0.009, 0.002],
}

\# Converting data into a DataFrame
df = pd.DataFrame(data)

\# Defining the independent variables (factors)
X = df[['Market_Returns', 'SMB', 'HML']]
y = df['Asset_Returns']

\# Adding a constant for the intercept
X = sm.add_constant(X)

\# Fitting a regression model to calculate factor exposures
model = sm.OLS(y, X).fit()
```

```
\# Displaying the model summary with factor exposures (betas)
print(model.summary())
```

The output from this analysis will provide the coefficients related to each factor, illuminating the asset's exposures to market risk, size, and value factors. These coefficients reveal how sensitive the asset is to variations in each specific factor, aptly clarifying the nature of these relationships.

The Interplay of Factor Exposure and Strategy Evaluation

Grasping both factor exposure and risk premia offers a significant strategic advantage in evaluating investment approaches. Investors equipped with the ability to accurately assess these elements can devise sophisticated strategies that effectively balance risk and return. For instance, if an investor targets growth stocks—characterized by their heightened exposure to growth factors—they must be mindful that the rewards represented by the growth premium need to surpass the accompanying volatility risks.

In conclusion, mapping out the complicated landscape of factor exposure and risk premia not only enhances our theoretical understanding but also provides investors and analysts with the actionable insights necessary for informed portfolio management decisions. As we move forward, we'll delve deeper into constructing factor models and the practical application of these frameworks within Python, equipping you with vital skills for success in quantitative finance.

Constructing Factor Models

Embarking on the journey of constructing factor models in quantitative finance unveils a wealth of insights into asset returns and their correlation with underlying risk factors. These models serve as indispensable tools for analysts and investors, allowing them to unravel the intricacies of asset performance. Imagine a financial vessel skillfully navigating turbulent waters; the various risk factors represent the unseen currents that may either propel or hinder its quest for investment success.

The Foundation of Factor Models

At their core, factor models are grounded in the premise that asset returns are fundamentally influenced by a range of systematic risk factors. These factors can be classified into two main categories: macroeconomic variables —such as interest rates and GDP growth—and firm-specific characteristics, including market capitalization and the value-growth orientation.

The first step in constructing a robust factor model involves carefully selecting the relevant factors. A well-known example is the Fama-French Three-Factor Model, which identifies three key factors:

1. **Market Risk** – The excess return of the market over a risk-free rate.
2. **Size (SMB)** – The historical tendency for smaller firms (small-cap stocks) to outperform their larger counterparts (large-cap stocks).
3. **Value (HML)** – The phenomenon where value stocks (characterized by lower price-to-book ratios) tend to deliver higher returns than growth stocks.

These fundamental factors not only serve as the building blocks for calculating excess returns but also enhance our understanding of how diversified portfolios respond to various market stimuli. To bring this concept to life, we will explore the process of implementing a factor model using Python.

Data Collection and Preparation

The journey of building a factor model begins with the careful collection and preparation of data. This process involves gathering historical asset returns along with the corresponding factor returns. For instance, let's consider a scenario where we examine a selection of small-cap stocks and their relationship with market returns, as well as specific size and value factors.

We can start by organizing our data in Python using the pandas library:

```python
import pandas as pd

\# Sample data representing stock and factor returns
data = {
  'stock_A_returns': [0.03, 0.04, 0.02, 0.05, 0.06],
  'stock_B_returns': [0.01, 0.03, 0.05, 0.01, 0.02],
  'market_returns': [0.02, 0.03, 0.02, 0.04, 0.05],
  'SMB': [0.005, -0.001, 0.003, 0.004, 0.002],
  'HML': [-0.002, 0.004, 0.001, 0.003, -0.001],
}

\# Creating a DataFrame
df = pd.DataFrame(data)
```

With our data meticulously organized, we can proceed to fit a linear regression model using the statsmodels library.

Estimating the Factor Model

The ordinary least squares (OLS) regression technique plays a pivotal role in quantifying how asset returns respond to the chosen risk factors. Let's take a closer look at how to estimate this model for stock A:

```python
import statsmodels.api as sm

\# Define the dependent variable (returns of stock A)
y = df['stock_A_returns']

\# Define the independent variables (factors)
X = df[['market_returns', 'SMB', 'HML']]
```

```
\# Adding a constant to the factors
X = sm.add_constant(X)

\# Fitting the model
model = sm.OLS(y, X).fit()

\# Displaying the results
print(model.summary())
```

The output from this regression will provide critical insights, including coefficients (or betas) that illustrate stock A's sensitivity to fluctuations in market returns, as well as the size and value factors. Moreover, we will obtain statistical significance measures.

Interpreting the Results

The coefficients derived from the regression output act as a navigational compass, illuminating the asset's risk exposures. For example, if the coefficient for market_returns is 1.3, it suggests that stock A is expected to experience a 1.3% increase in returns for every 1% increase in the market, indicating both elevated sensitivity and potential risk.

Statistical significance, often assessed through p-values, allows investors to discern whether observed relationships are real or merely the result of chance. Generally, a p-value below 0.05 indicates statistical significance, denoting that the factor has a substantive impact on the asset's returns.

Applications and Further Considerations

Effectively constructing factor models empowers investors to analyze investment strategies rooted in empirical evidence, rather than speculation. For example, by understanding whether a portfolio is heavily weighted towards small-cap stocks, an investor may decide to recalibrate their positions in response to anticipated market volatility.

To deepen our analysis, we can assess the model's fit through various metrics, such as Adjusted R-squared, which provides a comprehensive view of the proportion of variance in returns that can be explained by the selected factors.

Challenges in Factor Model Construction

Despite the benefits of constructing factor models, challenges exist. These include selecting the most appropriate factors, addressing multicollinearity (where some factors may be highly correlated), and frequently recalibrating models in rapidly evolving markets. Therefore, maintaining flexibility and rigor in factor selection and ongoing evaluation is essential for effective model implementation.

In conclusion, mastering the construction and interpretation of factor models equips analysts and investors with a powerful framework for navigating the complexities of financial returns. As markets continue to become more sophisticated, the importance of these quantitative methodologies will only continue to rise.

The Fama-French Three-Factor Model: A New Lens on Asset Pricing

In the dynamic realm of quantitative finance, gaining insight into the factors that drive asset pricing is essential for both investors and analysts. The Fama-French Three-Factor Model, introduced by renowned economists Eugene Fama and Kenneth French in the 1990s, offers a sophisticated alternative to the traditional Capital Asset Pricing Model (CAPM). Picture navigating a complex labyrinth of investment opportunities; the Fama-French model serves as a reliable guide, illuminating the paths to informed decision-making.

Delving into the Three Factors

At the core of the Fama-French framework lies a fundamental principle: asset returns are significantly influenced by systematic risk factors, categorized as follows:

1. **Market Risk**: A familiar concept for many investors, market risk reflects the excess return of the market over a risk-free rate. This factor highlights the extent to which an asset's returns are sensitive to fluctuations in the overall market. Essentially, it encapsulates the broader economic environment's impact on investment performance.
2. **Size (SMB)**: This factor, denoted as "SMB" (Small Minus Big), underscores the historical trend wherein smaller companies—commonly referred to as small-cap stocks—tend to outperform larger companies (large-cap stocks) over time. This phenomenon can be attributed to the higher risk associated with smaller firms, which are often less stable and more vulnerable to economic shifts.
3. **Value (HML)**: Represented by "HML" (High Minus Low), this factor elucidates the tendency for value stocks—characterized by lower price-to-book ratios—to deliver higher returns compared to their growth-oriented counterparts, which often boast inflated valuations. This dimension highlights the significant role that stock valuations play in driving market performance.

Building the Model

To construct the Fama-French Three-Factor Model, one begins by gathering and preparing relevant data pertaining to the model's key variables. Typically, this data includes the excess market return, as well as the SMB and HML values over a defined period. Let's explore a practical example that evaluates the performance of a hypothetical small-cap value stock in the context of these influential factors.

We start by importing essential libraries and generating simulated data:

```python
import pandas as pd
import numpy as np
import statsmodels.api as sm

# Simulating historical returns for a small-cap value stock and relevant market factors
np.random.seed(42)
data = {
    'stock_returns': np.random.normal(loc=0.015, scale=0.05, size=60),
    'market_returns': np.random.normal(loc=0.02, scale=0.04, size=60),
    'SMB': np.random.normal(loc=0.005, scale=0.02, size=60),
    'HML': np.random.normal(loc=0.003, scale=0.015, size=60)
}

# Creating a DataFrame from the simulated data
df = pd.DataFrame(data)
```

Having assembled our historical returns, we can now fit a regression model to explore the relationship between the stock's performance and the three identified factors:

```python
# Defining the dependent variable (stock returns)
y = df['stock_returns']

# Defining the independent variables (factors)
X = df[['market_returns', 'SMB', 'HML']]

# Adding a constant to the independent variables
X = sm.add_constant(X)

# Fitting the regression model
model = sm.OLS(y, X).fit()

# Displaying the regression results
print(model.summary())
```

The model's output reveals a wealth of insights, including

coefficients for each factor. For instance, if the coefficient for SMB is 0.8, it indicates that the small-cap value stock is projected to yield an additional 0.8% return for every 1% increase in returns of smaller companies relative to larger ones.

Interpreting the Results

Understanding the results produced by the regression is crucial for assessing the asset's performance. Each coefficient's statistical significance can be evaluated using p-values, where a p-value below 0.05 typically signifies that the associated factor has a meaningful impact on the stock's returns. Positive coefficients suggest that returns move in harmony with the factor, while negative coefficients indicate an inverse relationship.

For example, if our regression output yields the following coefficients:

- Market (excess return): 1.2
- SMB: 0.6
- HML: -0.3

These values imply that the stock is highly sensitive to market movements, positively influenced by smaller firms, yet underperforming when compared to value stocks. Such nuanced insights can greatly inform strategies for portfolio construction and risk management.

Practical Applications of the Fama-French Model

Utilizing the Fama-French model can empower investors to make more discerning investment choices. For instance, a risk-averse investor may lean toward stocks with lower exposure to the SMB and HML factors, particularly in uncertain market environments. Conversely, an aggressive investor might seize opportunities presented by small-cap outperformance during bullish trends.

Additionally, fund managers and analysts frequently apply

this model for backtesting investment strategies, assessing whether the incorporation of these factors can enhance returns relative to passive investment methods. The model's framework lays a foundation for further investigations into multi-factor investment strategies, potentially including additional variables such as momentum or profitability.

Challenges and Limitations

While the Fama-French Three-Factor Model is widely respected, it is not without its critiques. Notable limitations include:

- **Time-varying Factor Loadings**: The coefficients may fluctuate over time due to changes in market conditions, necessitating frequent recalibration and validation of the model.
- **Data Sensitivity**: The model's efficacy is contingent upon the quality and accuracy of the data employed. Flawed data can lead to misleading conclusions.
- **Exclusion of Additional Factors**: The model does not account for other dimensions of risk—such as momentum or liquidity—which can result in an incomplete understanding of asset price movements.

The Fama-French Three-Factor Model stands as a pivotal element in the field of quantitative finance, illuminating the intricate relationships between risk factors and asset returns. As we delve deeper into the world of factor models, grasping the implications of this foundational framework will equip investors with the strategic insights essential for navigating the complexities of tomorrow's financial markets.

Armed with this knowledge, individuals and institutions alike will be better prepared to explore multi-factor strategies, embracing advanced econometric techniques and machine learning methodologies that provide a more comprehensive understanding of asset behavior within our increasingly intricate financial landscape.

The Carhart Four-Factor Model: Broadening Perspectives in Asset Pricing

In the fast-paced world of quantitative finance, the pursuit of knowledge regarding asset returns has led to the evolution of intricate models that delve deeper than traditional analyses. One such significant advancement is the **Carhart Four-Factor Model**, conceived by Mark Carhart in 1997. This model builds upon the foundation laid by the Fama-French Three-Factor Model, introducing an essential fourth variable: the momentum factor. Picture stepping into a vibrant marketplace where returns are influenced not solely by core fundamentals, but also by recent price trends. The Carhart model encapsulates this dynamic interplay, offering a richer understanding of asset pricing.

Understanding the Four Factors

the Carhart model preserves the three foundational factors from the Fama-French framework while integrating momentum as its transformative component. Here's a closer look at each factor:

1. **Market Risk (Excess Return)**: Much like the Fama-French model, market risk reflects the overall return of the market above the risk-free rate. It remains a pivotal measure, indicating how an asset performs in relation to market fluctuations.

2. **Size (SMB)**: This factor, known as SMB (Small Minus Big), illustrates the historical trend wherein smaller companies have a propensity to generate higher returns compared to larger counterparts. This phenomenon often emerges from the heightened risks associated with smaller firms, which can deter some investors while enticing others willing to embrace the challenge.

3. **Value (HML)**: The value factor, indicated by HML (High Minus Low), reveals the tendency of value stocks—characterized by low price-to-book ratios—to outperform their growth-oriented counterparts. This factor underscores how valuation metrics can significantly affect investment performance.
4. **Momentum (WML)**: The newly introduced momentum factor, represented by WML (Winners Minus Losers), highlights the market's inclination to continue rewarding assets that have shown strong past performance, while those that have lagged behind often continue to struggle. This momentum effect suggests that prior performance can be a valuable predictor of future returns.

Constructing the Carhart Model

Utilizing the Carhart Four-Factor Model effectively involves a few key steps, beginning with the collection of historical data for each of these four factors. Below, we outline a practical approach to implementing this model using Python.

First, we prepare our dataset, which typically includes monthly returns for your selected stock, alongside data regarding market excess returns, SMB, HML, and WML for a defined timeframe. Here's a foundational code structure to get started:

```
```python import pandas as pd import numpy as np import statsmodels.api as sm

\# Generate sample data
np.random.seed(42)
data = {
        'stock_returns': np.random.normal(loc=0.015, scale=0.05, size=60), \# Simulated stock returns
    'market_excess_return': np.random.normal(loc=0.02, scale=0.04, size=60), \# Market excess return
    'SMB': np.random.normal(loc=0.005, scale=0.02, size=60), \# Size
```
```

```
factor
    'HML': np.random.normal(loc=0.003, scale=0.015, size=60), \#
Value factor
    'WML': np.random.normal(loc=0.01, scale=0.025, size=60), \#
Momentum factor
}

\# Creating a DataFrame
df = pd.DataFrame(data)
```

Next, we set up our regression analysis to assess the influence of these factors on stock returns:

```python
# Defining the dependent variable (stock returns)
y = df['stock_returns']

\# Defining the independent variables (factors)
X = df[['market_excess_return', 'SMB', 'HML', 'WML']]

\# Adding a constant for the regression model
X = sm.add_constant(X)

\# Fitting the model
model = sm.OLS(y, X).fit()

\# Displaying the regression results
print(model.summary())
```

Deciphering the Results

Once the regression model is executed, the results will yield coefficients for each independent variable, allowing for critical interpretations of their relationship with stock returns. For instance, consider the regression outputs:

- Market (excess return): 1.1
- SMB: 0.7
- HML: -0.2
- WML: 0.4

In this example, a market coefficient of 1.1 indicates that the stock returns are highly reactive to market movements. The SMB coefficient of 0.7 suggests a favorable alignment with the small-cap advantage, indicating potential additional returns as smaller firms outperform. Conversely, a negative HML value may reveal a relative underperformance against value stocks. Notably, a positive WML coefficient illustrates that past winners are likely to continue their upward trajectory, underscoring the model's emphasis on momentum.

Real-World Applications of the Carhart Model

The Carhart Four-Factor Model proves indispensable for portfolio managers, investors, and researchers alike.

For example, an investment strategy might be directed towards small-cap stocks characterized by high momentum, while remaining acutely aware of systemic risks through the market factor. Backtesting these strategies against historical data can yield meaningful insights, enhancing the investment decision-making process.

Moreover, fund managers can employ the Carhart model to analyze and communicate their performance in relation to expected returns derived from these factors.

Challenges and Limitations

Despite its strengths, the Carhart model is not without its critics. Some of the notable challenges include:

- **Data Dependency**: The model's predictive power hinges on the reliability of high-quality historical market data and precise factor definitions. Any inaccuracies can lead to skewed insights.
- **Market Dynamics**: The behaviors of factors can shift with evolving market conditions. Consequently, the model may require adjustments to its factors or coefficients to maintain relevance.

- **Oversimplification**: While comprehensive, the model does not encapsulate all potential risk factors, particularly those arising from broader macroeconomic changes, geopolitical factors, or unique market anomalies.

The Carhart Four-Factor Model stands as a pivotal development in the landscape of asset pricing, finely integrating the concept of momentum into the insightful framework established by Fama and French. This incorporation allows financial analysts and investors to deepen their understanding of market dynamics and the forces that drive asset performance. As we navigate the complexities of contemporary finance, the perspectives offered by the Carhart model serve as a powerful tool, empowering investors to make more precise and informed strategic decisions.

Implementing Multi-Factor Models in Python

Integrating multi-factor models into investment strategies represents a pivotal shift in the realm of quantitative finance. Unlike single-factor methods, multi-factor models leverage multiple variables to explain asset returns, thereby offering a more nuanced perspective on market behavior. This guide aims to provide a detailed, practical approach to implementing multi-factor models using Python, equipping you with the tools necessary to create, analyze, and backtest these models with real financial data.

Understanding the Framework: Key Models and Their Components

Before we embark on the coding journey, it's crucial to familiarize ourselves with the theoretical underpinnings of multi-factor models. Let's revisit two well-regarded frameworks: the Fama-French Three-Factor Model and the Carhart Four-Factor Model. Each of these models incorporates distinct factors that help investors forecast returns:

1. **Market Risk (R_m - R_f):** This is the excess return of the overall market relative to the risk-free rate.
2. **Size Effect (SMB - Small Minus Big):** Historical data supports the finding that smaller companies have consistently outperformed their larger counterparts.
3. **Value Factor (HML - High Minus Low):** This factor illustrates the tendency for undervalued stocks to deliver returns superior to those of overvalued stocks.
4. **Momentum (WML - Winners Minus Losers):** Momentum reflects the trend where assets that have performed well in the past tend to continue performing well in the near future.

Collecting and Preparing Data: Setting the Scene

The first step towards implementing these models is to gather relevant financial data. For demonstration purposes, let's analyze the performance of Apple Inc. (AAPL) by incorporating the aforementioned factors. Financial data sources like Yahoo Finance, Alpha Vantage, or Quandl can be excellent starting points.

Begin by setting up your environment and importing the necessary packages:

` ` `python import pandas as pd import numpy as np import yfinance as yf

```
\# Choose the stock and relevant market index
stock = 'AAPL'
market_index = '^GSPC' \# S&P 500 benchmark
start_date = '2015-01-01'
end_date = '2023-01-01'

\# Retrieving stock and market index data
stock_data = yf.download(stock, start=start_date, end=end_date)
['Adj Close']
```

market_data = yf.download(market_index, start=start_date, end=end_date)['Adj Close']

\# Computing daily returns
stock_returns = stock_data.pct_change().dropna()
market_returns = market_data.pct_change().dropna()

\# Consolidating the data into a single DataFrame
data = pd.DataFrame({'Stock Returns': stock_returns, 'Market Returns': market_returns})
```

*Augmenting the Dataset with Factor Returns*

Beyond just market returns, it's essential to include factor return data for SMB, HML, and WML. For our example, we will simulate these factors using random values to demonstrate how to incorporate them into our analysis.

```python # Simulating returns for the factors np.random.seed(42) data['SMB'] = np.random.normal(0, 0.01, len(data)) # Simulated Small Minus Big returns data['HML'] = np.random.normal(0, 0.01, len(data)) # Simulated High Minus Low returns data['WML'] = np.random.normal(0, 0.01, len(data)) # Simulated Winners Minus Losers returns
```

Constructing the Regression Model

With our dataset prepared, we can now construct a regression model using the statsmodels library. This model will help us determine the extent to which identified factors impact stock returns.

```python import statsmodels.api as sm

\# Set the dependent variable (stock returns)
y = data['Stock Returns']

\# Set the independent variables (factors)
X = data[['Market Returns', 'SMB', 'HML', 'WML']]

```
\# Adding a constant to the model
X = sm.add_constant(X)

\# Fitting the regression model
model = sm.OLS(y, X).fit()

\# Displaying the results summary
print(model.summary())
```

Decoding the Results

Upon executing the regression model, you'll receive a comprehensive output that includes coefficients for each factor, R-squared values, and p-values. Here's a guide on how to interpret these outputs:

- **Coefficient of Market Returns:** If this value is 1.2, it suggests that a 1% increase in market return correlates with a 1.2% rise in the stock's return.
- **Coefficient of SMB:** A positive coefficient (e.g., 0.5) indicates alignment with smaller company performance, hinting at a small-cap advantage.
- **Coefficient of HML:** A negative coefficient might suggest a weaker correlation with value stocks.
- **Coefficient of WML:** A positive value here signifies that the stock has benefited from momentum, confirming previous trends of price appreciation.

Backtesting the Model: Validating Performance

Once the model is established, backtesting is essential to assess performance based on historical data. This step is integral to uncovering how the stock would have performed using the model's predictions.

Let's outline a simple backtesting strategy that utilizes the regression model's coefficients to create a mock portfolio, rebalancing at regular intervals.

```python
# Developing a backtesting strategy
\# Calculate the weighted returns based on the regression coefficients
weights = model.params[1:] \# Excluding the constant term
port_returns = np.dot(data[['Market Returns', 'SMB', 'HML', 'WML']], weights)

\# Including the portfolio returns in the original DataFrame
data['Portfolio Returns'] = port_returns

\# Calculating cumulative returns for both the stock and the constructed portfolio
data['Cumulative Stock Returns'] = (1 + data['Stock Returns']).cumprod()
data['Cumulative Portfolio Returns'] = (1 + data['Portfolio Returns']).cumprod()

\# Visualizing the results
import matplotlib.pyplot as plt

plt.figure(figsize=(12, 6))
plt.plot(data['Cumulative Stock Returns'], label='AAPL Returns', color='blue')
plt.plot(data['Cumulative Portfolio Returns'], label='Portfolio Returns', color='red')
plt.title('Cumulative Returns: AAPL vs. Multi-Factor Portfolio')
plt.xlabel('Date')
plt.ylabel('Cumulative Returns')
plt.legend()
plt.show()
```

Real-World Considerations: Navigating the Landscape

The application of multi-factor models has several notable practical advantages:

- **Risk Management:** Investors gain insights into their

exposure to diverse risk factors, informing more thoughtful strategic choices.

- **Performance Analysis:** By dissecting how various factors impact returns, portfolio managers can enhance communication with stakeholders regarding strategy effectiveness.
- **Adaptability:** These models facilitate swift adjustments to strategies in response to evolving market dynamics and emerging factors.

Challenges in Implementation: Recognizing Hurdles

Despite their advantages, deploying multi-factor models is not without challenges. Accurate and high-quality factor data is essential since inaccuracies can lead to erroneous investment decisions. Additionally, understanding which factors to include—and how their definitions might need to evolve in accordance with market trends—requires ongoing research and validation.

Implementing multi-factor models with Python illustrates the intersection of finance, technology, and data science. As quantitative finance continues to advance, mastering these techniques will be an indispensable asset for any aspiring analyst in the field.

Backtesting Factor Strategies

Picture the vibrant atmosphere of London's financial district, where traders are often found immersed in screens, sifting through data to inform their decisions. Consider a trader intrigued by the prospects of developing a factor strategy based on the Fama-French three-factor model—comprising market risk, size, and value factors. Engaging in backtesting provides a crucial window into past performance, allowing the trader to glean insights that inform future strategies.

Understanding Backtesting Methodology

Embarking on backtesting necessitates a clear definition of the hypothesis to be tested. In the context of our Fama-French example, the hypothesis might propose that small, value stocks will consistently outperform larger, growth stocks over time. This guiding principle shapes the data collection process, requiring a compilation of historical price data alongside relevant factor metrics.

Step 1: Data Gathering

The cornerstone of effective backtesting lies in the acquisition of accurate data. For our scenario, historical price data for the selected stocks, as well as information regarding the Fama-French factors, can be sourced from reliable financial databases, such as Bloomberg or Yahoo Finance.

```python
import pandas as pd

\# Load Fama-French data
ff_factors = pd.read_csv('F-F_Research_Data_Factors.csv', parse_dates=True)
prices = pd.read_csv('stock_prices.csv', parse_dates=True)

\# Display the first few rows of the data for verification
print(ff_factors.head())
print(prices.head())
```

Step 2: Constructing the Portfolio

With the necessary data in hand, the next phase involves selecting a universe of stocks based on defined parameters, such as market capitalization (size) and book-to-market ratios (value). Python proves invaluable here, enabling efficient filtering of stocks according to these criteria.

```python
# Assuming stocks is a DataFrame containing available stocks value_stocks = stocks[stocks['book_to_market'] > 0.5] small_stocks = value_stocks[value_stocks['market_cap'] < 2e9] # Selecting
```

stocks with market cap under 2 billion

```
```

Step 3: Strategy Implementation

Having constructed the portfolio, we can now implement our trading strategy. Let's assume the strategy dictates a long position on small-cap value stocks initiated at the beginning of each month, with positions closed at month's end.

```python
def backtest_strategy(prices, start_date, end_date): profit_loss_history = [] for date in pd.date_range(start=start_date, end=end_date): monthly_prices = prices[prices['date'].dt.month == date.month] # Assume positions are calculated profit_loss = (monthly_prices['closing_price'].iloc[-1] - monthly_prices['closing_price'].iloc[0]) / monthly_prices['closing_price'].iloc[0] profit_loss_history.append(profit_loss) return profit_loss_history

\# Execute the backtest over a defined period
results = backtest_strategy(prices, '2010-01-01', '2020-01-01')
```

Step 4: Evaluating Performance

Once the strategy has been executed, the evaluation phase becomes vital. Here, we can utilize a variety of performance metrics, including:

- **Sharpe Ratio**: A measure of risk-adjusted returns.
- **Maximum Drawdown**: This assesses the peak-to-trough decline over a specific period.
- **Alpha and Beta**: These metrics indicate how the strategy's returns compare to those of market benchmarks.

This evaluation phase is critical not only to assess profitability but also to gauge the robustness and risk profile of the strategy.

```python
import numpy as np

def calculate_sharpe_ratio(returns, risk_free_rate=0.01):
    excess_returns = returns - risk_free_rate
    return np.mean(excess_returns) / np.std(excess_returns)

\# Calculate the Sharpe Ratio for the strategy's results
sharpe = calculate_sharpe_ratio(np.array(results))
print(f'Sharpe Ratio: {sharpe}')
```

Backtesting factor strategies provides a powerful framework for traders and analysts, transforming theoretical concepts into actionable plans that withstand the rigors of time. However, it's crucial to remember that while historical performance can guide future strategy, it is not an absolute predictor. Markets are dynamic, technology continues to advance, and new influential factors frequently emerge.

Through disciplined and thorough backtesting practices, you set the stage for the development of adaptable, evolving strategies. As financial aficionados often note, yesterday's successful strategies may falter today; thus, the continual refinement of strategies, fueled by fresh data and deeper analysis, is essential. As you delve into the world of factor investing, remain cognizant of the iterative nature of quantitative strategies, as each data point has the potential to reshape your insights as you navigate the complexities of financial markets.

Performance Metrics for Factor Models

In the sophisticated realm of quantitative finance, the success of multi-factor models lies not only in their theoretical underpinnings but significantly in the precision and lucidity with which they are executed and assessed. Performance metrics act as the navigational tools that empower analysts, helping them traverse the intricate investment landscape while providing insights that extend well beyond mere returns. A thorough evaluation of these metrics can make the difference between a successful investment strategy and one that falls short of expectations.

Visualize the bustling trading floors of New York City, where analysts in sharp suits immerse themselves in the data-rich environment. Here, the understanding and application of performance metrics transform raw numbers into insightful analyses that can shape real-world trading strategies. Picture a trader who relies on the Fama-French Three-Factor Model to devise a strategy. As this trader assesses portfolio performance, they leverage a range of critical performance metrics outlined below.

Delving into Key Performance Metrics

Performance metrics in finance can be grouped into several essential categories: risk-adjusted returns, absolute returns, and risk measures. While traditional measures like simple returns are vital, they provide an incomplete narrative unless paired with a deeper comprehension of the risks involved.

The Sharpe Ratio is a cornerstone of performance evaluation, encapsulating a strategy's risk-adjusted return. A higher Sharpe Ratio signifies a more favorable return in relation to risk.

```python
import numpy as np

def calculate_sharpe_ratio(returns, risk_free_rate=0.01):
    excess_returns = returns - risk_free_rate
    return np.mean(excess_returns) / np.std(excess_returns)

\# Simulating strategy returns
sample_returns = np.random.normal(0.01, 0.05, 100) \# Generating random returns
sharpe = calculate_sharpe_ratio(sample_returns)
print(f'Sharpe Ratio: {sharpe:.2f}')
```

In practice, if our trader calculates a Sharpe Ratio of 1.2 from their multi-factor strategy, it reflects a commendable generation of 1.2 units of return for each unit of risk assumed —an encouraging sign for potential investors.

2. Alpha and Beta

Alpha provides a direct insight into any excess return generated by a strategy over and above what is expected based on market movements (beta). Understanding alpha allows traders to assess how well their strategy performs relative to a benchmark index.

- **Alpha** can be computed using the following formula:

[\alpha = R_p - (R_f + \beta \times (R_m - R_f))]

Where: - (R_p) = portfolio return - (R_f) = risk-free rate - (R_m) = market return - (\beta) = portfolio's beta

```python def calculate_alpha(portfolio_return, risk_free_rate, beta, market_return): return portfolio_return - (risk_free_rate + beta * (market_return - risk_free_rate))

\# Example calculation
portfolio_return = 0.12
risk_free_rate = 0.01
beta = 1.1
market_return = 0.08

alpha = calculate_alpha(portfolio_return, risk_free_rate, beta, market_return)
print(f'Alpha: {alpha:.2f}')
```

When our trader determines an alpha of 0.03, it indicates their strategy has outperformed the market-adjusted expected return by 3%, highlighting their adeptness at strategy selection.

3. Maximum Drawdown

Another essential metric, **maximum drawdown**, captures the most significant decline from a peak to a trough before reaching a new peak. This measure is critical for evaluating a strategy's robustness during unfavorable market conditions, offering insights into potential worst-case scenarios that could affect investor sentiment.

```python
def calculate_max_drawdown(prices): cum_returns = (1 + prices).cumprod() peak = cum_returns.cummax() drawdown = (cum_returns - peak) / peak max_drawdown = drawdown.min() return max_drawdown

\# Simulating price returns
price_returns = np.random.normal(0.01, 0.02, 100) \# Generating simulated returns
max_dd = calculate_max_drawdown(price_returns)
print(f'Maximum Drawdown: {max_dd:.2%}')
```

In a scenario where the maximum drawdown is quantified at 20%, a trader might reassess their risk exposure to inform adjustments in their portfolio, striving to mitigate similar risks in the future.

*4. **Sortino Ratio***

While the Sharpe Ratio evaluates both upside and downside volatility, the **Sortino Ratio** narrows its focus to downside volatility, providing a clearer understanding of an investment's performance amid negative events. Analysts often prefer the Sortino Ratio, as it primarily concerns managing adverse returns without penalizing the strategy for volatility associated with positive returns.

The Sortino Ratio is calculated using the formula:

$$\text{Sortino Ratio} = \frac{R_p - R_f}{\sigma_d}$$

Where σ_d represents the downside standard

deviation of the portfolio's returns. This ratio proves invaluable when the asset's return distribution is asymmetric.

Accessing and interpreting these performance metrics equips traders with the necessary acumen to navigate the complexities of multi-factor investing effectively. Each metric offers a unique lens for assessing strategy performance, allowing traders to develop a more comprehensive understanding of risk and return.

As the financial landscape remains dynamic and ever-evolving, integrating a variety of performance metrics into analytical frameworks will be vital for discerning the true efficacy of multi-factor models. Ultimately, the blend of performance metrics illuminates the path ahead, guiding traders as they make informed, strategic decisions on their financial journeys.

The Simplification of Complexity

At the heart of any multi-factor model lies the assumption that various factors contribute to asset returns. However, the real world is far more intricate, shaped by a multitude of microeconomic and macroeconomic variables that influence price movements in unpredictable ways. The need to simplify in order to identify and quantify these factors can result in substantial omissions.

Consider a trader using the Fama-French Three-Factor Model, which takes into account market risk, size, and value. If this trader overlooks critical elements—such as momentum or relevant macroeconomic indicators—their forecasts may suffer from significant distortions.

Take, for example, a bond investor who undervalues the sensitivity of their assets to fluctuations in interest rates. Given that central banks continually adjust monetary policy based on a dynamic economic landscape, a trader relying solely on historical data devoid of real-time adjustments may find themselves ill-prepared for sudden rate shifts. Such unexpected volatility can disrupt portfolios dramatically, highlighting the imperative for ongoing model adaptation alongside comprehensive market analysis.

Factor Correlation and Multicollinearity

One significant concern affecting the efficacy of multi-factor models is factor correlation and the potential for multicollinearity. When multiple factors become intertwined, they can create redundancy in the information provided. For example, incorporating both profitability and value factors into a multi-factor framework may yield diminishing returns. If these factors are highly correlated, the extra return offered by one may not significantly differ from the other.

Imagine an analyst who discovers that size and value factors historically provide substantial returns. Yet, when integrated into a single model, the interaction may reduce the predictive power of the model overall, leading the analyst to place unwarranted faith in its forecasts. In this scenario, misguided confidence in the model's outputs could result in unexpected financial losses.

Data Quality and Overfitting

The principle of "garbage in, garbage out" rings especially true in the realm of multi-factor modeling, where the integrity of data is paramount. Subpar data quality can result in flawed factor definitions and unreliable predictions. Moreover, there is a persistent temptation to overfit models to historical data, compromising their future applicability.

Consider a quant trader who constructs a sophisticated model with numerous factors, meticulously fine-tuning it for exceptional historical performance. Unfortunately, this approach may backfire when the model is applied to new data, as it often fails to generalize. When subjected to forward-looking testing, the model might perform poorly, leading to disappointing results. Therefore, it is crucial for traders to strike a delicate balance between accurately fitting historical data while ensuring their models maintain robustness in the face of evolving market conditions.

Calibration and Model Sensitivity

Accurate calibration goes beyond merely using quality data. Multi-factor models may require continuous adjustments to factor definitions or their respective weights as market conditions change. A model's sensitivity to variations in parameter selection can lead to markedly different forecasts.

For example, if an investment strategist alters the weightings of factors based on a historical optimization, they face a potential pitfall if market dynamics shift unpredictably. During periods like the 2020 pandemic-driven market volatility, many historically reliable factors fell short. Traders who do not recalibrate their models promptly may inadvertently exacerbate their exposure to ineffective strategies, compromising performance during critical market transitions.

Regulatory and Ethical Considerations

The landscape of multi-factor investing is also laden with regulatory and ethical dimensions. A reliance on quantitative strategies may produce unintended consequences, especially as new regulations emerge, particularly regarding algorithm usage, data privacy, and issues related to market manipulation. Traders must remain vigilant about evolving regulations, ensuring that they uphold their fiduciary responsibilities.

Consider the firms using high-frequency trading algorithms that are subject to strict regulatory scrutiny. They must diligently audit their trading algorithms to ensure compliance with existing laws. This level of diligence serves as a safeguard against potential legal ramifications stemming from practices that might unwittingly manipulate asset prices or violate established norms.

In summary, while multi-factor models provide a strategic framework for unpacking the drivers of returns across varying market landscapes, their limitations should not be underestimated. A thorough understanding of model design complexities, data integrity, correlations, calibration, and regulatory constraints equips traders with the insights necessary for judicious application.

Navigating the landscape of quantitative finance requires a level of adaptability that transcends mere adherence to model predictions. Embracing these considerations ensures that traders and analysts can effectively harness the potential of multi-factor models, establishing robust frameworks to navigate the unpredictable nature of financial

Case Study: Factor Analysis in Equity Markets

As we explore the application of multi-factor models within equity markets, it's clear that theoretical insights must seamlessly integrate with practical considerations. This case study centers on a hypothetical investment firm, EquityInsights, focused on refining its portfolio management strategies by delving into the multifaceted drivers of stock returns.

Background: EquityInsights and Its Approach

Founded by a passionate team of quantitative finance experts, EquityInsights is headquartered in London, where it operates at the cutting edge of investment innovation. The firm is committed to transforming traditional investment strategies through optimization and data-driven methodologies. Their analytical framework prioritizes risk-adjusted returns while striving to minimize downside exposure, principles that resonate with the tenets of Modern Portfolio Theory (MPT).

To embark on this mission, EquityInsights selects the

Fama-French Three-Factor Model as the foundation for its analysis. This influential model encompasses three critical factors: market risk (beta), size—demonstrating the historical outperformance of smaller companies over larger counterparts—and value, which highlights the advantages of stocks with high book-to-market ratios relative to those with low ratios.

Data Collection and Preparation

EquityInsights kicks off its analysis by assembling a comprehensive dataset of historical stock prices spanning the last decade, sourced from reputable financial data providers such as Bloomberg and Yahoo Finance. This dataset is not limited to stock prices; it also incorporates essential factors including market capitalization, book-to-market ratios, and the performance metrics of relevant indices for benchmarking.

Utilizing the powerful Pandas library in Python, the team efficiently structures and manipulates their dataset. Their data preparation process entails the following key steps:

1. **Importing Required Libraries:**

```python import pandas as pd import numpy as np import yfinance as yf import matplotlib.pyplot as plt
```

1. **Fetching Historical Data:**

Using the yfinance library, the analysts download historical price data for their selected companies and corresponding indices.

```python tickers = ['AAPL', 'MSFT', 'GOOGL', 'AMZN', 'FB'] # Sample tech stocks price_data = yf.download(tickers, start='2012-01-01', end='2022-01-01')['Adj Close']
```

1. **Data Cleaning:**

Ensuring data integrity is crucial; therefore, missing values are filtered out, and the dataset is organized into a coherent format.

```python
price_data.dropna(inplace=True)
```

1. **Calculating Returns:**

Daily returns are calculated, providing a vital dataset for subsequent factor exposure analysis.

```python
returns = price_data.pct_change().dropna()
```

Implementing the Multi-Factor Model

With the data meticulously prepared, the analysts turn their attention to the Fama-French framework. They start by identifying the three pivotal factors to investigate:

1. **Market Risk (Beta):** This measures a stock's sensitivity to movements in the overall market.
2. **Size Factor (SMB):** Indicates the excess return of small-cap stocks relative to large-cap stocks, derived from market capitalization data.
3. **Value Factor (HML):** Captures the return differential between high book-to-market and low book-to-market stocks.

To extract these vital factors, the team integrates relevant data from Kenneth French's research into their analysis. This integration enables them to construct a regression model to explore how well each stock's returns are explained by these factors.

The linear regression model is articulated as:

[R_t = \alpha + \beta_1 \cdot (R_{m,t} - R_{f}) + \beta_2 \cdot SMB_t + \beta_3 \cdot HML_t + \epsilon_t]

Where: - (R_t): Return of the stock at time (t) - (R_{m,t}): Market return at time (t) - (R_f): Risk-free rate - (SMB_t): Size factor at time (t) - (HML_t): Value factor at time (t) - (\beta_1, \beta_2, \beta_3): Coefficients to estimate for the model

Analyzing Factor Exposure

EquityInsights employs the statsmodels library to assess the regression model for each stock, evaluating their exposure to the selected factors.

```python
import statsmodels.api as sm

\# Adding a constant for the intercept in the regression
X = sm.add_constant(fama_french_factors[['Market Excess Return',
'SMB', 'HML']])
model = sm.OLS(returns['AAPL'], X).fit()
print(model.summary())
```

Results Interpretation

The regression output provides coefficients for each factor, elucidating the stock's exposure:

- A **positive beta** indicates that the stock tends to move in sync with the market, whereas a **negative beta** signifies an inverse relationship.
- By analyzing the coefficients for SMB and HML, EquityInsights gains insight into whether a stock aligns more closely with small-cap or value stock trends.

For instance, if the regression output for AAPL reveals:

- **Market Beta**: 1.3 (signifying greater volatility compared to the broader market)
- **SMB**: 0.8 (indicating performance aligned with small-cap stocks)
- **HML**: -0.3 (indicating a divergence from value stocks)

These findings suggest that AAPL is positioned to outperform the market and exhibit characteristics typically associated with small-cap equities, while distancing itself from value stock dynamics.

Considerations for Active Management

EquityInsights uses their findings to recalibrate their equity portfolio, shifting allocations toward factors that demonstrate robust empirical returns, aligned with their risk appetite. They acknowledge the critical need for ongoing monitoring —economic conditions are transient, and the factors driving performance may evolve.

Investors keen on risk management should be mindful of the potential shifts in market dynamics that could alter correlation structures among stocks. Incorporating qualitative factors, such as anticipated interest rate modifications or geopolitical risks, can enrich the context surrounding investment decisions.

This case study vividly illustrates the potent application of multi-factor models in the equity market, illuminating both their analytical prowess and practical implications for investment strategies. The experiences of EquityInsights underscore the importance of an adaptable and integrated investment philosophy, merging solid quantitative analysis with insightful qualitative assessments.

As the financial landscape shifts, fostering an environment of continuous learning and improvement in analytical skills will empower equity investors to successfully navigate complexities, leveraging multi-factor strategies to enhance portfolio performance. Ultimately, adeptly applying these principles not only drives returns but also fortifies resilience against the inherent volatility of global financial markets.

CHAPTER 5: PORTFOLIO THEORY

Modern Portfolio Theory (MPT) first emerged in the 1950s, heralding a transformation in the world of investment management. Developed by the brilliant economist Harry Markowitz, MPT systematically introduced the principle of diversification, proposing that investors could strategically optimize their portfolios to achieve maximum returns for a given level of risk. This groundbreaking approach not only revolutionized portfolio construction and management but also laid the foundation for the quantitative finance practices that have become indispensable today.

The Core Principles of MPT

At the core of MPT is a fundamental tenet: the intricately linked relationship between risk and return. Investors are urged to strike an optimal balance between these two elements, which can be visualized through the concept of the efficient frontier. This frontier represents a collection of optimal portfolios that yield the highest expected returns for a defined level of risk, or the lowest risk for a given expected return. An understanding of this relationship is paramount for anyone aiming to engage in effective portfolio management.

Risk and Return: The Dynamic Duo

To clarify this principle, let's consider a fictional investor named Emma. Recently inheriting a substantial sum of money, Emma is keen to invest wisely. She faces a pivotal decision: invest all her funds in a single, high-growth technology stock, which promises significant returns but carries considerable volatility, or diversify her investments across various asset classes—stocks, bonds, and real estate—each exhibiting its own risk-return profile. MPT quantifies this decision-making process using statistical measures of risk, specifically variance and standard deviation. These metrics empower Emma, and investors like her, to make informed choices based on a clearer understanding of the associated risks.

Defining the Efficient Frontier

To visualize the efficient frontier, imagine a graph with expected portfolio returns plotted on the y-axis and portfolio risk (measured by standard deviation) on the x-axis. The curve that forms, representing the most favorable combinations of risky assets, is known as the efficient frontier. Portfolios that land on this curve are deemed efficient, meaning they provide the highest possible expected returns for their level of risk. Conversely, portfolios that fall below the curve are considered suboptimal, offering lower returns for the same level of risk or necessitating higher risk without adequate reward.

Example: Mapping an Optimal Portfolio

Let's delve deeper into Emma's investment strategy. Suppose she constructs a diversified portfolio comprising 60% stocks, 30% bonds, and 10% in real estate. When Emma plots her portfolio on the efficient frontier graph, she is pleased to find it occupies a spot on the curve, indicating that her investment strategy effectively balances risk and potential returns.

However, market conditions are always changing, and so

should Emma's portfolio. The principles of MPT encourage her to conduct regular assessments of risk and return, ensuring her portfolio remains in alignment with her investment goals while adapting to shifts in the market landscape.

The Role of Asset Correlations

An essential insight derived from MPT is the significance of asset correlations. The relationship between the returns of different assets—whether they tend to move in tandem (correlated) or move independently (uncorrelated)—has a profound impact on the overall risk profile of a portfolio. The objective is to combine assets that exhibit low or negative correlations, thereby lessening volatility.

For instance, during a downturn in the equities market, bonds may perform more favorably, providing stability to a diversified portfolio. This negative correlation illustrates why a diverse array of asset classes is vital for minimizing risk in an investor's portfolio.

Portfolio Optimization through Python

As we progress into the practical applications of these concepts, utilizing Python for portfolio optimization proves invaluable. Let us envision that Emma wishes to refine her portfolio further by evaluating how different asset allocations might impact her risk-return profile.

Here's a simple illustration of how Emma might initiate this process using the cvxpy library for optimization:

```python
import numpy as np import pandas as pd import cvxpy as cp

\# Assuming we have historical returns for various assets
returns = pd.DataFrame({
  'Stocks': [0.12, 0.15, 0.10],
  'Bonds': [0.04, 0.05, 0.03],
  'Real_Estate': [0.07, 0.09, 0.06]
})
```

```
\# Calculate expected returns and covariance matrix
expected_returns = np.mean(returns, axis=0)
cov_matrix = returns.cov()

\# Define portfolio weights
weights = cp.Variable(len(expected_returns))

\# Objective: maximize expected returns (for simplicity, we focus solely on returns)
objective = cp.Maximize(expected_returns @ weights)

\# Constraints: ensure weights sum to 1 and remain non-negative
constraints = [cp.sum(weights) == 1, weights >= 0]
problem = cp.Problem(objective, constraints)

\# Solve the optimization problem
problem.solve()

\# Output the results
optimal_weights = weights.value
print("Optimal portfolio weights:", optimal_weights)
```

In this scenario, Emma can dynamically adjust the expected returns based on shifting market conditions and fine-tune the constraints according to her risk tolerance. This empirical approach empowers her to construct a robust investment portfolio grounded in quantitative analysis.

Modern Portfolio Theory fundamentally reshaped the investment landscape, providing a critical framework for understanding risk and return. While it's important to recognize the theory's limitations—such as its reliance on historical data and the assumption of market efficiency—the principles of MPT remain essential for today's investors. For individuals like Emma, mastering and implementing MPT not only facilitates smarter investment choices but also equips them with the tools to navigate the complex, ever-evolving world of finance.

As we delve into advanced topics, including sophisticated asset allocation techniques and further utilization of Python for optimization, the foundational principles of MPT will continue to guide our strategies, underscoring their lasting impact in the domain of quantitative finance.

Risk and Return: Definitions and Concepts

The concepts of risk and return are woven together like threads in a complex tapestry. For anyone seeking to master the nuances of investment, especially within the tenets of Modern Portfolio Theory, grasping the relationship between these two elements is paramount. risk embodies the uncertainty surrounding an investment's future returns, whereas return signifies the profit or loss generated from that investment over a specific timeframe. This interplay profoundly influences investment choices, shapes strategies, and ultimately determines financial success.

Understanding Risk

Risk manifests in various forms, and its categorization is essential for effective investment management. In the financial arena, the most significant types of risk include:

1. **Market Risk**: Also referred to as systematic risk, this represents the potential for losses stemming from market-wide fluctuations that affect entire asset classes. For instance, during an economic recession, stocks may plummet across the board, impacting even well-performing companies. Diversification cannot fully shield investors from this pervasive risk, making it a crucial factor to consider when constructing portfolios.
2. **Credit Risk**: This encompasses the risk that a borrower may default on their financial obligations. For example, if an investor purchases bonds from a

company teetering on the brink of bankruptcy, the chances of default can result in significant losses —a stark reminder of the importance of assessing creditworthiness before investment.

3. **Liquidity Risk**: This risk arises when an investor struggles to buy or sell assets quickly without causing a substantial impact on their price. Small-cap stocks, for instance, often exhibit lower trading volumes, which can pose challenges when exiting a position, forcing the investor to accept less favorable pricing.
4. **Operational Risk**: Frequently underestimated, this risk pertains to potential failures within internal systems, processes, or human resources. Imagine a bank experiencing a technical malfunction that delays transactions; in volatile market conditions, such operational hiccups can exacerbate losses and create significant disruptions.

As we traverse the intricate landscape of investments, it is vital to keep these categories in mind. Yet, it's important to acknowledge that while risks cannot be eradicated entirely, they can certainly be managed. A strategic approach involves striking a balance among various types of risk to optimize returns.

Return: Measuring Performance

Return serves as the cornerstone for evaluating the financial performance of an investment over a designated period, typically expressed as a percentage. Accurately measuring return is essential for assessing investment performance relative to its inherent risks. Various methods exist for calculating return, each offering distinct insights:

- **Absolute Return**: This straightforward metric calculates the total profit or loss of an investment over time. For instance, if an investor purchases a stock for (100 and later sells it for)120, the absolute return amounts to 20%.

- **Relative Return**: This measures an investment's performance against a benchmark, such as a stock market index. If the S&P 500 yields a 10% return in a given year while an investor's portfolio returns 15%, the relative return indicates a 5% outperformance relative to the benchmark.
- **Annualized Return**: This metric standardizes returns over a year, facilitating easy comparisons across different assets or investment portfolios. For instance, if a (1,000 investment grows to)1,500 over three years, calculating the annualized return provides a clearer indicator of its performance over time.

The Risk-Return Trade-Off

Investors often grapple with the risk-return trade-off, a principle that asserts the potential for higher returns is typically accompanied by increased risk. Take, for example, Daniel, an enthusiastic investor weighing two opportunities. He is contemplating a government bond with a stable 3% yield versus a tech startup promising a striking 25% return.

While the allure of the tech startup's potential returns is compelling, it is inherently accompanied by considerable volatility and the risk of loss. On the other hand, the government bond, though offering a modest return, provides a comforting sense of stability. Ultimately, Daniel's decision hinges on his risk tolerance and overall investment objectives.

Visually, this risk-return dynamic can be captured in an upward-sloping curve, where the x-axis represents risk—quantified as standard deviation—and the y-axis illustrates expected returns. As investors move along this curve, they encounter progressively higher expected returns in tandem with increased risk.

Example: Building a Risk-Adjusted Portfolio

To navigate the complexities of risk while pursuing returns, diversification emerges as a critical strategy. Imagine Sarah, an investor with a well-diversified portfolio inclusive of stocks, bonds, and real estate. Suppose her portfolio boasts an expected return of 8% with a risk profile of 12%. Meanwhile, her analysis reveals a promising technology stock with an anticipated return of 18%, albeit with a risk level of 25%.

Before diving in, Sarah carefully evaluates the implications of adding this tech stock to her portfolio on her overall risk-return profile. The following Python snippet illustrates how she utilizes programming to assess her new portfolio's expected return and associated risk:

```python
import numpy as np

\# Current portfolio setup
weights_current = np.array([0.6, 0.3, 0.1]) \# allocations to stocks, bonds, and real estate
expected_returns_current = np.array([0.08, 0.04, 0.07]) \# returns for each asset class
cov_matrix_current = np.array([[0.01, 0.002, 0.001],
               [0.002, 0.01, 0.002],
               [0.001, 0.002, 0.01]]) \# covariance matrix for current assets

\# New asset details (the tech stock)
weight_tech_stock = 0.1
expected_return_tech_stock = 0.18
risk_tech_stock = 0.25

\# Updating portfolio weights
weights_new = np.append(weights_current, weight_tech_stock)

\# New expected returns array
expected_returns_new = np.append(expected_returns_current,
```

```
expected_return_tech_stock)

\# Calculate the new expected return of the portfolio
new_expected_return = np.dot(weights_new, expected_returns_new)

\# Update covariance matrix to include the new asset (simplifying for demonstration)
cov_matrix_new = np.zeros((4, 4))
cov_matrix_new[:3, :3] = cov_matrix_current
cov_matrix_new[3, 3] = risk_tech_stock ** 2

\# Portfolio variance calculation
portfolio_variance = np.dot(weights_new.T, np.dot(cov_matrix_new, weights_new))
portfolio_risk = np.sqrt(portfolio_variance)

print(f"New expected return: {new_expected_return:.2%}")
print(f"New portfolio risk: {portfolio_risk:.2%}")
```

Through this computational analysis, Sarah can gain valuable insights into how the addition of a tech stock affects her portfolio's expected return and risk profile. This capability to perform real-time calculations empowers investors like her to make informed decisions as market conditions fluctuate.

In conclusion, a profound understanding of risk and return is vital for any investor navigating the complexities of the financial landscape. Recognizing their intricate relationship —and adapting investment strategies accordingly—enables the creation of resilient, dynamic portfolios. The essence of investing lies not only in grasping these foundational concepts but also in integrating them into a comprehensive decision-making framework.

The Efficient Frontier: A Balancing Act

The Efficient Frontier embodies a dynamic collection of optimal portfolios that promise the highest expected return for a given level of risk or, conversely, the lowest risk for a specified return. Picture this as a curve on a graph where the x-axis denotes risk—measured by standard deviation—while the y-axis illustrates expected returns. Each point along this curve symbolizes a portfolio that an investor can assemble by varying combinations of assets.

To grasp the significance of the Efficient Frontier, consider the journey of Alex, an eager investor embarking on his financial adventure. Initially daunted by the sheer volume of investment options, Alex chooses to adopt a structured approach.

Through diligent analysis and exploration, Alex discovers that certain portfolios can deliver greater returns without significantly increasing risk. As he plots these portfolios on a graph, he uncovers the upward-sloping curve of the Efficient Frontier, revealing a critical insight: to aspire to higher returns, one must be willing to embrace greater risks. This curve distinctly separates the realm of attainable portfolios from those that remain elusive.

Example: Constructing the Efficient Frontier in Python

To make his insights tangible, Alex leverages the power of Python to simulate various portfolio combinations and visualize the Efficient Frontier. With a simplified set of assets, he creates code that generates potential portfolios and visually represents them:

```python import numpy as np import matplotlib.pyplot as plt

\# Simulated expected returns and covariance matrix for three assets
expected_returns = np.array([0.12, 0.08, 0.05]) \# Returns for Stock, Bond, and Commodity
cov_matrix = np.array([[0.02, 0.001, 0.0005],
              [0.001, 0.01, 0.002],
              [0.0005, 0.002, 0.001]])
```

```
\# Function to calculate portfolio performance
def portfolio_performance(weights):
    port_return = np.sum(weights * expected_returns)
    port_variance = np.dot(weights.T, np.dot(cov_matrix, weights))
    port_std_dev = np.sqrt(port_variance)
    return port_return, port_std_dev

\# Generate random portfolios
num_portfolios = 10000
results = np.zeros((3, num_portfolios))

for i in range(num_portfolios):
    weights = np.random.random(3)
    weights /= np.sum(weights)
    returns, std_dev = portfolio_performance(weights)
    results[0,i] = returns
    results[1,i] = std_dev
    results[2,i] = (returns - 0.05) / std_dev  \# Sharpe ratio

\# Plotting the Efficient Frontier
plt.figure(figsize=(10, 6))
plt.scatter(results[1,:], results[0,:], c=results[2,:], cmap='viridis',
marker='o')
plt.title('Efficient Frontier')
plt.xlabel('Risk (Standard Deviation)')
plt.ylabel('Expected Return')
plt.colorbar(label='Sharpe Ratio')
plt.grid()
plt.show()
```

Upon executing this code, Alex reveals the salient points on the graph, showcasing the Efficient Frontier's ascendant trajectory. This visual helps investors discern the most advantageous risk-return combinations available.

The Capital Market Line: Integrating Risk-

Free Asset and Market Portfolio

While the Efficient Frontier delineates the optimal risk-return trade-offs attainable through risky assets alone, the Capital Market Line introduces an essential dimension: the risk-free asset. Representing the ideal combination of risk-free investments—such as government treasury bills—with the market portfolio, the CML further enriches an investor's framework for decision-making.

Mathematically, the CML illustrates that by allocating a portion of capital to both the risk-free asset and the market portfolio, investors can cultivate a linear relationship between risk and return.

Visualizing the CML

Envision a line that emerges from the risk-free rate on the y-axis (denoting return) and extends tangentially from the Efficient Frontier's curve—this line is the Capital Market Line. The slope of this line signifies the market's price of risk, and is defined by the following equation:

$$\text{CML equation: } E(R_p) = R_f + \frac{E(R_m) - R_f}{\sigma_m} \sigma_p$$

Where: - ($E(R_p)$) = expected return of the portfolio - (R_f) = return on the risk-free asset - ($E(R_m)$) = expected return of the market portfolio - (σ_m) = standard deviation of returns of the market portfolio - (σ_p) = standard deviation of returns of the portfolio

As investors contemplate various asset allocations, they can compute their expected returns in relation to the risk introduced by the risk-free asset.

A Practical Example of the CML

Continuing with Alex's story, he estimates the risk-free rate at 3% and recalls his previous calculations showing that the expected market portfolio yield stands at 10%, with a standard deviation of 15%. This insight empowers him to plot the Capital Market Line:

```python
risk_free_rate = 0.03 market_return = 0.10
market_std_dev = 0.15

\# Generating CML points
x_cml = np.linspace(0, 0.2, 100)
y_cml = risk_free_rate + (market_return - risk_free_rate) /
market_std_dev * x_cml

plt.figure(figsize=(10, 6))
plt.plot(x_cml, y_cml, label='Capital Market Line', color='red')
plt.scatter(results[1,:], results[0,:], c=results[2,:], cmap='viridis',
marker='o')
plt.title('Efficient Frontier and Capital Market Line')
plt.xlabel('Risk (Standard Deviation)')
plt.ylabel('Expected Return')
plt.colorbar(label='Sharpe Ratio')
plt.legend()
plt.grid()
plt.show()
```

In this visualization, the interaction between the Efficient Frontier and the Capital Market Line illuminates the intricate relationship between risk and return, guiding Alex toward optimal strategies that incorporate both market and risk-free assets. This integration allows him to see the potential adjustments he could make to achieve his desired risk-return profile.

A comprehensive understanding of the Efficient Frontier and the Capital Market Line equips investors not only with theoretical insight but also with actionable strategies for constructing portfolios that maximize returns while effectively managing risks. As Alex's experience demonstrates, the real takeaway lies in recognizing how different asset allocations can impact performance, enabling investors to align their strategies with their unique risk tolerances and financial objectives.

The Foundations of Mean-Variance Optimization

Mean-variance optimization hinges on two pivotal concepts: the expected return and the variance (or standard deviation) of investment returns. The expected return is a valuable estimate of the average return an investor can anticipate from an asset, while variance quantifies the extent of variability around this expected return—effectively capturing the risk involved.

Consider Emma, an ambitious financial analyst based in London. With dreams of curating a resilient investment portfolio, she instinctively acknowledges that not all assets perform uniformly. Some stocks may skyrocket, while others may plummet; thus, Emma realizes that the key to successful investing lies in effectively balancing these contrasting risk-reward dynamics.

To illustrate her thought process, Emma identifies three promising assets:

- **Asset A:** Expected return of 10%, with a variance of 0.04.
- **Asset B:** Expected return of 6%, with a variance of 0.01.
- **Asset C:** Expected return of 8%, with a variance of 0.025.

The Mean-Variance Optimization Process

1. **Evaluating Return and Risk**: Emma embarks on her journey by calculating the expected return and variance of various asset combinations. She employs the following formulas:
2. **Expected Portfolio Return (E)**: [$E(R_p) = w_A \cdot E(R_A) + w_B \cdot E(R_B) + w_C \cdot E(R_C)$] Here,

(w) symbolizes the weight attributed to each asset in the portfolio.

3. **Portfolio Variance ((\sigma^2))**: [\sigma^2_p = w_A^2 \cdot \sigma^2_A + w_B^2 \cdot \sigma^2_B + w_C^2 \cdot \sigma^2_C + 2 \cdot w_A \cdot w_B \cdot \sigma_{AB} + 2 \cdot w_A \cdot w_C \cdot \sigma_{AC} + 2 \cdot w_B \cdot w_C \cdot \sigma_{BC}] In this equation, (\sigma_{ij}) denotes the covariance between assets (i) and (j).
4. **Determining Asset Weights**: As she meticulously adjusts the weights of the assets, Emma seeks to discover a combination that maximizes expected returns while minimizing the overall risk of her portfolio. This process involves analyzing multiple combinations of asset weights, allowing her to visualize the intricate relationship between risk and return.
5. **Harnessing Python for Portfolio Optimization**: To enhance her efficiency, Emma turns to Python, creating scripts that simplify the mean-variance optimization process. Below is an example of her approach:

```python import numpy as np import pandas as pd import matplotlib.pyplot as plt from scipy.optimize import minimize

```
\# Expected returns and variances
expected_returns = np.array([0.10, 0.06, 0.08])
cov_matrix = np.array([[0.04, 0.001, 0.002],
                       [0.001, 0.01, 0.0015],
                       [0.002, 0.0015, 0.025]])

\# Function to calculate portfolio performance
def portfolio_performance(weights):
  port_return = np.sum(weights * expected_returns)
  port_variance = np.dot(weights.T, np.dot(cov_matrix, weights))
```
```

```
    port_std_dev = np.sqrt(port_variance)
    return port_return, port_variance

\# Function to minimize (objective function)
def negative_sharpe_ratio(weights):
    return -portfolio_performance(weights)[0] / portfolio_performance(weights)[1]

\# Constraints and bounds
constraints = ({'type': 'eq', 'fun': lambda x: np.sum(x) - 1})
bounds = ((0, 1), (0, 1), (0, 1)) \# Asset weights must sum to 1

\# Initial guess for asset weights
initial_weights = np.array([1/3, 1/3, 1/3])

\# Optimization process
optimal_results = minimize(negative_sharpe_ratio, initial_weights, method='SLSQP', bounds=bounds, constraints=constraints)

optimal_weights = optimal_results.x
optimal_return, optimal_variance = portfolio_performance(optimal_weights)

print("Optimal Asset Weights:", optimal_weights)
print("Optimal Expected Return:", optimal_return)
print("Optimal Portfolio Variance:", optimal_variance)
```

By executing this code, Emma uncovers the optimal asset weights that strike a harmonious balance between expected returns and risk management. This computational approach affords her the agility to explore a variety of portfolio configurations, equipping her with the critical insights necessary for informed decision-making.

Practical Application of Mean-Variance Optimization

Armed with the knowledge she has gained, Emma constructs a portfolio that aligns seamlessly with her risk tolerance and investment objectives.

Moreover, Emma understands the importance of adaptability in the investment landscape. As market conditions evolve, she can modify her portfolio accordingly, leveraging the mean-variance optimization framework to reassess and realign her asset allocations with her shifting financial goals.

Grasping the concepts behind mean-variance optimization equips investors like Emma with a strategic methodology for portfolio construction.

As we advance through the intricacies of portfolio theory, the principles of mean-variance optimization will serve as a robust foundation for more sophisticated investment strategies. This framework not only illuminates the delicate interplay between risk and reward but also empowers investors to navigate the complexities of the financial landscape with confidence.

Asset Allocation Techniques

The Art of Diversification

Before embarking on the asset allocation journey, it's essential to understand the cornerstone principle of diversification. This strategy revolves around spreading investments across a myriad of financial instruments, sectors, and markets to mitigate risk. Picture a portfolio built solely on technology stocks: a downturn in that sector could devastate your financial standing. However, if that same portfolio also includes bonds, real estate, and commodities, the adverse impacts of a tech slump can be significantly alleviated.

Take the experience of Sarah, a London-based hedge fund manager, as a cautionary tale. In 2020, she heavily invested in travel stocks, anticipating a swift rebound as the world emerged from pandemic restrictions. Unfortunately, her optimism was misplaced, and as the travel sector continued to struggle, her portfolio suffered substantial losses. In hindsight, she recognized that a well-rounded approach—incorporating sectors like healthcare, utilities, and consumer staples—might have cushioned the blow during those unpredictable times.

Modern Portfolio Theory (MPT)

Developed by Nobel laureate Harry Markowitz in the 1950s, Modern Portfolio Theory (MPT) holds that investors seek to maximize expected returns for a given level of risk or, conversely, minimize risk for a targeted return. This elegant framework allows investors to identify a frontier of optimal portfolios, each offering the best possible expected return at specific risk levels—an essential balance of risk and reward.

Imagine an investor constructing a portfolio consisting of stocks, bonds, and commodities. Each asset class presents a unique risk-return profile, and blending them wisely positions the portfolio along the efficient frontier. The challenge, however, lies in pinpointing the optimal allocation, which is where tools like Python come into play.

Implementing MPT in Python

Leveraging Python alongside libraries such as NumPy and pandas can facilitate the implementation of MPT, making the modeling of investment portfolios both straightforward and efficient. Here's a glimpse of a simple implementation that calculates the expected return and risk of a diversified portfolio:

```python import numpy as np import pandas as pd import matplotlib.pyplot as plt

```
\# Sample data on asset returns
returns_data = {
    'Stocks': [0.1, 0.08, 0.12],
    'Bonds': [0.04, 0.05, 0.05],
    'Commodities': [0.05, 0.06, 0.03]
}
```
```

```
returns = pd.DataFrame(returns_data)

\# Calculate the average expected returns
expected_returns = returns.mean()

\# Compute the covariance matrix of returns
cov_matrix = returns.cov()

\# Function to calculate portfolio statistics
def portfolio_statistics(weights):
    portfolio_return = np.dot(weights, expected_returns)
    portfolio_volatility = np.sqrt(np.dot(weights.T, np.dot(cov_matrix, weights)))
    return portfolio_return, portfolio_volatility

\# Example allocation
weights = np.array([0.5, 0.3, 0.2]) \# 50% Stocks, 30% Bonds, 20% Commodities
expected_return, volatility = portfolio_statistics(weights)

print(f'Expected Return: {expected_return:.2%}')
print(f'Volatility: {volatility:.2%}')
```

This concise code snippet showcases how to effectively calculate expected return and volatility within a sample portfolio, offering a robust starting point for investors interested in conducting comprehensive analyses.

Strategic Asset Allocation

Strategic asset allocation involves establishing baseline allocations across various asset classes, periodically adjusted to align with market conditions. This long-term approach ensures portfolios remain in harmony with an investor's risk tolerance and overarching investment objectives. For instance, a young investor with a bold risk appetite may allocate 70% to equities and 30% to bonds. As retirement approaches, they might transition to a more conservative distribution of 40% equities and 60% bonds, reflecting a diminished capacity for risk.

The importance of making strategic adjustments cannot be overstated. A notable example involves a seasoned investment firm that routinely recalibrates its asset allocation based on economic indicators, adapting its bond-to-stock ratio in response to evolving interest rate forecasts.

Tactical Asset Allocation

In contrast to strategic asset allocation, tactical asset allocation enables short-term adjustments informed by market dynamics and macroeconomic trends. For instance, during the onset of a recession, an investor might proactively increase their bond holdings while reducing stock exposure. This adaptive strategy resembles a seasoned navigator adjusting their sails in response to shifting winds—it calls for both deep knowledge and practical experience.

Consider Mark, a New York-based investor, who quickly recognized economic distress early in the COVID-19 pandemic. He strategically shifted his holdings toward utilities and consumer goods—sectors that historically show resilience in downturns. This timely maneuver not only preserved his capital but positioned him advantageously for subsequent gains as the market began to stabilize.

Asset allocation is an intricate process that transcends mere capital distribution; it is an ongoing journey of understanding market dynamics, aligning individual goals, and navigating risk tolerance. Whether employing Modern Portfolio Theory, adopting strategic approaches, or making tactical adjustments, the fundamental aim remains the same: to construct a resilient portfolio capable of weathering diverse market conditions. The techniques outlined in this exploration serve as foundational tools that empower investors like Sarah and Mark to confidently traverse the complexities of the financial landscape, regardless of the challenges ahead.

Unleashing the Power of Python for Portfolio Optimization

In today's intricate financial landscape, efficient portfolio optimization stands out as a vital strategy for investors aiming to enhance their returns while mitigating risks. In this segment, we will explore how Python serves as a powerful ally in portfolio optimization, provide you with essential tools, and present practical examples to deepen your understanding of this valuable process.

The Integral Role of Python in Financial Analysis

Python's adaptability and extensive library ecosystem make it indispensable for financial analysts. The spectrum of tasks that Python can handle—from data manipulation to sophisticated mathematical modeling—allows analysts to integrate a variety of techniques seamlessly when optimizing portfolios. Libraries such as NumPy, which is ideal for numerical operations, pandas for data handling, and SciPy for optimization tasks create an all-encompassing framework that addresses every aspect of portfolio management.

Consider a mid-sized investment firm striving to enhance its portfolio optimization process, which has become a cumbersome endeavor filled with tedious manual calculations. This transformation not only streamlined operations but also significantly minimized human error, leading to more strategic investment decisions.

Laying the Groundwork for Portfolio Optimization

The journey to portfolio optimization begins with defining an investment universe—essentially the stocks or assets you intend to analyze. Following this, it's crucial to establish expected returns, risks, and correlations among the various assets involved. Let's break down how to achieve these objectives using Python.

1. Data Retrieval

Harnessing historical price data is essential for gaining valuable insights into asset performance. Here's how to easily retrieve stock price data using the yfinance library:

```python
import yfinance as yf
import pandas as pd

\# Define your asset universe
tickers = ['AAPL', 'MSFT', 'GOOGL', 'AMZN', 'FB']
data = yf.download(tickers, start="2018-01-01", end="2023-01-01")
['Adj Close']

\# Display the first few rows of the dataset
print(data.head())
```

This code snippet fetches adjusted closing prices for selected tech stocks over the past five years. Armed with this data, you can proceed to calculate the necessary returns, risks, and other key performance metrics.

2. Calculating Returns and Covariance

With your historical price data in hand, the next logical step is to compute daily returns and the covariance matrix—an essential tool for understanding the risk profile of your portfolio. Here's how to accomplish this:

```python
# Calculate daily returns returns =
data.pct_change().dropna()

\# Calculate the covariance matrix of returns
cov_matrix = returns.cov()

\# Display the covariance matrix
print(cov_matrix)
```

The covariance matrix will play a pivotal role when we evaluate the risk of different asset combinations later in the process.

Implementing Mean-Variance Optimization

At the core of portfolio optimization lies Mean-Variance Optimization. This technique assists investors in determining how to allocate their total assets to minimize risk while achieving a desired expected return.

3. Optimization Algorithm

To implement the optimization algorithm, we'll leverage the SciPy library. Our goal is to identify the asset proportions that minimize portfolio variance while achieving a designated return. Below is an example of how to do this:

```python
import numpy as np from scipy.optimize import minimize

\# Set initial weights
num_assets = len(tickers)
initial_weights = num_assets * [1.0 / num_assets] \# Equal weights

\# Define the objective function (portfolio variance)
def portfolio_variance(weights):
  return np.dot(weights.T, np.dot(cov_matrix, weights))

\# Constraints: weights must sum to 1
constraints = ({'type': 'eq', 'fun': lambda x: np.sum(x) - 1})

\# Bounds for each weight
bounds = tuple((0, 1) for asset in range(num_assets))

\# Perform optimization
optimal = minimize(portfolio_variance, initial_weights, method='SLSQP', bounds=bounds, constraints=constraints)

\# Display optimal weights
optimal_weights = optimal.x
print(f'Optimal Weights: {optimal_weights}')
```

This code utilizes the Sequential Least Squares Programming

(SLSQP) method to minimize variance while adhering to the constraint that all asset weights must sum to one. The output provides insights into how much capital should be allocated to each asset for effective risk management.

Evaluating the Optimized Portfolio

After discovering the optimal weights, it is crucial to evaluate the expected return and risk associated with the resulting portfolio. Understanding these metrics helps ensure that your optimized portfolio not only curtails volatility but also aligns with your return objectives. Here's how to perform those calculations:

```python
# Calculate expected portfolio return
expected_returns = returns.mean()
portfolio_return = np.dot(optimal_weights, expected_returns)

# Calculate expected portfolio volatility
portfolio_volatility = np.sqrt(portfolio_variance(optimal_weights))

print(f'Optimized Portfolio Expected Return: {portfolio_return:.2%}')
print(f'Optimized Portfolio Volatility: {portfolio_volatility:.2%}')
```

Equipped with these metrics, you can determine whether the optimized portfolio achieves the right balance between risk and expected returns.

Harnessing Python for portfolio optimization not only automates the investment process but also empowers analysts to make precise, data-driven decisions. As discussed in the case studies and illustrated through practical code examples, integrating technology in financial analysis is now more crucial than ever for achieving success in a competitive marketplace.

The Sharpe Ratio and Performance Attribution: A Comprehensive Guide

In the intricate landscape of finance, where meticulous calculations and data-driven insights underpin decision-making, the ability to accurately assess investment performance is essential. Among the various metrics available, the Sharpe Ratio stands out due to its clarity and relevance. In this exploration, we will dive into the nuances of the Sharpe Ratio, unpack the mechanics of performance attribution, and uncover how these concepts converge to create a detailed portrait of investment success.

Understanding the Sharpe Ratio

The Sharpe Ratio, conceptualized by Nobel laureate William F. Sharpe in 1966, is a fundamental metric in asset management, providing a systematic approach to risk-adjusted return evaluation. Essentially, it quantifies the return in excess of the risk-free rate per unit of volatility, effectively illustrating how well an investment rewards an investor for taking on risk.

Mathematically, the Sharpe Ratio is defined as follows:

$$\text{Sharpe Ratio} = \frac{R_p - R_f}{\sigma_p}$$

Where: - (R_p) represents the return of the portfolio, - (R_f) indicates the risk-free rate, and - (σ_p) denotes the standard deviation of the portfolio's excess return, a measure of its volatility.

The Components of the Sharpe Ratio

To leverage the Sharpe Ratio effectively, it is essential to grasp its fundamental components—this involves collating historical return data for the portfolio and the risk-free rate. The time frame for analysis can vary; daily, weekly, or monthly returns can be utilized depending on the investment horizon.

Let's look at a practical example utilizing Python to gather necessary data:

```python
import yfinance as yf import numpy as np

# Set the risk-free rate (for example, 10-Year Treasury Yield)
```

risk_free_rate = 0.0175 \# 1.75%

\# Retrieve historical price data for a portfolio (in this case, SPY)
portfolio_data = yf.download('SPY', start='2020-01-01', end='2023-01-01')['Adj Close']

\# Calculate daily returns
portfolio_returns = portfolio_data.pct_change().dropna()

\`\`\`

2. Calculating Expected Portfolio Return and Volatility

Once we have the daily returns, we can compute the average return and volatility as follows:

\`\`\`python # Average daily return expected_return = portfolio_returns.mean() * 252 # Annualize by multiplying by the number of trading days

\# Portfolio volatility
portfolio_volatility = portfolio_returns.std() * np.sqrt(252) \# Annualize the volatility

\`\`\`

3. Calculating the Sharpe Ratio

Now that we have all the necessary components, calculating the Sharpe Ratio becomes a straightforward process:

\`\`\`python # Calculate the Sharpe Ratio sharpe_ratio = (expected_return - risk_free_rate) / portfolio_volatility

print(f"Sharpe Ratio: {sharpe_ratio:.2f}")

\`\`\`

A Sharpe Ratio greater than one typically signals that the portfolio provides returns that are proportionate to the risk taken. Conversely, a ratio below one may suggest that the risk involved isn't justified by the returns, prompting investors to reassess their strategies.

Performance Attribution: Analyzing

Portfolio Success

While the Sharpe Ratio offers a robust framework for assessing risk-adjusted returns, performance attribution takes a closer look at the specific factors contributing to a portfolio's overall performance. Essentially, it seeks to answer the critical question: *What drives the portfolio's returns?*

Performance attribution can be categorized into four main components:

1. **Asset Allocation:** This evaluates how the distribution among different asset classes (e.g., equities, bonds, cash) affects overall performance.
2. **Security Selection:** This assesses the impact of individual security choices within an asset class on portfolio outcomes.
3. **Market Timing:** This examines how effectively the portfolio manager adjusted exposure to various asset classes based on prevailing market conditions.
4. **Interaction Effects:** This accounts for the combined impact of asset allocation and security selection on the overall performance.

A Practical Example of Performance Attribution

Imagine an investor following a fundamental approach to build a portfolio comprised of selected stocks while fluctuating allocations between equities and bonds based on market forecasts. A basic performance attribution analysis could be executed as follows:

```python # Sample data representation asset_classes = ['Stocks', 'Bonds'] returns = {'Stocks': 0.12, 'Bonds': 0.05} weights = {'Stocks': 0.7, 'Bonds': 0.3}

\# Performance attribution function
def performance_attribution(returns, weights):
  contribution = {}
  for asset in asset_classes:
```

```
    contribution[asset] = returns[asset] * weights[asset]
  return contribution

\# Analyze performance attribution
contributions = performance_attribution(returns, weights)
print("Performance Attribution Contributions:")
for asset, contrib in contributions.items():
  print(f"{asset}: {contrib:.2%} of total return")
```

This analysis enables investors to pinpoint which asset classes and specific investments significantly influenced overall performance. Was the robustness of stock returns due to astute selection, or was it merely a fortunate market movement? Such insights empower investors to refine their strategies by capitalizing on high-performing sectors while reevaluating underwhelming assets.

The synergy between the Sharpe Ratio and performance attribution enhances an investor's understanding of not only *how well* their portfolio is performing but also *why* it is achieving that performance.

As you harness the analytical capabilities of Python to conduct these evaluations, remember that the insights derived from these metrics can significantly influence your investment strategy.

Equipped with this foundational knowledge of the Sharpe Ratio and performance attribution, you are now prepared to elevate your investment strategies, making informed choices that align with your financial aspirations.

Uncovering Systematic Risk

Systematic risk, often referred to as market risk, encompasses the inherent uncertainties that affect the entire market or one of its segments. This type of risk is embedded in the broader economic framework and cannot be mitigated through diversification alone. Factors contributing to systematic risk include:

1. **Economic Fluctuations**: Variations in key economic indicators—such as GDP growth, unemployment rates, and inflation—significantly influence market performance.
2. **Geopolitical Dynamics**: Events like conflicts, international tensions, and major political shifts can lead to heightened market volatility, affecting all asset classes.
3. **Market Sentiment**: Collective investor behavior, increasingly swayed by news cycles and social media, can trigger wide-ranging market movements.

An illustrative example of systematic risk occurred during the global financial crisis of 2008. The collapse of major financial institutions, massive government bailouts, and plummeting consumer confidence resulted in a sharp downturn affecting virtually all asset classes, underscoring how interconnected and vulnerable investments can be to overarching economic forces.

To quantify systematic risk, investors commonly utilize metrics such as the beta coefficient:

[\text{Beta} = \frac{\text{Cov}(R_i, R_m)}{\text{Var}(R_m)}]

Where: - (R_i) represents the asset's return, - (R_m) signifies the market's return, - Cov indicates covariance, and - Var represents variance.

A beta of 1 suggests that an asset's price movement is aligned with that of the market. A beta greater than 1 indicates greater volatility relative to market fluctuations, while a beta less than 1 signifies reduced volatility.

```python import numpy as np import pandas as pd import yfinance as yf

\# Downloading market and stock data (for illustrative purposes,
```

```
consider a stock and S&P 500)
stock_symbol = 'AAPL'
market_symbol = '^GSPC'  \# S&P 500 as the market benchmark

\# Fetch historical data
stock_data = yf.download(stock_symbol, start='2020-01-01', end='2023-01-01')['Adj Close']
market_data = yf.download(market_symbol, start='2020-01-01', end='2023-01-01')['Adj Close']

\# Calculating daily returns
stock_returns = stock_data.pct_change().dropna()
market_returns = market_data.pct_change().dropna()

\# Calculate covariance and variance
covariance = np.cov(stock_returns, market_returns)[0][1]
market_variance = np.var(market_returns)

\# Calculate beta
beta = covariance / market_variance
print(f"Beta for {stock_symbol}: {beta:.2f}")
```

Understanding systematic risk is crucial for investors, as it informs strategic decisions—for instance, employing hedging techniques to mitigate potential downturns or reallocating investments towards more secure assets during periods of instability.

Delving into Unsystematic Risk

Conversely, unsystematic risk refers to risks associated with a specific asset or a small group of assets. These risks can arise from various factors, including:

1. **Company-Specific Performance**: Internal dynamics—such as leadership changes, product innovations, and operational challenges—can dramatically impact stock prices without any influence from broader market trends.

2. **Industry-Wide Changes**: Transformations within particular industries—attributed to technological breakthroughs, regulatory shifts, or mounting competition—create distinctive risk profiles across sectors.

Unlike systematic risk, unsystematic risk can often be mitigated through strategic diversification. For instance, an investor boasting a portfolio comprised of diverse stocks across various sectors can minimize the adverse impact of a poor-performing asset. If one company struggles, strong performances from other holdings can keep the overall portfolio steady.

A compelling example of unsystematic risk is illustrated by the contrasting fates of Blockbuster and Netflix. While Blockbuster remained stagnant in the face of the digital streaming revolution, Netflix embraced innovation and thrived. An investor who focused solely on cinema distribution would have suffered significant losses due to Blockbuster's decline, while seeing remarkable returns from Netflix.

Managing the Balance: Diversification and Risk Mitigation

With a clear understanding of both systematic and unsystematic risk, investors can implement diversified strategies to enhance portfolio resilience. While diversification significantly reduces unsystematic risk, it does not shield investors from systematic risks. A prudent approach may involve spreading investments across multiple asset classes—such as equities, fixed income, and commodities—while also diversifying geographically. This strategy limits exposure to fluctuations in any single market.

A practical demonstration of diversification can be achieved by constructing a mixed-asset portfolio using Python:

```python
# Sample asset returns data assets = { 'Stocks': np.random.normal(0.08, 0.12, 1000), 'Bonds': np.random.normal(0.04, 0.05, 1000), 'Real Estate': np.random.normal(0.07, 0.1, 1000) }

\# Simulating a random portfolio allocation
weights = np.random.dirichlet(np.ones(len(assets)), size=1)[0]

\# Calculate expected portfolio return and volatility
portfolio_return = sum(weights[i] * np.mean(assets[key]) for i, key in enumerate(assets.keys()))
portfolio_volatility = np.sqrt(sum(weights[i]**2 * np.var(assets[key]) for i, key in enumerate(assets.keys())))

print(f"Expected Portfolio Return: {portfolio_return:.2%}")
print(f"Portfolio Volatility: {portfolio_volatility:.2%}")
```

Navigating the complex terrain of finance necessitates not only recognizing the differences between systematic and unsystematic risk but also employing effective strategies for managing these risks.

Equipped with the insights provided in this exploration, you are now better positioned to tackle the intricacies of the market with confidence. Ensuring that every investment decision is grounded in a thorough comprehension of risk dynamics will distinguish you as a savvy investor in a competitive landscape.

Active vs. Passive Management: Navigating the Investment Landscape

Investing in financial markets can often feel like traversing a complex maze filled with a multitude of options and potential consequences. One of the most critical decisions any investor faces is whether to adopt active management or embrace a passive strategy. Each approach has its own strengths and weaknesses, shaping not only portfolio performance but also the investor's overall philosophy. To invest wisely in the unpredictable world of finance, a comprehensive understanding of the distinctions between active and passive management is essential.

The Philosophy Behind Active Management

Active management can be likened to a skilled conductor leading a vibrant orchestra, meticulously orchestrating investments with the aim of outperforming a benchmark index. This approach hinges on in-depth research, keen market insights, and timely decision-making, as portfolio managers actively buy and sell securities based on thorough analyses and market predictions. The primary objective? To "beat the market" by strategically timing purchases and sales, selecting individual stocks, bonds, or other investments believed to be positioned for growth.

A quintessential illustration of successful active management can be seen in hedge funds, which thrive on capitalizing on short-term price fluctuations. For instance, during the COVID-19 pandemic, numerous hedge funds swiftly adjusted their strategies, shorting heavily impacted sectors like travel and leisure while investing in technology companies that flourished during lockdown. These nimble pivots underscored the unique ability of active managers to adapt promptly to an ever-evolving market landscape.

Key Advantages of Active Management

1. **Potential for Higher Returns**: Skilled active managers can uncover market inefficiencies, identifying undervalued securities or emerging trends long before the broader market catches on.

2. **Flexibility in Asset Allocation**: Active managers have the freedom to modify their portfolios in response to changing market conditions, thereby managing risks effectively during downturns.

3. **Risk Control**: Through strategies like sector rotation and tactical asset allocation, active management offers the potential to protect against systematic risks, allowing for adjustments based on market dynamics.

The Challenges of Active Management

Despite its advantages, active management presents its own set of challenges:

1. **Higher Costs**: Engaging in active management often results in elevated fees—management fees, performance fees, and trading costs—that can significantly erode total returns. For example, a manager charging 2% annually, plus 20% on profits, can diminish a 10% portfolio growth down to merely 8% net yield.
2. **Market Timing Risks**: Active management necessitates a reliance on accurate market predictions, which can be a double-edged sword. A miscalculation regarding market direction can lead to substantial losses.
3. **Underperformance Risks**: Research from institutions like S&P Dow Jones Indices often reveals that, over extended periods, many active managers struggle to outperform their benchmark indices. After accounting for fees, the majority of active funds tend to lag behind simpler, less costly index funds.

The Passive Approach: Buy and Hold

In stark contrast to the dynamic nature of active management, passive investing can be visualized as nurturing a well-planned garden. Investors adopting a passive strategy typically embrace a "buy and hold" philosophy, acquiring a diversified array of asset classes that mirror a market index—such as the S&P 500—under the assumption that over time, the market will yield positive returns.

The remarkable ascent of passive investing can be traced back to the inception of index funds by Jack Bogle in the 1970s. These funds have surged in popularity, offering a simple, cost-effective means to achieve broad market exposure. Consider a passive investor who consistently contributes to an S&P 500 index fund over 20 years. Despite market fluctuations and downturns, historical performance suggests strong potential for meaningful gains over time, benefiting from the market's general upward trajectory.

Key Advantages of Passive Management

1. **Lower Costs**: Because passive funds involve minimal management and trading, they typically offer lower fees than their actively managed counterparts. This cost efficiency can lead to higher net returns over time.

2. **Simplicity and Transparency**: Passive investing is straightforward, enabling investors to grasp their holdings without extensive research or analytical work. Investors can focus on steady contributions rather than attempting to outsmart the market.

3. **Market Averaging**: Passive strategies tend to generate returns that are aligned with broader market performance, allowing investors to benefit from long-term market trends, regardless of economic fluctuations.

The Challenges of Passive Management

Despite its merits, passive management has its limitations:

1. **Limited Flexibility**: Passive strategies are inherently inflexible, automatically adjusting to match an index's composition. This may result in missed

opportunities in emerging markets or neglecting sectors that are underperforming.

2. **Market Risk Exposure**: Passive investors remain fully exposed to market downturns. During recessions or market crashes, like the 2008 financial crisis, the simultaneous plummet of all holdings can be detrimental.
3. **Lack of Active Response**: Unlike their active counterparts, passive strategies do not capitalize on short-term market fluctuations, which may prove disadvantageous during periods of high volatility.

Navigating the Best of Both Worlds

When it comes to choosing between active and passive management, factors such as personal preferences, risk tolerance, and financial objectives play a pivotal role. Some investors may relish the excitement and potential of higher returns associated with active strategies, while others may gravitate towards the ease and cost-effectiveness of passive investing.

A blended approach could prove advantageous. For instance, an investor might allocate a portion of their portfolio to actively managed funds, aiming for higher returns during market fluctuations, while concurrently investing in low-cost index funds for a foundation of stability and market exposure. This strategy embodies the best of both worlds, enabling adaptability while maintaining cost efficiency.

In summary, the discourse surrounding active versus passive investment management is both intricate and nuanced. Each strategy carries its unique set of advantages and disadvantages, offering investors a distinctive opportunity to tailor their portfolios according to personal aspirations and market insights. Whether one opts for the thrill of active trading or the tranquility of passive strategies, the key lies in aligning investment approaches with individual financial goals and risk preferences. With a blend of knowledge and practical experience, every investor can navigate their financial path—finding balance in the realms of active and passive investment management.

Case Study: Building an Optimal Portfolio

Investing is an intricate art form, much like a master chef skillfully blending flavors to create a culinary masterpiece. Each ingredient contributes to the overall dish, and in the realm of investment, constructing an optimal portfolio involves a careful balance of various elements to achieve desirable returns while managing risk effectively. This case study invites you to embark on a journey through the multifaceted world of portfolio construction, incorporating theoretical foundations alongside practical Python techniques to bring these concepts to life.

Understanding the Essentials of Portfolio Construction

Before delving into the intricacies of portfolio creation, it's essential to grasp the fundamental principles outlined in Modern Portfolio Theory (MPT). MPT posits that investors can construct portfolios that maximize expected returns for a given level of risk, effectively navigating the delicate trade-offs between risk and reward.

Key Components of an Optimal Portfolio

1. **Risk Tolerance**: The first step in crafting an optimal portfolio is discerning how much risk you're willing to assume. This is inherently individual—shaped by personal financial goals, investment time horizons, and comfort with market fluctuations.

2. **Asset Allocation**: This strategy involves selecting the appropriate mix of asset classes—such as equities,

bonds, and alternative investments—to strike a desired balance between risk and return. A well-diversified portfolio that spans different sectors and geographies can significantly mitigate risk.

3. **Expected Return**: To construct an optimal portfolio, you need to estimate the expected return of different assets. This estimation is informed by a thorough analysis of historical performance, macroeconomic indicators, and current market trends.
4. **Correlations**: Understanding how asset returns relate to one another is critical.

Demonstrating the Process with Python

Now, let's dive into a practical example of constructing an optimal portfolio using Python. Consider an investor aiming for a 7% annual return while staying within a risk threshold of 10%. The available asset classes are:

- **Equities**: Historical returns of 10% with a standard deviation of 15%
- **Bonds**: Historical returns of 4% with a standard deviation of 5%
- **Real Estate Investment Trusts (REITs)**: Historical returns of 8% with a standard deviation of 12%

Steps to Construct the Portfolio

1. **Setting Up the Python Environment**: To initiate our analysis, we'll need to set up our environment with essential libraries such as numpy, pandas, and matplotlib.

```python
import numpy as np import pandas as pd
import matplotlib.pyplot as plt
```

1. **Defining Asset Characteristics**: Next, we define

the expected returns, standard deviations, and the correlation matrix for each asset class.

```python
# Expected Returns returns = np.array([0.10, 0.04, 0.08]) # Corresponding to Equities, Bonds, REITs # Standard Deviations std_dev = np.array([0.15, 0.05, 0.12]) # Correlation Matrix correlation_matrix = np.array([[1, 0.2, 0.3], [0.2, 1, 0.2], [0.3, 0.2, 1]])
```

1. **Calculating the Covariance Matrix**: To comprehend the relationships between assets, we calculate the covariance matrix using the standard deviations and correlation coefficients.

```python
cov_matrix = np.outer(std_dev, std_dev) * correlation_matrix
```

1. **Optimizing Portfolio Weights**: We create a function that generates random portfolio weights while ensuring they sum to 1. This function will also calculate the expected return and volatility associated with these weights.

```python
def portfolio_performance(weights): portfolio_return = np.sum(weights * returns) portfolio_std_dev = np.sqrt(np.dot(weights.T, np.dot(cov_matrix, weights))) return portfolio_return, portfolio_std_dev
```

1. **Simulating Random Portfolios**: To explore the efficient frontier, we'll generate a multitude of portfolio combinations and plot the potential returns against their associated risks.

```python
num_portfolios = 10000
results = np.zeros((3, num_portfolios))

for i in range(num_portfolios):
  weights = np.random.random(3)
  weights /= np.sum(weights)
  returns, std_dev = portfolio_performance(weights)
  results[0, i] = returns
  results[1, i] = std_dev
  results[2, i] = results[0, i] / results[1, i] \# Sharpe Ratio

plt.scatter(results[1, :], results[0, :], c=results[2, :], cmap='viridis')
plt.xlabel('Risk (Standard Deviation)')
plt.ylabel('Return')
plt.title('Efficient Frontier')
plt.colorbar(label='Sharpe Ratio')
plt.show()
```

Analyzing the Results

Upon visualizing our results, we can identify the portfolio that maximizes the Sharpe ratio, illuminating the efficient frontier—a cornerstone of MPT. To pinpoint the optimal portfolio weights, we can either employ advanced techniques like gradient ascent or evolutionary algorithms. Alternatively, we can utilize optimization libraries like SciPy to identify the maximum Sharpe ratio more directly.

```python
from scipy.optimize import minimize

def minimize_volatility(weights):
  return portfolio_performance(weights)[1]

constraints = ({'type': 'eq', 'fun': lambda weights: np.sum(weights) - 1})
bounds = tuple((0, 1) for x in range(len(returns)))

optimal = minimize(minimize_volatility, [1/len(returns)]
```

```
* len(returns), method='SLSQP', bounds=bounds,
constraints=constraints)
optimal_weights = optimal.x
```

Crafting an optimal portfolio transcends mere technicality; it embodies a harmonious blend of art and science, merging financial theory with the realities of the market. Through this case study, we've explored key concepts such as risk tolerance, diversification, and correlations, while using Python as a versatile tool for analysis.

As you navigate your investment journey, cultivate an eagerness to explore different strategies, applying these principles to design a portfolio that resonates with your personal financial aspirations. Whether you perceive investing as an exhilarating endeavor or a methodical process, remember that the essence of portfolio management rests in making informed choices that steer you toward your financial goals.

CHAPTER 6: RISK MANAGEMENT TECHNIQUES

Financial risk refers to the potential for loss of financial capital or the failure to achieve anticipated returns. This uncertainty arises from a multitude of factors, including market volatility, economic shifts, and the inherent unpredictability of individual assets.

Categories of Financial Risk

1. **Market Risk**: This category encompasses the potential for losses due to fluctuations in market prices. For instance, a sudden plunge in stock values following a disappointing earnings report exemplifies market risk. It is divided into two subcategories: systematic and unsystematic risks. Systematic risk affects the entire market and is typically mitigated through diversification, while unsystematic risk pertains to individual assets and can often be alleviated through in-depth analysis.

2. **Credit Risk**: This risk arises from the possibility that a borrower may default on their financial obligations, failing to repay their debts. Consider the scenario

of lending money to a friend who frequently delays payment; similarly, in finance, if a corporation or government entity defaults on bond payments, investors face credit risk. Credit ratings serve as a barometer for this risk, indicating the likelihood of default.

3. **Liquidity Risk**: The inability to buy or sell an asset without causing a significant impact on its price characterizes liquidity risk. Picture a quaint antique shop in a small town—a rare item may exist, but finding a buyer willing to pay its worth can be a challenge. In financial markets, insufficient liquidity can widen bid-ask spreads and hinder investors from executing trades with efficiency.
4. **Operational Risk**: This risk stems from failures in internal processes, systems, or human resources. Just like a Manhattan restaurant encountering logistical difficulties in sourcing ingredients, a financial institution can incur losses due to managerial mishaps, technology breakdowns, or even fraudulent activities.
5. **Currency Risk**: For investors engaged in transactions across different currencies, fluctuations can significantly affect returns when converted back to the base currency. For instance, a Canadian investor purchasing shares of a US-based tech firm may see their profitability impacted by changes in USD/CAD exchange rates.

Measuring Financial Risk

Effectively quantifying risk is essential in finance; without appropriate metrics, decision-making can become increasingly nebulous. Various models assist in this task, ranging from historical analyses to sophisticated mathematical frameworks.

Value at Risk (VaR)

One of the most widely used methodologies is Value at Risk (VaR), which estimates the potential loss in the value of a portfolio over a specified time frame, adjusted for a given confidence level. For example, if a portfolio's one-day VaR is (1 million at a 95% confidence level, there is a 5% chance that the portfolio could lose more than)1 million in a single day.

Here's a practical Python example to illustrate how to compute VaR using daily historical returns:

```python
import numpy as np

\# Simulating daily returns of a portfolio
returns = np.random.normal(0, 0.01, 1000)  \# Sample data

\# Function to calculate VaR at a specified confidence level
def calculate_var(returns, confidence_level=0.95):
  return np.percentile(returns, 100 * (1 - confidence_level))

var_95 = calculate_var(returns)
print(f"95% VaR: {-var_95:.2f}")
```

Stress Testing and Scenario Analysis

Stress testing is a vital tool for financial institutions, enabling them to evaluate the resilience of their portfolios during extreme market conditions. This practice can be likened to a marathon runner pushing their limits to prepare for unforeseen challenges.

In Python, one might simulate various stress scenarios to assess their potential impacts on a portfolio:

```python
# Function to perform stress testing on a portfolio def stress_test(portfolio, shocks): results = [] for shock in shocks: new_returns = portfolio * (1 + shock) results.append(new_returns) return results
```

```
portfolio = np.array([1.02, 0.98, 1.05]) \# Example portfolio values
shocks = [-0.1, -0.2, -0.3] \# Simulating 10%, 20%, and 30% market downturns

stressed_portfolios = stress_test(portfolio, shocks)
for stress in stressed_portfolios:
  print(stress)
```

The Importance of Understanding Financial Risk

Grasping the nuances of financial risk confers significant advantages, empowering investors to make informed decisions. This knowledge allows them to identify, analyze, and mitigate scenarios that might threaten their financial goals.

In a volatile world where geopolitical events and economic fluctuations can trigger market instability at a moment's notice, mastering the art of financial risk management becomes crucial for navigating these tumultuous waters.

Conclusion

As we conclude our exploration of financial risk, it becomes clear that effective navigation through the financial landscape necessitates more than mere instinct; it requires a thorough understanding of the diverse risks that may lie ahead. Just as a skilled sailor adjusts their sails to harness the wind's energy, investors too must be agile, equipped with knowledge, strategic tools, and the insight to foresee potential challenges.

This foundational understanding prepares us for our next discussion, where we'll delve deeper into specific risk measurement tools and methodologies, enhancing our toolkit for managing financial exposures in an ever-evolving market environment.

What Is Value at Risk (VaR)?

Value at Risk is a statistical measure that estimates the potential loss in value of an asset or portfolio over a specific time frame, given a certain confidence interval. Picture an investment portfolio responding to the fluctuations of stock prices, interest rates, or currency values—VaR effectively encapsulates the worst-case scenario within a designated period under normal market conditions.

For example, consider a portfolio with a one-day VaR of (100,000 at a 95% confidence level. This calculation implies there is a 5% chance that the portfolio could experience losses exceeding)100,000 within just one day. In this sense, VaR establishes a critical boundary for acceptable losses, arming investors with essential insights into their risk exposure.

How Is VaR Calculated?

Multiple methodologies are available for calculating VaR, each with unique strengths suited to different contexts. The three most prominent methods include:

1. **Historical Simulation**: This approach uses historical returns to project potential future outcomes, based on the assumption that past market behavior informs future risks. For instance, if a portfolio's returns over several days have been -2%, 1%, and 3%, these actual historical results serve as the foundation for future simulations.
2. **Variance-Covariance Method**: A more streamlined parametric approach, this method presumes a normal distribution of returns. Its straightforward nature makes it a popular choice among finance professionals.
3. **Monte Carlo Simulation**: This advanced technique harnesses random sampling and statistical modeling

to estimate a broad range of possible outcomes.

Example of VaR Calculation Using Python

As quantitative finance evolves, tools like Python play a crucial role in efficiently calculating VaR. Below is a basic implementation using the Historical Simulation method:

```
python import numpy as np import pandas as pd

\# Simulating daily returns for a hypothetical portfolio
np.random.seed(42) \# Ensures reproducibility
daily_returns = np.random.normal(0.001, 0.02, 1000) \# Mean return: 0.1%, standard deviation: 2%

\# Creating a DataFrame to store the returns
portfolio_returns = pd.DataFrame(daily_returns, columns=['Returns'])

\# Calculating VaR at the 95% confidence interval
confidence_level = 0.95
var_95 = -np.percentile(portfolio_returns['Returns'], (1 - confidence_level) * 100)
print(f"95% Value at Risk (VaR): \({var_95:.2f}")
```

This code snippet generates simulated daily portfolio returns based on a normal distribution and calculates the 95% VaR, providing valuable insights into the potential losses investors might face.

Understanding VaR Results

Interpreting VaR results is essential for effective risk management. A lower VaR value denotes a less risky profile, while a higher value signals increased risk exposure. However, it's important to recognize the limitations of VaR—the methodology does not account for the magnitude of losses that may occur beyond the specified percentile.

For instance, if an investor encounters a VaR of)50,000 at a

99% confidence interval, they can expect that losses should stay below this threshold approximately 99 out of 100 days. Yet, extreme market events, characterized by tail risks and distributions with fat tails, can lead to unexpected and substantial losses that VaR fails to predict.

The Role of VaR in Risk Management Frameworks

Integrating VaR into comprehensive risk management frameworks significantly enhances its effectiveness. Financial professionals can pair VaR with stress testing, which examines hypothetical adverse conditions to gauge the potential impact on portfolios.

During stress testing, practitioners simulate extreme scenarios—such as geopolitical crises or sudden market shocks—to identify vulnerabilities within their investment strategies.

As we delve deeper into the realm of financial risk, grasping the intricacies of Value at Risk through its various methodologies and applications becomes vital. VaR not only provides a statistically robust approach to estimating potential losses but also serves as a foundational element of a comprehensive risk management strategy.

Understanding Monte Carlo Simulations

The name "Monte Carlo simulation" pays homage to the legendary casino in Monaco, where luck plays a crucial role—akin to the stochastic nature of the simulations we seek to create. Fundamentally, a Monte Carlo simulation involves executing a model numerous times with random inputs, generating a spectrum of outcomes. This method shines particularly in scenarios that are influenced by a multitude of unpredictable variables, allowing analysts to assess complex systems with greater clarity.

How Monte Carlo Works

The process of conducting a Monte Carlo simulation begins with the establishment of a mathematical model that encapsulates the investment or system under evaluation. Key parameters and variables are identified, and random values are generated for these inputs based on their respective probability distributions, such as normal, log-normal, or uniform distributions. The model is then replicated thousands, or even millions, of times to yield a comprehensive distribution of possible outcomes. This array of results equips analysts to evaluate the likelihood of various scenarios and better understand associated risks.

For instance, when assessing a new investment project, factors such as prospective revenues, costs, and market conditions might each follow distinct probability distributions. Executing a Monte Carlo simulation enables stakeholders to gauge the volatility of potential cash flows, thereby informing more strategic investment decisions.

Applications in Financial Risk Analysis

Monte Carlo simulations have diverse applications within the realm of financial risk analysis, particularly in the following key areas:

1. **Value at Risk (VaR):** By simulating thousands of potential portfolio returns, analysts can ascertain the probability of a loss surpassing a defined threshold within a specified time frame.

2. **Option Pricing:** While the Black-Scholes model has long been a standard in derivatives pricing, Monte Carlo simulations provide a versatile alternative when confronting complex derivatives or exotic options that resist traditional methods.

3. **Stress Testing:** Financial institutions utilize simulations to evaluate portfolios' responses to extreme market conditions or shocks, such as

economic recessions or abrupt shifts in interest rates.

4. **Project Valuation:** In capital budgeting and project finance, Monte Carlo simulations can critically assess the uncertainties and risks shadowing cash flow projections.
5. **Portfolio Optimization:** As investment managers craft optimal asset allocations, simulations enable them to consider risk factors that conventional mean-variance optimization methods may overlook.

Implementing Monte Carlo Simulations in Python

Now, let's shift gears and immerse ourselves in a hands-on example illustrating the implementation of Monte Carlo simulation for risk analysis using Python. Our focus will be on calculating the Value at Risk (VaR) for a straightforward portfolio.

Step 1: Setting Up the Environment

Before we delve into the code, ensure that you have the requisite libraries installed. NumPy and Matplotlib are essential for numerical calculations and data visualization, respectively. If you haven't installed them yet, you can do so using the following command:

```bash
pip install numpy matplotlib
```

Step 2: Simulation Code

Next, we will define a function to simulate the returns of the portfolio:

```python
import numpy as np import matplotlib.pyplot as plt

\# Define parameters for the simulation
num_simulations = 10000  \# Total number of Monte Carlo
```

```
simulations
initial_portfolio_value = 100000 \# Initial value of the portfolio
mean_daily_return = 0.001 \# Expected average daily return (0.1%)
daily_volatility = 0.02 \# Daily standard deviation of returns (2%)

\# Executing the Monte Carlo simulations
simulated_returns = np.random.normal(mean_daily_return,
daily_volatility, (num_simulations, 1))
simulated_portfolio_value = initial_portfolio_value * (1 +
simulated_returns).cumprod()

\# Calculating the 5% Value at Risk (VaR)
VaR_5_percent = np.percentile(simulated_portfolio_value, 5)

\# Visualizing the results
plt.figure(figsize=(12, 6))
plt.hist(simulated_portfolio_value, bins=50, alpha=0.75,
color='blue')
plt.axvline(VaR_5_percent, color='red', linestyle='dashed',
linewidth=2)
plt.title('Monte Carlo Simulation of Portfolio Returns')
plt.xlabel('Portfolio Value')
plt.ylabel('Frequency')
plt.legend(['5% VaR Threshold', 'Simulated Returns'])
plt.grid()
plt.show()

\# Displaying the Value at Risk
print(f"Value at Risk (5%): \({initial_portfolio_value -
VaR_5_percent:.2f}")
```

Step 3: Explanation of the Code

The code begins by importing the required libraries and setting key parameters including the number of simulations, initial portfolio value, mean daily returns, and expected volatility. Utilizing the normal distribution, we generate thousands of simulated returns, which are then compounded to compute the portfolio value over the simulated period.

After running the simulations, we calculate the 5% Value at Risk using the np.percentile function, which identifies a significant threshold that highlights potential loss entities. The results are then visualized, showcasing the distribution of simulated portfolio values along with a dashed line marking the VaR threshold.

Conclusion

Monte Carlo simulation stands as a formidable tool in the financial analyst's arsenal, enabling them to navigate the complex waters of risk assessment with a clearer perspective. While the example we have covered only scratches the surface, the foundational concepts illustrated here are broadly applicable across a myriad of financial contexts, unveiling insights that traditional statistics may overlook.

As we move forward into subsequent sections, an in-depth understanding of these simulations will enrich our discussions on advanced statistical methodologies and financial analysis using Python, equipping you with the knowledge to tackle challenges with increased confidence and acumen.

Demystifying Stress Testing

Stress testing is a method of simulating severe yet plausible adverse market conditions to assess how portfolios would perform under such duress. The primary goal of stress testing is to evaluate the resilience of financial institutions against a spectrum of stress factors, ranging from economic recessions to market shocks.

Take, for example, the financial crisis of 2008. Many institutions were unprepared for the extent of the credit market collapse. The aftermath revealed that comprehensive stress testing protocols could have offered insights that might have mitigated the crisis's impact.

Key Components of a Stress Test

1. **Identification of Risks**: The initial step in stress testing involves thoroughly identifying the risks facing the portfolio, such as credit, market, liquidity, and operational risks.
2. **Defining Scenarios**: Following risk identification, analysts craft scenarios that represent potential adverse conditions. These scenarios can be grounded in historical data, hypothetical events, or regulatory stipulations.
3. **Modeling Effects**: Analysts employ financial models to simulate the impact of these scenarios on portfolio performance, calculating potential losses, changes in portfolio value, and other pertinent metrics.
4. **Evaluating Results**: The final step involves assessing the outcomes of the stress tests to gauge their implications for capital adequacy and liquidity—insights that guide strategic decision-making.

The Importance of Scenario Analysis

While closely related to stress testing, scenario analysis broadens the focus by evaluating various combinations of factors and their potential future trajectories. Rather than solely concentrating on extreme conditions, scenario analysis involves creating multiple detailed scenarios to explore a wide array of possible outcomes.

For instance, consider a portfolio heavily weighted in technology stocks. If analysts construct scenarios that include not only a rapid sector downturn but also geopolitical tensions affecting supply chains, the resultant insights will provide a more nuanced understanding of the portfolio's vulnerabilities compared to a single stress test focusing solely on a market decline.

Steps in Conducting Scenario Analysis

1. **Scenario Development**: Develop plausible economic scenarios based on macroeconomic trends, industry behaviors, and historical data.
2. **Effect Estimation**: Use analytical models to estimate the potential impact each scenario could have on the portfolio, including alterations in revenues, valuations, and risk factors.
3. **Integrating Findings**: Finally, amalgamate the results from multiple scenarios to shape effective risk management strategies and investment decisions.

Practical Application with Python

To contextualize stress testing and scenario analysis, let's walk through a practical example using Python that simulates a stress test for a hypothetical equity portfolio.

Step 1: Environment Setup

Begin by ensuring you have the necessary libraries installed. If you haven't installed Pandas and Matplotlib yet, you can do so using the following command:

```bash
pip install pandas matplotlib
```

Step 2: Sample Portfolio and Baseline Data

Let's define a sample portfolio containing shares from three distinct companies, along with their current market values:

```python
import pandas as pd
import numpy as np
import matplotlib.pyplot as plt

# Sample portfolio with shares and current values
portfolio = {
    'Company A': 50000,  # value in USD
    'Company B': 30000,
```

'Company C': 20000,
}

\# Correlation matrix reflecting historical correlations among assets
corr_matrix = np.array([[1.0, 0.8, 0.5],
[0.8, 1.0, 0.3],
[0.5, 0.3, 1.0]])

\# Create a DataFrame for better visualization
portfolio_df = pd.DataFrame(list(portfolio.items()), columns=['Company', 'Value'])
print(portfolio_df)
` ` `

Step 3: Define Stress Scenarios

Next, we will establish two potential stress scenarios: one illustrating a significant market downturn and another representing escalating geopolitical tensions.

` ` `python # Define stress scenarios that negatively impact returns stress_scenarios = { 'Market Downturn': [-0.25, -0.1, -0.15], # returns in percentages 'Geopolitical Tension': [-0.15, -0.2, -0.05], }

\# Create a DataFrame to structure scenarios
scenarios_df = pd.DataFrame(stress_scenarios, index=portfolio_df['Company'])
print(scenarios_df)
` ` `

Step 4: Calculate Portfolio Impact

We will now calculate the potential value of the portfolio after applying the stress scenarios.

` ` `python # Calculate portfolio value under each stress scenario portfolio_values = {}

for scenario, returns in stress_scenarios.items():

```
    portfolio_value_after_stress = sum(portfolio[company] * (1 + returns[i]) for i, company in enumerate(portfolio.keys()))
  portfolio_values[scenario] = portfolio_value_after_stress

\# Create a Results DataFrame
results_df = pd.DataFrame(list(portfolio_values.items()), columns=['Scenario', 'Portfolio Value After Stress'])
print(results_df)
```

Step 5: Visualizing Results

To facilitate a clearer understanding of the impacts from different stress scenarios, let's visualize the results.

```python
# Plotting the portfolio value under different stress scenarios plt.figure(figsize=(10, 5)) plt.bar(results_df['Scenario'], results_df['Portfolio Value After Stress'], color=['red', 'orange']) plt.title('Impact of Stress Scenarios on Portfolio Value') plt.xlabel('Scenarios') plt.ylabel('Portfolio Value (USD)') plt.grid(axis='y') plt.xticks(rotation=45) plt.show()
```

The implementation of stress testing and scenario analysis underscores the critical importance of preparedness in the face of adverse financial conditions.

In the subsequent sections, we will delve deeper into quantitative risk management techniques, further enriching your toolkit for comprehensive financial analysis and risk assessment.

The Importance of Credit Risk Modeling

Credit risk modeling provides a structured framework for lenders and investors to estimate the likelihood of borrower default. In an era characterized by a plethora of financial products—ranging from corporate bonds to sophisticated credit derivatives—the ability to accurately assess credit risk is not just desirable; it is imperative. Proper evaluations can prevent financial losses, enhance portfolio optimization, and ensure compliance with regulatory requirements.

Consider a bank deliberating the approval of a substantial corporate loan. A meticulously designed credit risk model empowers the bank to gauge the creditworthiness of the borrower, aiding in decisions about loan approval as well as shaping the terms and interest rates of the loan.

Core Elements of Credit Risk Models

1. **Default Probability Estimation**: This vital aspect involves calculating the likelihood of a borrower defaulting on their obligations within a designated timeframe. Various statistical approaches, including logistic regression and machine learning techniques, are harnessed to derive these probabilities.

2. **Loss Given Default (LGD)**: LGD quantifies the expected loss for the lender in the event of a borrower default. This figure takes into account several factors, including recovery rates, collateral values, and the specific structure of the debt.

3. **Exposure at Default (EAD)**: EAD represents the total exposure a lender faces from a borrower at the point of default. Accurately estimating EAD is essential for a comprehensive assessment of credit risk.

4. **Risk Assessment Framework**: A robust credit risk model integrates quantitative assessment with qualitative insights, considering factors such as the borrower's management quality, prevailing market conditions, and overall industry health.

Methodologies in Credit Risk Modeling

Equipped with an understanding of the fundamental components, we can explore the diverse methodologies at the forefront of credit risk modeling.

Utilizing Logistic Regression for Default Probability

Logistic regression remains a cornerstone statistical technique for forecasting default probabilities.

Demonstrating Logistic Regression with Python

Let's illustrate this concept using a hypothetical dataset comprising borrower features and their respective default status. We will leverage logistic regression to predict default probabilities.

Step 1: Setting Up the Programming Environment

First, ensure you have the necessary libraries installed:

```bash
pip install pandas numpy scikit-learn
```

Step 2: Importing Libraries and Data

Next, we import the needed libraries and load our dataset.

```python
import pandas as pd import numpy as np from sklearn.model_selection import train_test_split from sklearn.linear_model import LogisticRegression from sklearn.metrics import classification_report, confusion_matrix

\# Loading sample dataset
data = pd.read_csv('credit_data.csv') \# This dataset should contain borrower features and a binary 'default' column
```

Step 3: Data Preprocessing

Before proceeding with logistic regression, we need to cleanse our data by addressing missing values, encoding categorical variables, and dividing the dataset into training and testing subsets.

```python
# Handling missing values
```

data.fillna(data.mean(), inplace=True)

\# Encoding categorical variables
data = pd.get_dummies(data, drop_first=True)

\# Defining features and the target variable
X = data.drop('default', axis=1)
y = data['default']

\# Splitting the data into training and testing sets
X_train, X_test, y_train, y_test = train_test_split(X, y, test_size=0.3, random_state=42)

```

*Step 4: Training the Logistic Regression Model*

Now, we can train our logistic regression model using the training dataset.

```python model = LogisticRegression() model.fit(X_train, y_train)

```

Step 5: Evaluating Model Performance

Following the training phase, we will evaluate the model's accuracy by applying it to the test dataset.

```python y_pred = model.predict(X_test)

print(confusion_matrix(y_test, y_pred))
print(classification_report(y_test, y_pred))

```

The displayed output will illuminate the model's proficiency, detailing metrics such as accuracy, precision, recall, and the F1 score, thereby enabling analysts to assess the effectiveness of their credit risk evaluations.

Advanced Machine Learning Techniques

As technology evolves, machine learning techniques—such as random forests, gradient boosting, and neural networks
```

—are increasingly prominent in credit risk modeling. These advanced methodologies excel at capturing intricate non-linear relationships within the data and often surpass traditional approaches in terms of performance.

For instance, employing a random forest classifier allows analysts to leverage the predictive strengths of multiple decision trees, thereby improving the accuracy of default predictions and uncovering insights into feature importance.

Incorporating Qualitative Insights: The Role of Expert Judgment

While quantitative models are critical, it is equally essential to integrate qualitative factors into the credit risk assessment process. Economic trends, macroeconomic forecasts, and the unique circumstances of individual borrowers can profoundly influence default probabilities.

Real-World Application of Credit Risk Modeling with Python

Step 1: Building an Advanced Credit Risk Model

Integrating both quantitative and qualitative data can significantly enhance credit risk evaluations. Below is an advanced example demonstrating the combination of logistic regression with sophisticated machine learning techniques.

```python
from sklearn.ensemble import RandomForestClassifier

\# Implementing a Random Forest model for predicting defaults
rf_model = RandomForestClassifier(n_estimators=100, random_state=42)
rf_model.fit(X_train, y_train)

\# Model Evaluation
rf_pred = rf_model.predict(X_test)
print(confusion_matrix(y_test, rf_pred))
print(classification_report(y_test, rf_pred))
```

```
```

Step 2: Analyzing Feature Importance

One remarkable benefit of utilizing random forests is the ability to assess feature importance, enabling financial analysts to identify which factors carry the most weight in determining default risk.

```python
import matplotlib.pyplot as plt

feature_importances = rf_model.feature_importances_
features = X.columns

\# Visualizing feature importance
plt.figure(figsize=(10, 5))
plt.barh(features, feature_importances)
plt.title('Feature Importance in Credit Risk Prediction')
plt.xlabel('Importance Score')
plt.ylabel('Features')
plt.show()
```

Credit risk modeling is an indispensable asset in the financial sector, equipping institutions to evaluate borrower creditworthiness and expertly manage potential losses.

Operational risk has emerged as a critical area of focus for institutions aiming to maintain resilience and integrity within their operations. Distinct from credit and market risks, operational risk arises from inadequacies or failures in internal processes, systems, people, or external events. For instance, consider a scenario where a bank's software experiences a glitch, compromising sensitive client data. The repercussions could be severe—reputational damage, regulatory penalties, and a significant loss of client trust. This underscores the necessity of a comprehensive and proactive operational risk assessment for any financial institution.

Understanding Operational Risk

Operational risk encompasses a wide variety of potential threats, including:

- **Process Failures**: Inefficiencies or errors within key operational processes can stem from procedural misalignment, leading to financial losses or compliance breaches.
- **System Failures**: Technical failures, whether in software or hardware, can disrupt daily operations and result in significant downtimes.
- **Human Errors**: Mistakes made by personnel—whether due to negligence, insufficient training, or poor communication—can expose institutions to various risks.
- **External Events**: Factors such as natural disasters, cyber-attacks, and geopolitical shifts can introduce significant disruptions to financial operations.

Given the multifaceted nature of these risks, constructing a comprehensive risk assessment framework becomes essential.

The Importance of Operational Risk Assessment

Operational risk assessments serve as vital tools through which organizations can identify, evaluate, and proactively mitigate risks.

Benefits of Robust Operational Risk Assessment

1. **Enhanced Decision-Making**: Armed with clear insights into their operational risks, organizations can make informed decisions regarding resource allocation and operational enhancements.
2. **Compliance Assurance**: Financial institutions face stringent regulatory requirements; effective risk assessments provide a systematic approach to

ensuring adherence to these guidelines.

3. **Reputation Management**: By conducting proactive assessments, institutions can prevent incidents that may harm their public image and client trust.
4. **Financial Protection**: Quantifying and mitigating operational risks equips organizations to defend themselves against unexpected financial losses.

Methodologies for Operational Risk Assessment

Operational risk assessment is not a monolithic process; it encompasses various methodologies that can be customized to meet the specific needs of an organization. Let's explore several widely recognized approaches.

Risk and Control Self-Assessment (RCSA)

RCSA is an inclusive process that encourages employees across multiple departments to identify pertinent risks and evaluate the effectiveness of existing controls. This bottom-up approach fosters a culture of accountability, ensuring that risks are acknowledged and addressed at all organizational levels.

Implementing RCSA

To successfully execute an RCSA, institutions can follow these structured steps:

1. **Identify Risks**: Teams collaborate to brainstorm and catalogue potential risks originating from their workflows.
2. **Evaluate Controls**: The effectiveness of current controls is assessed in relation to the identified risks.
3. **Formulate Action Plans**: For risks deemed inadequately mitigated by existing controls, teams propose actionable strategies to address them.

In a recent RCSA workshop at a London-based investment bank, the trade settlement team identified human error as a significant vulnerability. They promptly scheduled targeted training sessions, resulting in a remarkable 30% reduction in transaction errors.

Scenario Analysis

Scenario analysis is a technique that evaluates potential operational risk events through realistic mock-ups. This method assesses the potential impact of such events and the adequacy of controls in place to mitigate them.

Conducting Scenario Analysis

1. **Defining Scenarios**: Teams create scenarios that reflect plausible operational disruptions while considering historical data and emerging threats.
2. **Impact Assessment**: Each scenario is analyzed based on its potential financial repercussions, frequency of occurrence, and the effectiveness of existing controls.
3. **Action Planning**: Institutions craft contingency plans to address identified vulnerabilities.

For example, an asset management firm may simulate the operational effects of a cyber-attack, such as a ransomware incident. This analysis could lead to enhanced cybersecurity protocols and a fortified incident response strategy, thereby reducing vulnerability and improving overall resilience.

Key Risk Indicators (KRIs)

KRIs are quantifiable metrics that signal potential levels of operational risk. They provide a tangible means for organizations to monitor risk behaviors over time.

Developing KRIs

To establish comprehensive KRIs, organizations should:

1. **Identify Metrics**: Determine operational aspects closely related to potential risks, such as transaction volumes or error rates.

2. **Set Thresholds**: Define acceptable operational levels for each metric.
3. **Monitor and Report**: Regularly track KRIs and communicate any instances where thresholds are breached.

For instance, a retail bank may track monthly fraud attempts on its online platform as a KRI. A significant spike above the predetermined threshold could indicate a heightened risk, prompting a thorough review of security measures.

Implementing Operational Risk Assessment with Python

In our technology-driven era, organizations are increasingly leveraging tools like Python to streamline operational risk assessments. Python's flexibility facilitates the automation of various risk evaluation processes, enhancing both efficiency and accuracy.

Example: Automating KRI Monitoring

Consider a financial institution looking to automate its KRI monitoring system. The following is a simplified implementation using Python and its powerful pandas library.

Step 1: Importing Libraries

```python
import pandas as pd import numpy as np
```

Step 2: Simulating KRI Data

```python
# Creating a sample dataset to simulate KRI data data = { 'Month': ['2022-01', '2022-02', '2022-03', '2022-04', '2022-05'], 'Fraud_Attempts': [12, 15, 10, 20, 25], # Example measurement of fraud attempts } kri_data = pd.DataFrame(data)
```

Step 3: Setting Threshold and Monitoring

```python
threshold = 20 # Define your KRI threshold
kri_data['Alert'] = kri_data['Fraud_Attempts'] > threshold
print(kri_data)
```

Output Analysis

Upon executing the above code, the output will indicate whether any month saw a number of fraud attempts exceeding the established threshold. Should an alert trigger, it allows risk management professionals to investigate the underlying causes behind this uptick in activity.

Conclusion

Operational risk assessment is essential for financial institutions seeking to thrive amid increasing complexity and uncertainty.

Understanding Liquidity Risk

Liquidity risk typically presents itself in two primary forms: market liquidity risk and funding liquidity risk.

1. **Market Liquidity Risk**: This type refers to the difficulty in buying or selling assets without significantly affecting their market prices. Several factors contribute to market liquidity risk, including trading volumes, bid-ask spreads, and prevailing market conditions. For example, during financial crises, like that of 2008, liquidity can evaporate swiftly, forcing institutions to sell assets at steep discounts.

2. **Funding Liquidity Risk**: Conversely, funding liquidity risk arises when a financial institution cannot meet its short-term obligations due to a lack of sufficient liquid assets. This risk often intensifies during periods of economic uncertainty,

where lenders may hesitate to extend credit. A classic scenario is a bank experiencing a sudden surge in deposit withdrawals, leaving it unable to liquidate assets swiftly enough to fulfill its obligations.

The Importance of Effective Liquidity Risk Management

A proactive liquidity risk management strategy is vital for maintaining an institution's financial integrity and fostering market confidence. A well-structured liquidity risk framework can yield numerous benefits:

- **Ensures Regulatory Compliance**: Regulatory bodies, such as those governing the Basel III guidelines, impose stringent liquidity requirements to shield against systemic risks. A robust liquidity management strategy assures compliance with these essential standards.
- **Enhances Institutional Reputation**: Organizations recognized for sound liquidity management are likely to gain increased trust from investors, regulators, and clients, contributing to long-term operational success.
- **Facilitates Strategic Decision-Making**: Effective oversight of liquidity enables firms to adeptly navigate adverse market conditions and strategically prepare for future liquidity needs.

Liquidity Risk Assessment Methodologies

To adeptly manage liquidity risks, financial institutions often utilize various methodologies tailored to their operational contexts and risk profiles. Here are some widely adopted approaches:

The Liquidity Coverage Ratio (LCR) assesses an institution's capacity to survive a 30-day liquidity crisis.

Implementing LCR Assessment

The LCR is calculated through a systematic process:

1. **Identifying HQLA**: Compile a comprehensive list of assets considered high quality, meaning they can be easily converted to cash without significant price impact, such as government bonds.
2. **Calculating Net Cash Outflows**: Estimate expected cash outflows over the assessment period, making adjustments for anticipated cash inflows.
3. **Computing LCR**: The calculation is performed using the following formula:

[LCR = \frac{HQLA}{Net Cash Outflows}]

For instance, consider an investment bank in New York that assesses its liquidity based on current market conditions. If its HQLA amounts to)500 million and net cash outflows are estimated at (300 million, its LCR would be calculated at 1.67, well above the regulatory minimum of 1.00.

Stress Testing

Stress testing simulates various adverse scenarios to assess how effectively an institution can weather potential liquidity strains. This method involves evaluating diverse market conditions, including sudden interest rate shifts, unexpected market shocks, and increased outflows.

Conducting a Stress Test

To implement an effective stress test, institutions can follow these steps:

1. **Defining Scenarios**: Identify a wide array of stress scenarios, such as economic recessions or counterparty defaults.
2. **Analyzing Potential Impact**: For each scenario, evaluate its possible impact on cash flows and overall funding conditions.
3. **Reviewing and Adjusting**: Based on stress test

outcomes, refine liquidity strategies to bolster resilience.

For instance, during a recent stress testing exercise, a European bank simulated a sudden spike in credit spreads. The analysis revealed a potential liquidity shortfall of €200 million within six months, prompting proactive measures to enhance its HQLA reserves and diversify funding sources.

Cash Flow Projections

Cash flow projections provide a forward-looking view of liquidity requirements.

Creating Effective Cash Flow Projections

To develop accurate cash flow projections, institutions can:

1. **Collect Historical Data**: Review past inflows and outflows to identify trends and seasonality.
2. **Adjust for Future Expectations**: Modify projections based on anticipated changes in operations, economic trends, and market dynamics.
3. **Review Regularly**: Continuously evaluate these projections in reaction to fluctuations in market conditions and business operations, thus enabling agile responses to shifting liquidity needs.

Consider a large corporate treasurer who anticipates cash inflows from client payments totaling)3 million in the upcoming quarter, alongside forecasted operating outflows of (2.8 million. This results in a positive cash flow of)200,000, reflecting a solid liquidity position that allows for strategic operational adjustments or potential expansions.

Leveraging Python for Liquidity Risk Management

As technology increasingly shapes financial risk management, Python emerges as a powerful tool for conducting liquidity risk assessments. Below is a simplified example of using

Python to calculate the LCR.

Example: Calculating LCR using Python

Step 1: Importing Libraries

```python
import pandas as pd
```

Step 2: Creating a DataFrame for HQLA and Cash Flows

```python
# Sample data for HQLA and Net Cash Outflows
data = { 'Assets': ['Government Bonds', 'Cash Reserves', 'Corporate Bonds'], 'Values': [250000, 150000, 100000], # HQLA values }

hql_df = pd.DataFrame(data)
net_cash_outflows = 300000 \# Projected cash outflows
```

Step 3: Calculating Total HQLA and LCR

```python
# Calculate total HQLA total_hql = hql_df['Values'].sum()

\# Calculate LCR
lcr = total_hql / net_cash_outflows
print(f"Total HQLA: \({total_hql}")
print(f"Liquidity Coverage Ratio (LCR): {lcr:.2f}")
```

Output Analysis

Executing this Python script provides crucial insights into an institution's liquidity status. For example, if total HQLA reaches)500,000 while net cash outflows amount to (300,000, the script yields an LCR of 1.67, indicating a robust liquidity position that aligns with regulatory expectations.

In our upcoming discussions, we will explore the pivotal role of stress testing and scenario analysis in liquidity risk management, delving deeper into proactive strategies that strengthen institutions against unexpected market fluctuations. The future will involve integrating quantitative skills with strategic foresight, creating a comprehensive approach to liquidity management that is in harmony with modern regulatory demands and market realities.

The financial markets can often resemble stormy seas, filled with unpredictable waves of uncertainty that can rise and fall with little warning. This volatility presents challenges not only to novice investors but also to seasoned financial professionals. To combat the inherent risks associated with price fluctuations, hedging strategies have emerged as essential tools for market participants seeking to protect their investments. In this discussion, we will explore various hedging strategies utilizing derivatives, highlighting their mechanics, advantages, and real-world applications.

Understanding Derivatives in Risk Mitigation

Derivatives come in multiple forms, including options, futures, forwards, and swaps, each possessing unique functionalities and risk profiles. At the heart of these instruments lies the ability to either speculate on future price movements or hedge against undesirable outcomes affecting market valuations.

Options empower buyers with the right, though not the obligation, to purchase or sell an asset at a predetermined price within a specified timeframe. They generally fall into two categories: call options, which confer the right to buy, and put options, which provide the right to sell.

A Real-World Example of Hedging with Options

Imagine an investor who holds a substantial position in Apple Inc. (AAPL), currently priced at)150. With an upcoming earnings report on the horizon, the investor foresees potential volatility and decides to purchase a put option with a strike price of (145, set to expire in three months. This strategic decision acts as an insurance policy against a significant decline in Apple's stock price.

- If Apple's stock price drops to)130, the investor can exercise the option, selling shares at (145, thus limiting potential losses.
- Conversely, if the stock price surges to)160, they can let the option expire without further action, retaining the upside potential from the price appreciation.

This straightforward yet impactful strategy showcases how options can serve as protective measures for investors, ensuring they remain shielded from drastic declines.

2. Futures Contracts

Futures contracts obligate involved parties to buy or sell an asset at a designated future date for a price agreed upon today. These contracts are standardized and traded on exchanges, making them an effective instrument for hedging against price fluctuations in commodities, currencies, and financial products.

A Real-World Example of Hedging with Futures

Consider a Colombian coffee producer expecting a harvest in six months. With the current market price sitting at (2.00 per pound, the producer fears a potential price drop that could significantly diminish revenues. To hedge against this risk, the farmer sells futures contracts for 10,000 pounds of coffee at the current price.

- If the price of coffee plummets to)1.50 at harvest time, the farmer can sell their actual harvest at this lower price but profits from the futures contract profits will offset the revenue shortfall.
- If coffee prices rise to (2.50 during this period, the farmer may incur losses from the futures contracts but benefits by selling their harvest at the higher

market price, achieving an overall neutral financial outcome.

Futures contracts thus offer a robust mechanism for producers and consumers to effectively manage exposure to volatile prices.

3. Swaps

Swaps entail the exchange of cash flows between two parties based on agreed terms. The most prevalent form is the interest rate swap, where one party pays a fixed interest rate while receiving a floating rate in return, or vice versa.

A Real-World Example of Hedging with Swaps

Consider a corporation holding a variable-rate loan tied to LIBOR (London Interbank Offered Rate). With interest rates projected to rise, the company faces escalating payment obligations, signaling a potential hedging opportunity. The CFO initiates an interest rate swap agreement with a financial institution.

- Under this agreement, the company pays a fixed interest rate while receiving payments based on the floating LIBOR rate.
- If interest rates indeed rise, the floating payments received will counterbalance the increased costs of the variable-rate loan, effectively stabilizing cash flow and providing a safeguard against rising rates.

Swaps exemplify how organizations can manage interest rate exposure without needing to restructure the underlying debt instruments.

Assessing the Effectiveness of Hedging Strategies

While hedging strategies can effectively curtail risk, they are not without limitations and come with associated costs and complexities:

1. **Derivative Costs**: Purchasing options, entering futures contracts, or engaging in swaps often entails upfront expenses, which may erode profits if the anticipated risks do not materialize.
2. **Complexity and Precision**: Accurately determining the ideal quantity and types of derivatives for effective hedging necessitates sophisticated analysis and forecasting, often employing complex mathematical models and simulations.
3. **Over-Hedging Risks**: Striking the right balance is crucial, as over-hedging can result in diminished returns or even losses during favorable market conditions.

Practical Application: Crafting a Hedging Strategy

To develop a cohesive hedging strategy utilizing derivatives, financial professionals should adopt a structured approach:

1. **Risk Assessment**: Conduct an in-depth analysis of the specific risks linked to asset portfolios, including market price fluctuations, interest rate volatility, and foreign exchange exposure.
2. **Selection of Derivative Instruments**: Based on identified risks, stakeholders must carefully choose from options, futures, or swaps that align with their hedging goals.
3. **Execution**: Once the strategy is established, executing trades with precision while considering market conditions is vital.
4. **Continuous Monitoring and Adjustment**: Regular assessment of hedging effectiveness is essential, requiring adjustments as market dynamics shift or as exposure levels evolve.

Example of a Comprehensive Hedging Strategy

Returning to our Apple Inc. investor, imagine they also hold a diversified equity portfolio that may experience broader market volatility. Here's how a multi-layered hedging strategy might look:

- **Step 1: Identify Risks**: The investor acknowledges the potential impact of market volatility on their broader stock portfolio.
- **Step 2: Utilize Index Options**: To safeguard against declines in major indices like the S&P 500, the investor purchases put options on SPY (the S&P 500 ETF).
- **Step 3: Implement Futures Contracts on Indices**: In addition to put options, the investor could sell S&P 500 futures contracts for heightened protection against systemic risks.
- **Step 4: Ongoing Evaluation**: Regularly reviewing the strategy's effectiveness and adjusting positions based on market trends and performance is imperative.

Incorporating hedging strategies using derivatives can provide investors and organizations with effective protection against the uncertainties of financial markets, safeguarding their investments from unexpected fluctuations. A thorough understanding of how options, futures, and swaps function within this landscape is crucial for establishing a solid risk management framework.

Demystifying Risk Models

Risk models play a pivotal role in quantifying exposure to various financial risks, including market, credit, operational, and liquidity risks. Their significance extends beyond merely assessing potential losses; these models also aid in devising strategies to manage or mitigate such losses effectively. One of the most widely recognized methodologies is Value at Risk (VaR), which provides a statistical framework to estimate the maximum expected loss over a specified time frame at a selected confidence level.

For instance, if a bank states that its VaR is)1 million at a 95% confidence level, it indicates that there is a 95% probability that losses will not exceed (1 million over the next day. In addition to VaR, techniques such as Monte Carlo simulations and stress testing offer further insights into potential risk exposure, enabling a more comprehensive understanding of market behavior.

Setting Up Your Python Environment

Before diving into the code, it's crucial to establish the right environment. Organizing your workspace using a virtual environment can help you manage dependencies efficiently. Here are the steps to set it up:

```bash
# Create a virtual environment to keep packages organized python -m venv quant_finance_env

# Activate the environment (Windows) quant_finance_env \Scripts\activate

# Activate the environment (macOS/Linux) source quant_finance_env/bin/activate

# Install essential libraries for financial analysis pip install numpy pandas scipy matplotlib seaborn
```

Essential Python Libraries for Risk Modeling

1. **NumPy**: Enables efficient numerical computations and array manipulations.
2. **Pandas**: Provides powerful data manipulation and analysis tools.
3. **SciPy**: Includes functions for scientific and technical calculations, particularly probability distributions and statistical functions.
4. **Matplotlib/Seaborn**: Essential for data visualization, helping you interpret results with clarity.

Implementing Value at Risk (VaR) in Python

We'll delve into a practical implementation of a VaR model using historical price data, allowing us to gain a deeper understanding of risk exposure. Our approach will involve calculating daily returns as a precursor to simulating VaR.

Step 1: Importing Historical Data

To begin, we need access to historical stock price data. For demonstration purposes, we'll utilize the Pandas library to read a CSV file containing daily closing prices for a particular stock.

```python
import pandas as pd

\# Load historical stock price data from a CSV file
data = pd.read_csv('AAPL_stock_prices.csv')  \# Make sure the file is correctly referenced
data['Date'] = pd.to_datetime(data['Date'])
data.set_index('Date', inplace=True)

\# Display the first few rows of the data
print(data.head())
```

Step 2: Calculating Daily Returns

The next step involves calculating daily returns, which are fundamental to our VaR calculations.

```python
# Compute daily returns based on closing prices
data['Return'] = data['Close'].pct_change()
data.dropna(inplace=True)

\# Display the first few daily returns
print(data['Return'].head())
```

Step 3: Computing VaR

With daily returns calculated, we can now compute VaR at a

specified confidence level, such as 95%.

```python
# Define the confidence level for VaR calculation
confidence_level = 0.95

# Compute the VaR
VaR = -data['Return'].quantile(1 - confidence_level)

print(f"The VaR at the {confidence_level * 100}% confidence level is: {VaR:.4%}")
```

This code snippet determines the VaR as a percentage, illustrating the maximum expected loss over the defined period.

Step 4: Visualizing Returns and VaR

Visual representation of return distributions can enhance understanding and highlight the implications of VaR.

```python
import matplotlib.pyplot as plt
import seaborn as sns

# Create a histogram to visualize the returns
plt.figure(figsize=(10, 6))
sns.histplot(data['Return'], bins=50, kde=True)
plt.axvline(-VaR, color='r', linestyle='--', label='VaR (95%)')
plt.title('Distribution of Daily Returns')
plt.xlabel('Daily Return')
plt.ylabel('Frequency')
plt.legend()
plt.show()
```

In this plot, the distribution of daily returns is illustrated, with a red dashed line indicating the VaR threshold, effectively demonstrating potential loss in a clear visual format.

Advanced Risk Modeling Through Monte Carlo Simulations

While VaR offers a snapshot of potential loss, it doesn't capture the full spectrum of possible outcomes. Monte Carlo simulations provide a framework for modeling various scenarios, thereby enriching our understanding of risk under differing conditions.

Step 1: Setting Up the Simulation

We start by defining crucial parameters for the simulation, including expected returns, volatility, and the number of simulations.

```python
import numpy as np

\# Establish parameters for the Monte Carlo simulation
num_simulations = 10000
num_days = 252  \# Representing one year of trading days
expected_return = data['Return'].mean()
volatility = data['Return'].std()

\# Create an array to hold simulated price paths
simulated_prices = np.zeros((num_days, num_simulations))
simulated_prices[0] = data['Close'][-1]  \# Start from the last known price

for t in range(1, num_days):
  random_returns = np.random.normal(expected_return, volatility, num_simulations)
        simulated_prices[t] = simulated_prices[t - 1] * (1 + random_returns)

\# Display a preview of the simulated prices
print(simulated_prices)
```

Step 2: Analyzing Simulation Results

After executing the simulations, we will analyze the final outcomes, focusing on the potential prices at the end of the simulation period.

```python
# Extract the final price distribution from simulations
final_prices = simulated_prices[-1]

# Calculate the expected price and VaR
mean_price = final_prices.mean()
VaR_simulation = np.percentile(final_prices, 5)  # 95% confidence interval

print(f"Expected price after {num_days} days: {mean_price:.2f}")
print(f"VaR from Monte Carlo simulation: {data['Close'][-1] - VaR_simulation:.2f}")
```

Step 3: Visualizing Simulation Outcomes

Finally, creating a visual representation of the simulation results enhances comprehension of the range of potential outcomes.

```python
plt.figure(figsize=(10, 6)) plt.hist(final_prices, bins=50, alpha=0.7) plt.axvline(VaR_simulation, color='r', linestyle='--', label='VaR (95%) Simulation') plt.axvline(mean_price, color='g', linestyle='--', label='Expected Price') plt.title('Simulated Final Prices Distribution') plt.xlabel('Final Price') plt.ylabel('Frequency') plt.legend() plt.show()
```

This visualization exhibits the distribution of final simulated prices, clarifying the range of possible outcomes and reinforcing the understanding of risk in uncertain markets.

Conclusion

By implementing risk models in Python, we unlock a dynamic approach to understanding and managing financial risks. Through our exploration of Value at Risk and Monte Carlo simulations, we have equipped ourselves with effective methodologies for assessing potential losses and navigating the complexities of financial markets.

Strategy Overview: The Moving Average Crossover Approach

Imagine a straightforward yet effective trading strategy centered on moving averages—specifically, the crossover technique. In this methodology, traders buy a stock when its short-term moving average surpasses its long-term moving average, signaling an upward momentum. Conversely, they sell or short the stock when the reverse occurs. This approach harnesses the power of trend detection and offers straightforward signals to mitigate potential losses.

To contextualize our analysis, let's apply this strategy to historical data from Tesla Inc. (TSLA). The objective is to evaluate the strategy's performance while closely examining the associated risks, such as potential drawdowns, volatility, and Value at Risk (VaR).

Data Acquisition and Preparation

Our analysis starts with gathering the necessary historical stock price data. Here, the Pandas library plays a crucial role, enabling seamless acquisition and manipulation of financial datasets. For this case study, we will download our data using the yfinance library, which simplifies the retrieval of stock market data.

Step 1: Setting Up the Environment

Let's ensure our Python environment is equipped with the libraries required for our comprehensive analysis.

```bash
# Install required libraries pip install yfinance numpy pandas matplotlib seaborn
```

Step 2: Downloading Historical Data

Next, we'll leverage the yfinance library to fetch TSLA's stock price data for the past two years.

```python
import yfinance as yf import pandas as pd

\# Download historical price data for Tesla
data = yf.download('TSLA', start='2021-01-01', end='2023-01-01')

\# Display the first few rows of the dataset
print(data.head())
```

Step 3: Calculating Moving Averages

To implement our trading strategy, we will calculate the short-term (20-day) and long-term (50-day) moving averages. These metrics are essential for establishing our buy and sell signals.

```python
data['Short_MA'] = data['Close'].rolling(window=20).mean() data['Long_MA'] = data['Close'].rolling(window=50).mean()

\# Visualizing the Moving Averages
import matplotlib.pyplot as plt

plt.figure(figsize=(14, 7))
plt.plot(data['Close'], label='TSLA Close Price', color='blue')
plt.plot(data['Short_MA'], label='20-Day Moving Average', color='red')
plt.plot(data['Long_MA'], label='50-Day Moving Average', color='green')
plt.title('TSLA Price and Moving Averages')
plt.legend()
plt.show()
```

Step 4: Generating Trading Signals

With moving averages calculated, we can now generate our trading signals, assigning a "1" for a buy signal and a "-1" for a sell signal.

```python
data['Signal'] = 0 data['Signal'][20:] =
```

np.where(data['Short_MA'][20:] > data['Long_MA'][20:], 1, -1) data['Position'] = data['Signal'].diff() # Shift signals by 1 to avoid look-ahead bias

\# Visualizing Trading Signals
plt.figure(figsize=(14, 7))
plt.plot(data['Close'], label='TSLA Close Price', color='blue', alpha=0.5)
plt.plot(data[data['Position'] == 1].index,
    data['Short_MA'][data['Position'] == 1],
    '^', markersize=10, color='g', label='Buy Signal')
plt.plot(data[data['Position'] == -1].index,
    data['Short_MA'][data['Position'] == -1],
    'v', markersize=10, color='r', label='Sell Signal')
plt.title('TSLA Price with Trading Signals')
plt.legend()
plt.show()
```

## Risk Assessment Metrics

### Step 5: Calculating Performance Metrics

Now, let's evaluate our strategy's performance through several metrics, including total returns, maximum drawdown, and volatility.

*Total Returns Calculation*

We will begin by calculating the total returns generated by the strategy.

```python data['Market_Returns'] = data['Close'].pct_change() data['Strategy_Returns'] = data['Market_Returns'] * data['Signal'].shift(1) # Apply signals to market returns

\# Cumulative returns for market and strategy
cumulative_market_returns = (1 + data['Market_Returns']).cumprod() - 1
cumulative_strategy_returns = (1 + data['Strategy_Returns']).cumprod() - 1

```
\# Plotting the cumulative returns
plt.figure(figsize=(14, 7))
plt.plot(cumulative_market_returns, label='Market Returns',
color='blue')
plt.plot(cumulative_strategy_returns, label='Strategy Returns',
color='orange')
plt.title('Cumulative Returns: Market vs Strategy')
plt.legend()
plt.show()
```

Maximum Drawdown

Next, we will compute the maximum drawdown—a critical metric that assesses the potential decline from a peak to a trough during a given period. This provides vital insights into the risk of significant losses.

```python
def max_drawdown(returns): cumulative_returns = (1 + returns).cumprod() peak = cumulative_returns.cummax() drawdowns = (cumulative_returns - peak) / peak max_drawdown_value = drawdowns.min() return max_drawdown_value

\# Calculating maximum drawdown for the strategy
strategy_max_drawdown =
max_drawdown(data['Strategy_Returns'])
print(f'Maximum Drawdown for the Strategy:
{strategy_max_drawdown:.2%}')
```

Step 6: Value at Risk (VaR) Calculation

To deepen our risk assessment, we will calculate the Value at Risk (VaR) using a historical simulation method. VaR is a crucial metric that estimates potential losses over a specified time frame.

```python
confidence_level = 0.95 var = -
```

data['Strategy_Returns'].quantile(1 - confidence_level)

print(f'The Value at Risk (VaR) at the {confidence_level*100}% confidence level is: \){var:.2%}')

```
```

Step 7: Visualizing Strategy Risk and Returns

To consolidate our risk assessment, visualizing the drawdown alongside our cumulative returns can provide critical insights into the strategy's performance during various market conditions.

```python
plt.figure(figsize=(14, 7)) plt.plot(data['Strategy_Returns'].cumsum(), label='Cumulative Strategy Returns', color='orange') plt.fill_between(data.index, strategy_max_drawdown, color='red', alpha=0.3, label='Max Drawdown') plt.title('Cumulative Returns vs Max Drawdown') plt.legend() plt.show()
```

Our examination of the hypothetical moving average trading strategy has revealed valuable insights into its risk and return profile.

Recognizing the implications of these metrics empowers traders and financial analysts to refine their strategies and make informed decisions. This case study illustrates how Python can be an indispensable tool in risk assessment, transforming complex data into actionable insights for navigating the intricate landscape of quantitative finance.

Looking ahead, we will explore additional methodologies and strategies to further reinforce the importance of rigorous risk analysis in achieving sustained financial success.

CHAPTER 7: MACHINE LEARNING IN FINANCE

Picture yourself as a trader in the vibrant and fast-paced world of New York City, a true epicenter of global finance. From your modern office with a captivating view of the skyline, you are inundated with a constant flow of market data: stock prices oscillating wildly, economic indicators flashing signals of change, and real-time news updates cascading across your screen. In this hectic environment, making swift and informed decisions is paramount. Increasingly, the key to navigating this dynamic landscape lies in machine learning—an invaluable partner enhancing analytical precision in quantitative finance.

machine learning (ML) is a subset of artificial intelligence that enables algorithms to discern patterns and forecast outcomes from vast amounts of data. These algorithms thrive on extensive datasets, which feed them the historical context necessary for training. As they process new information, they continuously refine their predictive capabilities—an advantage that is crucial in the relentless pace of financial markets.

To better understand the role of machine learning in finance, let's explore some fundamental concepts:

1. **Supervised Learning**: In this framework, models are trained on labeled datasets where both inputs and outputs are defined. Imagine feeding your model historical stock prices along with the actual price movements that followed. The objective is for the model to uncover the hidden patterns that could foresee future price changes. When faced with new, unseen data, it can generate predictions that mirror the instinct of an experienced trader reading the ebb and flow of the market. In practical terms, Python libraries like scikit-learn are commonly utilized for implementing supervised learning algorithms.

```python
from sklearn.model_selection import train_test_split
from sklearn.linear_model import LinearRegression
import pandas as pd

# Load historical stock prices
df = pd.read_csv('historical_stock_prices.csv')
X = df[['feature1', 'feature2', 'feature3']] # Input features
y = df['target_price'] # Target variable

# Splitting dataset into training and testing sets
X_train, X_test, y_train, y_test = train_test_split(X, y, test_size=0.2, random_state=42)

# Creating and training the model
model = LinearRegression()
model.fit(X_train, y_train)

# Making predictions
predictions = model.predict(X_test)
```

1. **Unsupervised Learning**: In contrast to supervised learning, unsupervised learning deals with

unlabeled data where the outcomes are unknown. This methodology excels in clustering and anomaly detection—critical tasks in the financial realm. For instance, clustering algorithms like k-means are excellent for segmenting clients based on risk profiles or investment behaviors. Additionally, anomaly detection proves invaluable for identifying fraudulent transactions or unusual market behaviors.

```python
from sklearn.cluster import KMeans

\# Using relevant financial data
X = df[['feature_a', 'feature_b']] \# Features for clustering
kmeans = KMeans(n_clusters=3)
kmeans.fit(X)

\# Assigning clusters back to the original data
df['cluster'] = kmeans.labels_
```

1. **Reinforcement Learning**: This sophisticated area of machine learning emulates a learning agent through trial and error, which may resonate deeply with seasoned traders. In this context, the algorithm learns to make decisions based on rewards or penalties resulting from its actions—much like a trader hones their strategy based on market experiences. In the financial landscape, reinforcement learning can revolutionize trading strategies, enabling them to adapt in real-time to fluctuating market conditions.
2. **Feature Engineering**: Often an overlooked component, feature engineering is vital for elevating the effectiveness of machine learning algorithms. Just as a proficient analyst selects key performance indicators (KPIs) to monitor, one must meticulously

choose or construct features from the available data. This may include calculating moving averages, volatility indices, or even deriving sentiment scores from news articles—each invaluable in signaling trends within a trading strategy.

3. **Model Evaluation**: After developing a model, gauging its performance is a critical step. While conventional metrics like accuracy, precision, recall, and F1 scores provide insight, the finance sector often demands more intricate evaluations, such as Sharpe Ratios for trading models. Moreover, ensuring that the model generalizes well to unseen data is essential; thus, cross-validation techniques emerge as indispensable tools in this assessment process.
4. **Ethical Considerations**: As we embrace the use of machine learning in finance, we must confront essential ethical concerns. Issues surrounding data privacy, algorithmic bias, and the transparency of predictive models should be forefront in our discussions, ensuring that the integrity and trustworthiness of our financial systems are upheld.

The intersection of quantitative finance and machine learning is a rapidly evolving terrain, with ML proving to be a transformative force. As we navigate the complexities of trading strategies, portfolio management, and risk assessment, adopting these advanced methods is akin to wielding a double-edged sword—immensely powerful yet requiring cautious navigation.

Supervised vs. Unsupervised Learning

As we venture deeper into the fascinating world of machine learning, we encounter two essential paradigms that play a crucial role in shaping strategies within quantitative finance: supervised and unsupervised learning. Each of these methodologies unlocks the potential of data, guiding us towards meaningful insights and informed decisions, akin to navigating the bustling streets of Wall Street with a finely tuned compass.

Supervised Learning: A Guided Approach

At the heart of supervised learning lies a structured framework where models learn from labeled datasets—comprised of input variables (features) paired with corresponding outputs (targets). This approach resembles the guidance provided by an experienced mentor to a novice trader, illuminating the path towards optimal decision-making.

The aim of supervised learning is to uncover patterns from historical data that can be applied to predict future events. Picture a scenario where you're tasked with forecasting stock prices based on a rich tapestry of historical trends, trading volumes, and economic indicators. The process involves training a model on past data, enabling it to discern the relationships between inputs and their corresponding outcomes—ultimately forecasting future stock prices.

To illustrate this concept, let's walk through an example utilizing a linear regression model, implemented in Python with the help of the powerful scikit-learn library:

```python
from sklearn.model_selection import train_test_split
from sklearn.linear_model import LinearRegression
import pandas as pd

\# Load historical stock prices
df = pd.read_csv('historical_stock_prices.csv')
X = df[['feature1', 'feature2', 'feature3']] \# Input features
y = df['target_price'] \# Target variable

\# Splitting dataset into training and testing sets
X_train, X_test, y_train, y_test = train_test_split(X, y, test_size=0.2, random_state=42)

\# Creating and training the linear regression model
```

```
model = LinearRegression()
model.fit(X_train, y_train)

\# Making predictions on the test set
predictions = model.predict(X_test)

\# Evaluating model performance
from sklearn.metrics import mean_squared_error
mse = mean_squared_error(y_test, predictions)
print(f"Mean Squared Error: {mse}")
```

In this Python snippet, we begin by loading our dataset, carefully distinguishing between features and the target variable. The train_test_split function then divides the data into training and testing subsets, laying the groundwork for evaluating the model's effectiveness. The linear regression model captures the underlying correlations, enabling predictions of future stock prices. The Mean Squared Error (MSE) becomes an essential metric to gauge the accuracy of these predictions.

Unsupervised Learning: Discovering Hidden Patterns

In contrast to its supervised counterpart, unsupervised learning takes an exploratory approach, navigating vast fields of data to unveil hidden structures and patterns that may not be immediately discernible. This technique is especially relevant in finance, where the complexity of market behaviors often calls for a deeper understanding of latent relationships.

Consider unsupervised learning as a market analyst sifting through a mountain of unstructured data—be it customer transactions, trading patterns, or social media sentiment—aiming to categorize and delineate intrinsic characteristics. This methodology proves ideal for tasks such as market segmentation or detecting anomalies in trading behaviors.

A widely-used technique in this realm is **clustering**, which organizes data points into groups based on inherent similarities. For example, one might wish to classify clients into distinct profiles based on their investment behaviors. The K-means clustering algorithm is a popular choice for this purpose. Let's visualize this concept using Python:

```python
from sklearn.cluster import KMeans
import matplotlib.pyplot as plt

\# Assume 'df' contains financial features for clustering
X = df[['feature_a', 'feature_b']] \# Features for clustering
kmeans = KMeans(n_clusters=3) \# Specifying the number of clusters
kmeans.fit(X)

\# Assigning cluster labels back to the original dataset
df['cluster'] = kmeans.labels_

\# Visualizing the clusters
plt.scatter(df['feature_a'], df['feature_b'], c=df['cluster'], cmap='viridis')
plt.xlabel('Feature A')
plt.ylabel('Feature B')
plt.title('K-Means Clustering of Financial Data')
plt.show()
```

In this example, K-means effectively identifies three distinct clusters within the dataset, which can be visualized through a scatter plot. Each cluster represents a unique segment characterized by similar investment patterns—insights that are invaluable for tailoring personalized investment strategies or gaining a deeper understanding of market dynamics.

Bridging the Paradigms

While supervised and unsupervised learning present unique methodologies, they are far from isolated in application. In many real-world scenarios, successful financial analysis often integrates both techniques, capitalizing on their individual strengths to generate richer insights.

For instance, consider an investment firm that employs supervised learning to forecast stock price movements while simultaneously utilizing unsupervised learning to segment clients based on their trading behaviors. This dual approach enables the firm to offer personalized investment strategies that resonate with individual client profiles, enhancing satisfaction and optimizing investment portfolios.

In summary, a firm grasp of these machine learning paradigms equips you with the tools required to tackle financial complexities with greater precision and foresight. As the financial landscape evolves, embracing these methodologies will ensure that you remain well-prepared to seize the challenges and opportunities that lie ahead.

Feature Selection and Engineering

When it comes to finance, the vast ocean of available data can feel as chaotic as New York's Times Square during peak tourist season—an overwhelming flood of numbers, trends, and signals clamoring for your attention. In this environment, discerning which variables hold real significance can illuminate pathways to critical insights. This necessity leads us to explore feature selection and engineering, vital processes that enhance the effectiveness of machine learning models by narrowing focus to the most impactful information.

Feature Selection: The Art of Choosing Wisely

Feature selection is the disciplined process of identifying and retaining a specific subset of relevant features from a larger dataset. This pruning is essential for several reasons: it boosts model efficiency, cuts computational costs, and reduces the risk of overfitting by filtering out noise. Just as a photographer adjusts the lens to capture a clearer image, financial analysts refine their models by concentrating on variables that truly influence market behavior.

To illustrate, let's consider a dataset aimed at predicting stock price movements. Features might include historical prices, trading volumes, interest rates, and even geopolitical events.

Here's a practical Python example showcasing the use of feature importance scores derived from a Random Forest model:

```python
import pandas as pd from sklearn.ensemble import RandomForestClassifier from sklearn.model_selection import train_test_split import matplotlib.pyplot as plt

\# Load dataset
df = pd.read_csv('stock_data.csv')
X = df.drop('target', axis=1) \# Features
y = df['target']             \# Target variable

\# Splitting dataset into training and testing sets
X_train, X_test, y_train, y_test = train_test_split(X, y, test_size=0.3, random_state=42)

\# Fitting the Random Forest model
rf_model = RandomForestClassifier(n_estimators=100, random_state=42)
rf_model.fit(X_train, y_train)

\# Getting feature importances
importances = rf_model.feature_importances_
feature_names = X.columns

\# Visualizing the feature importances
plt.figure(figsize=(10, 6))
plt.barh(feature_names, importances, color='skyblue')
plt.xlabel('Feature Importance')
plt.title('Feature Importance from Random Forest Model')
plt.show()
```

In this example, we load the stock dataset and segregate it into training and testing subsets. The Random Forest algorithm then identifies which features significantly influence the target variable. The subsequent visualization provides clear insights into feature importance, allowing analysts to prioritize their focus and refine future analyses.

Feature Engineering: Transforming Raw Data into Insight

While feature selection hones in on pre-existing variables, feature engineering is about innovation—creating new variables from raw data to unlock fresh perspectives. Think of it as a culinary artist transforming a simple array of ingredients into a stunning gourmet dish.

Several popular techniques in feature engineering include:

1. **Creating Interaction Terms:** Often, relationships between variables reveal insights that individual variables alone cannot. For example, the interaction between trading volume and price changes can offer deeper understanding of market behavior.
2. **Temporal Features:** Financial data is steeped in timing.
3. **Lagged Variables:** In time series analysis, including past values as features—commonly known as lagged variables—can greatly enhance a model's predictive comprehension. For instance, using the previous day's closing price as a predictor can add valuable context.

Here's how to create a few new features using an existing dataset:

```python # Assume 'df' has a 'date' column and a 'close' column for closing prices df['date'] = pd.to_datetime(df['date']) df['day_of_week'] = df['date'].dt.dayofweek # 0=Monday, 6=Sunday df['month'] = df['date'].dt.month df['lagged_close'] = df['close'].shift(1) # Previous day's close

\# Drop NA values that arise due to shifting
```

```
df.dropna(inplace=True)
```

With this code snippet, we introduce three new features: 'day of week', 'month', and 'lagged close'. These additions enrich the dataset, potentially leading to more nuanced and robust model predictions.

Bridging the Concepts

The interplay between feature selection and engineering creates fertile ground for advanced financial analysis using machine learning. Imagine a hedge fund leveraging both processes: initially sifting to identify only the most consequential features while subsequently enhancing the dataset with thoughtfully engineered variables. This comprehensive approach empowers firms to develop strategies that are not only data-driven but finely attuned to the intricacies of market dynamics.

Ultimately, mastering feature selection and engineering elevates your analytical capabilities, allowing you to cut through the clutter of financial data and focus on what truly matters. As you refine these skills, your aptitude for interpreting market signals and anticipating stock price movements will sharpen, positioning you as a formidable participant in the evolving landscape of quantitative finance.

In conclusion, feature selection and engineering are not just technical skills; they are pivotal tools for uncovering the full potential of your financial analyses. As the data landscape continues to expand, proficiency in these methodologies ensures that you are not only equipped to navigate its complexities but also poised to seize the countless opportunities it presents.

Regression Techniques in Finance

The captivating realm of finance thrives on the power to forecast trends and uncover correlations. Picture navigating the bustling London subway during rush hour: every stop reveals a tide of commuters, much like the endless stream of data points that analysts encounter in financial datasets. To derive meaningful insights from this complexity, practitioners deploy regression techniques—essential tools that facilitate the exploration of relationships among various financial variables.

Understanding Regression Models: A Brief Overview

regression analysis seeks to model relationships between a dependent variable—such as stock prices—and one or more independent variables, which could be factors such as trading volumes, earnings reports, or broader economic indicators.

In the finance sector, regression models are versatile; they extend from forecasting future stock prices to evaluating the effectiveness of trading strategies. The two predominant types of regression models utilized in finance are linear regression and multiple regression.

Linear Regression: A Foundation for Financial Analysis

Linear regression operates under the assumption that a relationship exists between the independent and dependent variables, expressed in a linear fashion. While it may appear straightforward, this model lays a crucial foundation for apprehending more intricate modeling techniques.

To illustrate, let's delve into a practical example of utilizing linear regression to project a stock's price based on historical pricing data and trading volumes. Here's how this can be executed in Python:

```
```python import pandas as pd from sklearn.linear_model import LinearRegression import matplotlib.pyplot as plt

\# Load historical stock price data
df = pd.read_csv('historical_stock_data.csv')

\# Define independent variables and the dependent variable
```
```

```
X = df[['trading_volume', 'previous_day_close']] \# Features
y = df['current_day_close']              \# Target variable

\# Initialize and fit the linear regression model
model = LinearRegression()
model.fit(X, y)

\# Display the coefficients
print("Intercept:", model.intercept_)
print("Coefficients:", model.coef_)

\# Predicting values
predictions = model.predict(X)

\# Visualizing the results
plt.scatter(df['trading_volume'], df['current_day_close'], color='blue', label='Actual values')
plt.scatter(df['trading_volume'], predictions, color='red', label='Predictions')
plt.xlabel('Trading Volume')
plt.ylabel('Current Day Close')
plt.title('Linear Regression: Predictions vs Actual Values')
plt.legend()
plt.show()
```

Through this code, we analyze historical stock data to forecast the current day's closing price based on trading volume and the preceding day's closing value. The output elucidates both the intercept and coefficients, revealing the degree of impact each feature exerts on the target variable. Visualizing the results provides an intuitive grasp of our model's performance.

Multiple Regression: Diving Deeper

While linear regression is excellent for basic analyses, the intricacies of the financial landscape often necessitate more complexity. Multiple regression rises to this challenge by accommodating several independent variables simultaneously, effectively elucidating how multiple factors coalesce to influence financial outcomes.

For instance, if our goal is to comprehend how interest rates, inflation, and consumer sentiment collectively affect stock returns, we can extend our model as follows:

```python
# Incorporating additional features for multiple regression X = df[['trading_volume', 'previous_day_close', 'interest_rate', 'inflation_rate', 'consumer_sentiment']] y = df['current_day_close']

\# Fitting the multiple regression model
model.fit(X, y)

\# Predicting values
predictions = model.predict(X)

\# Displaying all coefficients
print("Intercept:", model.intercept_)
print("Coefficients:", model.coef_)
```

By integrating diverse features, we attain a nuanced understanding of market dynamics, empowering analysts to construct robust financial models that serve as reliable pillars for trading strategies or investment decisions.

Regression Diagnostics: Ensuring Model Validity

Harnessing regression analysis encompasses more than just computing coefficients; evaluating their validity is paramount. Residual analysis plays a vital role in this context. Residuals, the differences between actual and predicted values, provide critical insights into model performance. An effective regression model should exhibit randomly scattered residuals, indicating that the examined relationships have been accurately captured.

```python
# Analyzing the residuals residuals = y - predictions
```

```
plt.figure(figsize=(10, 6))
plt.scatter(predictions, residuals, color='purple')
plt.axhline(0, color='red', linestyle='--')
plt.title('Residuals vs Predicted Values')
plt.xlabel('Predicted Values')
plt.ylabel('Residuals')
plt.show()
```

A lack of discernible patterns in this plot bolsters the idea of model adequacy, suggesting that the model has appropriately captured the underlying relationships. In contrast, identifiable patterns may hint at omitted variables or inappropriate model specifications.

Advanced Regression Techniques: Navigating Complexity

As the landscape of finance evolves, practitioners increasingly gravitate toward advanced regression methods like Ridge and Lasso regression. These techniques incorporate regularization mechanisms to penalize large coefficients, which helps mitigate issues of multicollinearity while enhancing model generalizability.

Here's a succinct illustration of employing Ridge regression in Python:

```python
from sklearn.linear_model import Ridge

\# Initializing Ridge regression with a specified alpha (regularization strength)
ridge_model = Ridge(alpha=1.0)
ridge_model.fit(X, y)
ridge_predictions = ridge_model.predict(X)

\# Coefficients from Ridge model
print("Ridge Intercept:", ridge_model.intercept_)
print("Ridge Coefficients:", ridge_model.coef_)
```

By executing this code, you will observe how regularization modifies the coefficients, thereby augmenting their relevance and effectiveness within the financial framework.

In exploring regression techniques, it becomes evident that these models are foundational components of quantitative finance.

Ultimately, mastering regression analysis equips financial professionals with the capability to extract insightful narratives from vast datasets—an essential skill in navigating the evolving landscape of machine learning and data-driven investment strategies.

Classification Methods for Financial Predictions

In the ever-evolving landscape of financial markets, uncertainty is a constant companion. As financial analysts sift through an avalanche of data, the ability to extract meaningful insights becomes increasingly crucial. This is precisely where classification methods shine, serving as exceptional tools for predicting discrete outcomes that can guide decision-making. Picture yourself navigating the vibrant streets of Manhattan, where each individual represents a data point, each with its own narrative. Just as you read the crowd's intentions, classification techniques empower us to forecast market behaviors using past trends as a lens.

Understanding Classification: Crafting Categorical Models

classification is about predicting distinct categories based on quantitative inputs. Within the realm of finance, this could involve discerning whether a stock's value will increase or decrease, identifying transactions as genuine or fraudulent, or assessing varying levels of credit risk. Central to classification is supervised learning, where models are trained on labeled datasets—this enables them to uncover patterns and relationships that inform future predictions.

Logistic Regression: The Cornerstone of Classification

Logistic regression stands out as a foundational technique in the classification toolkit. While its title includes "regression," it fundamentally serves the purpose of classification by estimating the probability that a specific input belongs to a particular category. This technique is invaluable when predicting events such as loan defaults based on an individual's financial history.

For instance, let's assume we want to determine the likelihood that a bank customer will default on a loan based on factors like income, credit score, and total debt. Here's a practical implementation of logistic regression in Python:

```python
import pandas as pd from sklearn.linear_model import LogisticRegression from sklearn.model_selection import train_test_split from sklearn.metrics import confusion_matrix, classification_report

\# Load customer data
df = pd.read_csv('customer_data.csv')

\# Define features and target variable
X = df[['income', 'credit_score', 'debt']]
y = df['default'] \# 0: No default, 1: Default

\# Split dataset into training and testing sets
X_train, X_test, y_train, y_test = train_test_split(X, y, test_size=0.3, random_state=42)

\# Initialize and fit logistic regression model
logistic_model = LogisticRegression()
logistic_model.fit(X_train, y_train)

\# Predictions and evaluation
predictions = logistic_model.predict(X_test)
print(confusion_matrix(y_test, predictions))
print(classification_report(y_test, predictions))
```

In this example, we assess the model's capacity to predict loan defaults based on customer characteristics. The resulting confusion matrix and classification report provide a comprehensive look at the model's performance, revealing precision, recall, and F1-score—each metric an essential indicator of its ability to correctly identify defaulters while minimizing false positives.

Decision Trees: Visualizing Financial Choices

Decision trees offer a visually intuitive means of classification, employing a series of bifurcations to guide decision-making based on feature values. This method resonates with our natural decision-making processes, allowing stakeholders to visualize the logical pathways leading to specific classifications.

Let's consider using decision trees to predict whether a stock will outperform the market based on its historical performance metrics:

```python
from sklearn.tree import DecisionTreeClassifier
from sklearn import tree import matplotlib.pyplot as plt

\# Load stock data
df = pd.read_csv('stock_performance_data.csv')

\# Define features and target variable
X = df[['previous_close', 'trading_volume', 'market_sentiment']]
y = df['outperform'] \# 0: Does not outperform, 1: Outperform

\# Split dataset
X_train, X_test, y_train, y_test = train_test_split(X, y, test_size=0.3,
random_state=42)

\# Initialize and fit Decision Tree model
tree_model = DecisionTreeClassifier()
tree_model.fit(X_train, y_train)

\# Visualize the tree
```

```
plt.figure(figsize=(15,10))
tree.plot_tree(tree_model, filled=True)
plt.title('Decision Tree for Stock Outperformance Prediction')
plt.show()
```

The decision tree diagram not only clarifies the model's classification process but also enhances interpretability.

Random Forest Classifier: Boosting Classification Competence

While decision trees are powerful, they can sometimes be prone to overfitting, especially amid noisy data or when many features are involved. Random forests tackle this challenge by constructing an ensemble of decision trees, each trained on different subsets of data. This ensemble approach pools predictions from multiple trees, enhancing both accuracy and resilience against overfitting.

Here's how to implement a random forest classifier to predict credit risk:

```python
from sklearn.ensemble import RandomForestClassifier

\# Initialize and fit Random Forest model
rf_model = RandomForestClassifier(n_estimators=100, random_state=42)
rf_model.fit(X_train, y_train)

\# Predictions and evaluation
rf_predictions = rf_model.predict(X_test)
print(confusion_matrix(y_test, rf_predictions))
print(classification_report(y_test, rf_predictions))
```

Employing a random forest significantly reduces the likelihood of overfitting while amplifying predictive performance. Its collective approach captures a wider range of data insights, enabling deeper interpretations of risk factors.

Support Vector Machines (SVM): Finding the Optimal Margin

Support vector machines present yet another sophisticated classification technique, particularly effective in high-dimensional spaces.

For example, consider employing SVM to classify stocks as either "high-risk" or "low-risk" based on various performance metrics and fundamental factors:

```python
from sklearn.svm import SVC

\# Initialize and fit SVM model
svm_model = SVC(kernel='linear')
svm_model.fit(X_train, y_train)

\# Predictions and evaluation
svm_predictions = svm_model.predict(X_test)
print(confusion_matrix(y_test, svm_predictions))
print(classification_report(y_test, svm_predictions))
```

The outcomes will offer perspectives on how effectively SVM can fulfill classification tasks in finance, showcasing the model's competence in meticulously differentiating classes even within intricate datasets.

Evaluating Model Performance: A Vital Component

As we explore diverse classification methodologies, assessing model performance becomes paramount. Relying solely on accuracy can be misleading—especially with imbalanced datasets where one class predominates. Therefore, complementary metrics—including F1-score, precision, recall, and area under the ROC curve (AUC-ROC)—provide a holistic view of a model's performance capacities.

```python
from sklearn.metrics import roc_auc_score

\# Compute AUC-ROC score
```

```
roc_auc = roc_auc_score(y_test, rf_predictions) \# Using the Random Forest model
print("AUC-ROC Score:", roc_auc)
```

This score offers critical insights into a model's efficacy in distinguishing between positive and negative outcomes, serving as a guide for potential refinements.

As we navigate the complex realm of finance, classification methodologies emerge as invaluable tools for deriving categorical predictions. From foundational logistic regression to nuanced ensemble methods like random forests and SVMs, these diverse approaches equip analysts to tackle the challenges posed by dynamic markets and varied data streams.

Ultimately, mastering classification techniques empowers financial analysts to transform vast amounts of information into actionable strategies—enabling them to traverse the unpredictable waters of finance with confidence and precision. Armed with these capabilities, analysts are positioned not only as interpreters of data but also as strategic navigators within the continuously evolving financial landscape.

Clustering Analysis for Market Segmentation

As the landscape of modern finance continues to evolve, it brings with it an abundance of data that necessitates a new approach to understanding market dynamics. Amidst an array of analytical techniques available to financial professionals, clustering analysis is particularly noteworthy for its role in market segmentation.

Imagine strolling through the vibrant streets of London's retail districts, where each shop is tailored to meet the needs and preferences of distinct customer demographics. Just as retailers craft targeted offers based on shopping habits, financial analysts can utilize clustering analysis to segment clients or assets, enabling more precise investment strategies and customized marketing initiatives.

Understanding Clustering: The Power of Unsupervised Learning

clustering analysis falls under the realm of unsupervised learning—a technique where the model discerns patterns and structures within a dataset devoid of prior labels or classifications. In contrast to supervised learning, which relies on labeled data to predict outcomes, clustering allows analysts to explore data intuitively, activating natural groupings that might otherwise go unnoticed.

Consider the objective of categorizing a customer base into meaningful segments. This can enhance product offerings and better assess varying risk profiles. Clustering methodologies, such as K-means and hierarchical clustering, provide practical solutions, each with unique advantages that cater to different segmentation requirements.

K-means Clustering: Simplified Grouping

K-means clustering stands out as one of the most widely adopted techniques, lauded for its straightforward implementation and computational efficiency. The algorithm follows an iterative process that assigns data points to the nearest cluster, recalibrates the cluster centroids, and continues refining the groupings until a stable state is achieved.

To illustrate K-means clustering in action, consider the case of segmenting customers based on their financial behaviors. The following Python code snippet demonstrates how to implement K-means clustering:

```python
import pandas as pd import matplotlib.pyplot as plt from sklearn.cluster import KMeans from sklearn.preprocessing import StandardScaler

\# Load customer financial data
```

```
df = pd.read_csv('customer_financial_data.csv')

\# Feature selection (e.g., annual income, spending score)
X = df[['annual_income', 'spending_score']]

\# Standardization of features
scaler = StandardScaler()
X_scaled = scaler.fit_transform(X)

\# Determining the optimal number of clusters using the Elbow
method
wcss = []
for i in range(1, 11):
  kmeans = KMeans(n_clusters=i, random_state=42)
  kmeans.fit(X_scaled)
  wcss.append(kmeans.inertia_)

\# Plotting the Elbow method results
plt.plot(range(1, 11), wcss)
plt.title('Elbow Method for Optimal k')
plt.xlabel('Number of Clusters')
plt.ylabel('WCSS')
plt.show()

\# Based on the plot, let's say we choose 3 clusters
kmeans = KMeans(n_clusters=3, random_state=42)
y_kmeans = kmeans.fit_predict(X_scaled)

\# Visualizing the clusters
plt.scatter(X_scaled[y_kmeans == 0, 0], X_scaled[y_kmeans == 0, 1],
s=100, c='red', label='Cluster 1')
plt.scatter(X_scaled[y_kmeans == 1, 0], X_scaled[y_kmeans == 1, 1],
s=100, c='blue', label='Cluster 2')
plt.scatter(X_scaled[y_kmeans == 2, 0], X_scaled[y_kmeans == 2, 1],
s=100, c='green', label='Cluster 3')
plt.scatter(kmeans.cluster_centers_[:, 0], kmeans.cluster_centers_[:,
1], s=300, c='yellow', label='Centroids')
plt.title('Customer Segments using K-means Clustering')
plt.xlabel('Annual Income (Standardized)')
```

```
plt.ylabel('Spending Score (Standardized)')
plt.legend()
plt.show()
```

In this scenario, the Elbow method aids in determining the ideal number of clusters for the customer dataset, facilitating a balanced division that accurately mirrors different segments.

Hierarchical Clustering: Just Like Family Trees

While K-means offers a straightforward methodology, hierarchical clustering provides a nuanced perspective by constructing a tree-like structure that visually encapsulates the relationships among data points. This approach can yield either a series of nested clusters or a more simplified grouping, depending on the specific analytical needs of the user.

A practical application of hierarchical clustering might involve analyzing the correlation between various stocks based on historical price movements. The following Python code illustrates how to implement hierarchical clustering:

```python
import seaborn as sns from scipy.cluster.hierarchy import dendrogram, linkage

\# Load stock price data
stock_data = pd.read_csv('stock_price_data.csv')

\# Create a linkage matrix
Z = linkage(stock_data[['stock_A', 'stock_B', 'stock_C', 'stock_D']], method='ward')

\# Dendrogram visualization
plt.figure(figsize=(10, 7))
dendrogram(Z, labels=stock_data.columns)
plt.title('Hierarchical Clustering Dendrogram')
plt.xlabel('Stocks')
plt.ylabel('Distance')
```

```
plt.show()
```

The resulting dendrogram serves as a comprehensive overview of how the stocks relate to one another. Analysts can identify clusters of stocks that behave similarly, a valuable insight that can inform diversification strategies within an investment portfolio.

Evaluating Clustering Performance: Beyond Visuals

While clustering analysis offers significant insights, assessing the quality of the clustering outcomes is vital. Employing internal validation metrics such as the Silhouette Score or the Davies-Bouldin Index can provide a quantitative measure of cluster effectiveness. The Silhouette Score, for example, evaluates both intra-cluster cohesion and inter-cluster separation, with a value close to 1 indicating that the clusters are well-defined.

```python
from sklearn.metrics import silhouette_score

# Calculate the Silhouette Score
silhouette_avg = silhouette_score(X_scaled, y_kmeans)
print("Silhouette Score for K-means:", silhouette_avg)
```

By coupling visual assessments with quantitative evaluations, financial analysts can establish a thorough understanding of clustering effectiveness, validating the strategic decisions derived from these insights.

In summary, clustering analysis proves to be an invaluable asset in the realm of market segmentation within finance. As financial markets grow increasingly intricate and unpredictable, harnessing the power of clustering enhances the analyst's toolkit, empowering them to navigate these complexities with confidence.

Equipped with these advanced analytical capabilities,

professionals transition from being mere data interpreters to becoming strategic architects, capable of constructing robust frameworks that not only embrace the volatility of finance but also leverage it to secure a competitive edge. As you continue to refine your skills in implementing clustering techniques, remember that every dataset presents a narrative waiting to be uncovered—an invitation to enrich your financial strategies and elevate your practice.

Neural Networks and Deep Learning Applications

The world of finance operates in a realm of constant change and intricacy, where the ability to analyze vast amounts of data quickly can make all the difference. Herein lies the transformative power of neural networks and deep learning models—these advanced algorithms not only adapt to shifting market conditions but excel at tackling the multifaceted challenges faced by financial professionals. Much like a skilled trader who deftly interprets a flurry of market signals, financial analysts today are increasingly harnessing these sophisticated techniques for predictive analytics, risk management, and portfolio optimization.

Neural networks are designed to emulate the way human brains function, utilizing interconnected nodes—akin to neurons—to process information across various layers. This structure allows them to uncover intricate patterns within data sets, making neural networks exceptionally proficient in navigating the expansive and diverse landscape of financial markets. Picture the bustling streets of New York City: while chaos might reign on the surface, beneath lies a sophisticated web of routines and patterns guiding every moment. Neural networks illuminate these hidden structures, offering clarity amid the noise.

Understanding Neural Networks: A Gentle Introduction

Neural networks consist of three main parts: an input layer that receives initial data, one or more hidden layers that perform complex computations, and an output layer that provides predictions or classifications. Each connection between nodes is assigned a weight, reflecting its significance in influencing the final output. During the training phase, the network undergoes a process known as backpropagation, where it adjusts these weights based on prediction errors, rigorously improving its accuracy with each iteration.

To illustrate, let's consider the task of predicting stock prices using historical data. A straightforward neural network architecture could include an input layer with various financial indicators (like previous closing prices, trading volume, and market sentiment), multiple hidden layers for detecting intricate relationships, and an output layer that forecasts future prices.

Here's a code snippet that lays out a basic neural network for stock price prediction using Python with the TensorFlow library:

```python
import numpy as np import pandas as pd from sklearn.model_selection import train_test_split from tensorflow.keras.models import Sequential from tensorflow.keras.layers import Dense

\# Load your dataset
data = pd.read_csv('stock_prices.csv')

\# Prepare your data - assume 'price' is the target variable
X = data.drop('price', axis=1).values \# Features
y = data['price'].values \# Target variable

\# Split the data into training and testing sets
X_train, X_test, y_train, y_test = train_test_split(X, y, test_size=0.2,
random_state=42)

\# Build a simple neural network model
model = Sequential()
model.add(Dense(64, input_dim=X_train.shape[1],
activation='relu')) \# Input layer + hidden layer
```

```
model.add(Dense(32, activation='relu')) \# Additional hidden layer
model.add(Dense(1)) \# Output layer

\# Compile the model
model.compile(loss='mean_squared_error', optimizer='adam')

\# Train the model
model.fit(X_train, y_train, epochs=100, batch_size=10)

\# Evaluate the model on test data
loss = model.evaluate(X_test, y_test)
print('Model Loss:', loss)
```

This code encapsulates the fundamental steps required to design, train, and assess a neural network for financial prediction. The parameters chosen for your neural architecture—from the number of layers to activation functions—can dramatically impact overall model performance, making fine-tuning a necessary aspect of the analytical process.

Diving Deeper: Exploring Advanced Neural Network Architectures

While basic neural networks are foundational, more advanced architectures can significantly enhance performance, particularly in complex scenarios. Notably, Convolutional Neural Networks (CNNs) and Recurrent Neural Networks (RNNs) have gained traction in finance for their unique strengths.

1. **Convolutional Neural Networks (CNNs): Generalizing Patterns**

Traditionally associated with image analysis, CNNs are finding fascinating applications in the financial domain, especially when time series data is treated as visual representations. For instance, they can be employed to conduct market sentiment analyses by interpreting price charts as images, thus enabling them to identify trends and anomalies with remarkable precision.

Consider the scenario where a CNN is tasked with foreseeing stock movements based on visual cues from candlestick charts. Here's how you might set up a basic CNN using TensorFlow:

```python
from tensorflow.keras import layers

\# Assuming you have preprocessed your data into 'X' and 'y'
X = X.reshape(X.shape[0], 64, 64, 1) \# Reshape data for CNN (64x64 images)

cnn_model = Sequential()
cnn_model.add(layers.Conv2D(32, (3, 3), activation='relu', input_shape=(64, 64, 1)))
cnn_model.add(layers.MaxPooling2D(pool_size=(2, 2)))
cnn_model.add(layers.Flatten())
cnn_model.add(layers.Dense(64, activation='relu'))
cnn_model.add(layers.Dense(1)) \# Output layer

cnn_model.compile(optimizer='adam', loss='mean_squared_error')
cnn_model.fit(X_train, y_train, epochs=100, batch_size=10)
```

1. **Recurrent Neural Networks (RNNs): Capturing Temporal Dynamics**

RNNs are specifically designed to capture temporal dependencies in sequential data, making them particularly suitable for time series analysis. Their unique feedback loop architecture empowers them to remember and learn from past inputs, enabling a more nuanced understanding of trends and cycles that traditional models often overlook.

Among RNNs, Long Short-Term Memory (LSTM) networks stand out by effectively managing long-range dependencies, which is crucial for financial forecasting. Here's a code example demonstrating the use of an LSTM for stock price prediction:

```python
from tensorflow.keras.layers import LSTM

\# Reshape the input into 3D array for LSTM
X = X.reshape(X.shape[0], X.shape[1], 1)

lstm_model = Sequential()
lstm_model.add(LSTM(50, return_sequences=True,
input_shape=(X.shape[1], 1)))
lstm_model.add(LSTM(50))
lstm_model.add(Dense(1))

lstm_model.compile(loss='mean_squared_error', optimizer='adam')
lstm_model.fit(X_train, y_train, epochs=100, batch_size=10)
```

Evaluating Performance: Going Beyond Accuracy

While the creation of models is crucial, the ability to evaluate and interpret their performance is equally important. Metrics such as Mean Absolute Error (MAE), Root Mean Squared Error (RMSE), and R-squared values provide insights into the accuracy of model predictions. Gaining proficiency in these metrics is essential for understanding how well a model can generalize to unseen data, allowing you to make informed refinements as necessary.

```python
from sklearn.metrics import mean_squared_error

\# Evaluate and calculate RMSE
y_pred = lstm_model.predict(X_test)
rmse = np.sqrt(mean_squared_error(y_test, y_pred))
print('Root Mean Squared Error:', rmse)
```

The embrace of neural networks transforms analysts from mere data processors into forward-thinking strategists, equipped with innovative tools to navigate the complexities of finance. Mastering these techniques invites you to redefine how financial phenomena are understood, interpreted, and acted upon. In an age where data is the new gold, deep learning not only signifies a technical evolution but marks a profound shift in the art and science of quantitative finance.

Model Evaluation and Validation Techniques

In the fast-paced world of finance, where decisions can lead to enormous gains or significant losses, the importance of model evaluation and validation cannot be overstated. As machine learning algorithms become increasingly sophisticated, establishing

The Symbiosis of Machine Learning and Financial Data

Navigating the Data Landscape

To successfully integrate machine learning with financial data, it is crucial to first understand the diverse nature of financial data itself. It comes in multiple forms—ranging from time series data like stock prices and trade transactions to unstructured formats such as news articles that might influence investor sentiment. Each type carries unique challenges and advantages.

Take stock price data, for example. This classic time series data is characterized by continuous sequential time stamps, which inherently exhibit trends, seasonality, and volatility. These patterns require sophisticated machine learning algorithms capable of interpretation. Meanwhile, extracting insights from social media or news articles necessitates the application of natural language processing (NLP), where understanding context and sentiment is vital for gauging market impacts.

The Importance of Data Preprocessing

Before applying machine learning algorithms, it is imperative to preprocess financial data to make it suitable for analysis. The preprocessing phase involves critical steps, which can be summarized as follows:

1. **Data Cleaning:** Financial datasets often contain inaccuracies or extraneous information. Rigorous data cleaning ensures that noise is minimized, allowing for more effective model training. For instance, an analyst may encounter erroneous entries in transaction records that need correction to maintain integrity.
2. **Normalization:** Since various financial metrics can have disparate ranges, normalization techniques—such as Min-Max scaling or Z-score standardization—are employed to standardize these metrics, enhancing the performance of machine learning models.
3. **Feature Selection:** Identifying relevant features that significantly influence desired outcomes (e.g., stock price fluctuations) is crucial. Techniques such as Recursive Feature Elimination (RFE) can help pinpoint the most informative features, streamlining the model's efficiency.
4. **Handling Missing Values:** Gaps in financial data often arise due to system errors or non-reporting. Analysts must strategically address these missing entries through imputation or deletion, being cautious to avoid introducing bias that could skew results.
5. **Dataset Splitting:** Finally, dividing the data into training and testing subsets is essential to validate model performance. A common practice involves using 80% of the data for training and 20% for testing, providing a reliable framework for evaluating a model's effectiveness on previously unseen data.

Selecting the Right Algorithms

Once the preprocessing is complete, the next step is to choose appropriate machine learning algorithms tailored to the specific financial objectives. Several notable algorithms can be particularly effective:

- **Regression Algorithms:** These are ideal for predicting continuous outcomes, such as stock prices, with options ranging from basic Linear Regression to more complex versions like Random Forest Regression.
- **Classification Algorithms:** These are essential for forecasting categorical outcomes, such as determining whether stock prices will rise or fall. Popular choices include Logistic Regression, Support Vector Machines (SVM), and Decision Trees.
- **Clustering Algorithms:** These can uncover hidden patterns within data sets. For instance, K-Means clustering is particularly useful for grouping clients based on trading behaviors, paving the way for more personalized financial services.

Crafting an Effective Machine Learning Pipeline

To truly leverage the power of machine learning in finance, a structured pipeline is fundamental. A typical pipeline consists of the following components:

1. **Data Collection:** Employ APIs to gather financial data efficiently. For example, leveraging Python libraries like yfinance allows for the seamless retrieval of historical stock prices:

```python
import yfinance as yf

\# Fetching historical stock prices for Apple
data = yf.download('AAPL', start='2020-01-01', end='2021-01-01')
print(data.head())
```

1. **Preprocessing:** Follow the aforementioned cleaning and preparation steps.
2. **Model Selection:** Choose and instantiate the appropriate model based on your analytical needs. For stock return predictions, a Random Forest model might be suitable:

```python
from sklearn.ensemble import RandomForestRegressor

\# Define the model
model = RandomForestRegressor()
```

1. **Training the Model:** Fit the model to the training data, adjusting hyperparameters as necessary to optimize performance.

```python
X_train, y_train = training_data[features], training_data[target] model.fit(X_train, y_train)
```

1. **Evaluating the Model:** After training, it's crucial to assess the model's performance using the test dataset. Metrics such as Mean Absolute Error (MAE) or accuracy for classification tasks provide insights into effectiveness.

```python
from sklearn.metrics import mean_absolute_error

y_pred = model.predict(X_test)
mae = mean_absolute_error(y_test, y_pred)
print(f'Mean Absolute Error: {mae}')
```

1. **Iterating for Improvement:** Depending on initial outcomes, revisit various pipeline steps—refining feature selection, tweaking algorithms, and

exploring alternative models to enhance prediction accuracy.

Real-World Application: Predictive Analytics in Action

Among the most impactful uses of integrating ML with financial data is predictive analytics, particularly for hedge funds looking to refine their trading strategies.

For instance, imagine a scenario where a hedge fund employs a machine learning model trained on five years of historical data to project price movements over the upcoming month. After several iterations and refinements, the predictive accuracy of the model reaches an impressive 85%. This remarkable performance could significantly influence the fund's trading strategies, enabling improved profitability while mitigating associated risks.

Final Thoughts

The integration of machine learning with financial data stands as a powerful, transformative force in the finance sector. A comprehensive understanding of data preprocessing, algorithm selection, and evaluation techniques empowers analysts to unlock invaluable insights, leading to the development of advanced financial models poised to meet future challenges.

As we look ahead, the convergence of machine learning and finance is bound to expand, fueled by the ever-growing volume of data and the pressing need for informed decision-making strategies. Adopting this shift will not only elevate the capabilities of financial analysts but also catalyze groundbreaking innovations that redefine our interactions with financial data.

Case Study: Harnessing Predictive Analytics for Stock Movement

In the dynamic world of finance, uncertainty pervades, yet predictive analytics has emerged as a formidable tool to help investors navigate this volatile landscape. This case study will illuminate how predictive analytics can be effectively utilized to forecast stock movements, thereby transforming complex data analysis into actionable trading strategies.

Laying the Groundwork: Data Collection and Preparation

Our journey begins with the essential task of data gathering. For this examination, we will explore the historical stock prices of our hypothetical company, Tech Innovators Inc. This fictitious entity has captured the interest of investors due to its pioneering developments in artificial intelligence and cloud computing technologies.

```python
import yfinance as yf
import pandas as pd

\# Define the stock symbol and time frame
stock_symbol = "TII"  \# TII represents Tech Innovators Inc.
data = yf.download(stock_symbol, start='2021-01-01', end='2023-01-01')

\# Display the initial rows of the dataset
print(data.head())
```

This dataset provides significant insights, featuring key columns such as "Open," "High," "Low," "Close," and "Volume." From these metrics, we will extract carefully crafted features that will serve as inputs for our predictive model.

Cultivating Insights: The Importance of Feature Engineering

Feature engineering is critical in enhancing the predictive power of our analytical initiatives. In this case, we will derive several key features from the raw stock data:

1. **Daily Returns:** By calculating the percentage change in stock prices from one day to the next, we gain insights into the stock's volatility.

```python
data['Daily Return'] = data['Close'].pct_change()
```

```

1. **Moving Averages:** Utilizing simple moving averages (SMA) over distinct periods (e.g., 20-day and 50-day) helps discern trends in stock behavior.

```python data['20 Day SMA'] = data['Close'].rolling(window=20).mean() data['50 Day SMA'] = data['Close'].rolling(window=50).mean()
```

1. **Volume Changes:** Examining fluctuations in trading volume may indicate shifts in market interest or potential price movements.

```python data['Volume Change'] = data['Volume'].pct_change()
```

Once the features are engineered, we must ensure their accuracy while also addressing any missing values that could hinder our analysis. Engaging in data cleaning and preprocessing is vital for providing our model with high-quality inputs.

Selecting the Ideal Model: Algorithmic Choices

In the realm of stock movement predictions, supervised learning techniques are commonly employed, particularly regression models. For this case study, we will utilize a Random Forest Regressor, a robust method adept at handling non-linear relationships and effectively managing interactions among features.

To kickstart our modeling process, we will divide our dataset into a training set for model fitting and a test set for subsequent evaluation, ensuring we preserve enough unseen data for accurate performance assessment:

```python from sklearn.model_selection import

train_test_split

\# Dropping any rows with NaN values
cleaned_data = data.dropna()

\# Define features and target variable
features = cleaned_data[['20 Day SMA', '50 Day SMA', 'Volume Change']]
target = cleaned_data['Close'].shift(-1) \# Predicting the closing price for the next day

\# Splitting the data
X_train, X_test, y_train, y_test = train_test_split(features, target[:-1], test_size=0.2, random_state=42)
` ` `

Here, the target variable is the "Close" price of the stock for the next day, while our features comprise the derived indicators we previously computed.

*Training and Evaluating the Model*

With our data now prepared and partitioned, we can proceed to train our Random Forest model. A crucial aspect of this stage is hyperparameter tuning, enabling us to fine-tune the model for optimal predictive performance:

` ` `python from sklearn.ensemble import RandomForestRegressor from sklearn.metrics import mean_absolute_error

\# Instantiate the model
model = RandomForestRegressor(n_estimators=100, random_state=42)

\# Fit the model using the training data
model.fit(X_train, y_train)

\# Conduct predictions on the test set
y_pred = model.predict(X_test)

\# Evaluate the model's accuracy

```
mae = mean_absolute_error(y_test, y_pred)
print(f'Mean Absolute Error: {mae}')
```

The Mean Absolute Error (MAE) serves as a straightforward metric that reflects the model's predictive efficacy. A lower MAE indicates a higher precision in our forecasts.

Visualizing Results: Gaining Deeper Insights

To enhance our understanding, let's visualize the results.pyplot as plt

plt.figure(figsize=(14, 7)) plt.plot(y_test.index, y_test, label='Actual Prices', color='blue') plt.plot(y_test.index, y_pred, label='Predicted Prices', color='orange') plt.xlabel('Date') plt.ylabel('Stock Price') plt.title('Comparison of Actual and Predicted Stock Prices for Tech Innovators Inc.') plt.legend() plt.show() ```

This visualization provides stakeholders with clarity on how predictive analytics can inform trading strategies and facilitate better-informed decision-making based on the model's predictions.

Real-World Implications: Driving Informed Decisions

The implications of leveraging predictive analytics extend far beyond theoretical discussions. In practical trading strategies, these insights can steer investment decisions, thereby minimizing risks and maximizing profitability. For example, if our model predicts a substantial rise in stock prices, investors may opt to accumulate shares, positioning themselves to benefit from future gains.

Consider the approaches employed by hedge funds, which often leverage predictive models using extensive historical data. These sophisticated analyses empower them to identify market trends, exploit inefficiencies, and optimize asset allocations based on anticipated price movements.

Incorporating predictive analytics into stock price forecasting underscores the transformative potential of data-driven decision-making within finance. The meticulous progression—from data collection and preparation through feature engineering, modeling, and evaluation—reflects a comprehensive framework that equips financial analysts for success.

As machine learning techniques and data availability continue to evolve, the horizon promises even more advanced models capable of integrating not just historical stock data but also macroeconomic indicators, sentiment analysis derived from news articles, and real-time market conditions. Financial professionals who embrace these innovations will be well-equipped to navigate the complexities of an ever-evolving quantitative finance landscape, turning potential volatility into informed strategy and opportunity.

CHAPTER 8: ADVANCED TOPICS IN STATISTICAL METHODS

At the heart of Bayesian statistics lies Bayes' Theorem, which delineates how the probability of a hypothesis can be adjusted as new information is encountered. Think of Bayesian inference as a dynamic two-step cycle: establishing a prior belief and updating that belief.

1. **Prior Belief**: Initially, analysts harbor prior knowledge or beliefs regarding the likelihood of certain financial events—this is referred to as the "prior distribution." For instance, a portfolio manager may assess that a particular stock has a 60% probability of experiencing a positive return based on historical performance.

2. **Updating Belief**: When new data becomes available, such as more recent earnings reports or unexpected geopolitical developments, the prior belief is updated to create a "posterior distribution." This reflects a synthesis of the prior information and the likelihood

of the new evidence.

Mathematically, Bayes' Theorem is expressed as:

$$P(H|E) = \frac{P(E|H) \cdot P(H)}{P(E)}$$

Where: - $P(H|E)$ represents the posterior probability (the belief after incorporating new evidence). - $P(E|H)$ denotes the likelihood (the probability of observing the evidence given the hypothesis). - $P(H)$ signifies the prior probability (the initial belief before new evidence). - $P(E)$ is the marginal likelihood (the overall probability of the evidence).

With this foundation, analysts can iteratively refine their forecasts in reaction to unfolding information, positioning Bayesian statistics as a vital tool in financial decision-making.

Applications in Finance: Harnessing the Power of Bayesian Methods

The versatility of Bayesian statistics has led to its adoption across varied domains within finance, including risk assessment, portfolio optimization, and predictive modeling. Let's delve deeper into how these methods can enhance analytical capabilities in each area.

Bayesian statistics significantly bolsters risk management by enabling a more nuanced evaluation of the uncertainties associated with financial instruments. For example, a hedge fund manager seeking to estimate a stock's volatility may find that relying solely on historical data is inadequate. Instead, they can incorporate fresh market intelligence into their volatility estimates.

Example: Consider a stock, XYZ Corp, with a historical volatility rate of 25%. Following the release of quarterly earnings that exceeded market expectations, our manager receives information indicating an upward trend in volatility due to impending regulatory changes. Utilizing Bayesian techniques, they can recalibrate their volatility estimate:

```python
import numpy as np
import matplotlib.pyplot as plt
from scipy.stats import norm

\# Prior distribution (historical volatility assumptions)
prior_mu = 25 \# Prior mean
prior_sigma = 5 \# Prior standard deviation

\# New evidence indicating increased future volatility
new_evidence_mu = 35
new_evidence_sigma = 10

\# Calculate the posterior distribution
posterior_mu = (prior_mu / prior_sigma**2 + new_evidence_mu / new_evidence_sigma**2) / (1 / prior_sigma**2 + 1 / new_evidence_sigma**2)
posterior_sigma = np.sqrt(1 / (1 / prior_sigma**2 + 1 / new_evidence_sigma**2))

\# Visualize the distributions
x = np.linspace(0, 100, 100)
plt.plot(x, norm(prior_mu, prior_sigma).pdf(x), label='Prior Distribution', linestyle='--')
plt.plot(x, norm(posterior_mu, posterior_sigma).pdf(x), label='Posterior Distribution', linestyle='-')
plt.title('Prior vs. Posterior Distribution of Volatility')
plt.xlabel('Volatility (%)')
plt.ylabel('Density')
plt.legend()
plt.show()
```

This code provides a visual contrast between prior assumptions and the revised risk evaluation, illustrating the efficacy of Bayesian methods in generating refined assessments.

Portfolio Optimization

In the realm of portfolio management, Bayesian statistics

enrich the investment decision-making process by integrating uncertainty into asset allocation strategies. Rather than relying solely on historical returns, analysts can harness Bayesian frameworks to construct a more resilient understanding of expected returns and their corresponding uncertainties.

Picture a portfolio manager tasked with optimizing asset allocation across multiple sectors.

Example: The manager might estimate that the expected return on equities follows a normal distribution centered around 8% with a standard deviation of 2%. Should recent data from market surveys indicate a sharply positive shift in market sentiment, their model can be updated accordingly:

```python
# Define prior expectations based on historical analysis
prior_return = 0.08
prior_volatility = 0.02

\# New market sentiment adjustments
new_market_return = 0.1  \# Revised expectation reflecting current conditions
new_market_volatility = 0.015

\# Compute updated posterior expectations
posterior_return = (prior_return / prior_volatility**2 + new_market_return / new_market_volatility**2) / (1 / prior_volatility**2 + 1 / new_market_volatility**2)
posterior_volatility = np.sqrt(1 / (1 / prior_volatility**2 + 1 / new_market_volatility**2))

print(f"Updated Expected Return: {posterior_return*100:.2f}%")
print(f"Updated Volatility: {posterior_volatility*100:.2f}%")
```

This approach creates a dynamic portolio management strategy, allowing the manager to respond to market changes with agility and precision.

Predictive Modeling

Bayesian methods shine in predictive modeling, where they facilitate a more comprehensive approach to forecasting by incorporating uncertainty directly into projections. This capacity helps mitigate overfitting, a significant challenge frequently encountered in conventional statistical techniques.

Example: A financial analyst intends to forecast the future price of a stock, dependent on various economic indicators.

Using the pymc3 library, the analyst might construct a Bayesian regression model as follows:

```python
import pymc3 as pm
import numpy as np
import matplotlib.pyplot as plt

# Simulated dataset representing economic indicators influencing stock prices
np.random.seed(42)
n_samples = 100
x_data = np.random.normal(loc=10, scale=1, size=n_samples) # Economic indicators
true_intercept = 5
true_slope = 0.5
y_data = true_intercept + true_slope * x_data + np.random.normal(scale=1, size=n_samples) # Stock prices

with pm.Model() as model:
  intercept = pm.Normal('intercept', mu=0, sigma=10)
  slope = pm.Normal('slope', mu=0, sigma=1)
  sigma = pm.HalfNormal('sigma', sigma=1)

   mu = intercept + slope * x_data
         Y_obs = pm.Normal('Y_obs', mu=mu, sigma=sigma, observed=y_data)

   trace = pm.sample(2000, return_inferencedata=False)

# Analyze and visualize the results
pm.plot_trace(trace)
plt.show()
```

` ` `

This code allows the analyst to assess the posterior distributions of key parameters, providing a robust framework that encapsulates the unpredictability inherent to stock price movements.

As a powerful framework for data analysis, Bayesian statistics has the potential to redefine financial analysis in an increasingly complex and volatile market.

Looking ahead, we expect a proliferation of Bayesian techniques as computational advancements and real-time data access become more readily available. Financial professionals who integrate Bayesian statistics into their practices will be well-equipped to tackle emerging challenges and seize opportunities in intricate financial landscapes.

Furthermore, the synergy of Bayesian methodologies with cutting-edge technologies, such as machine learning, holds promise for unlocking even greater analytical potential. As you journey through the world of quantitative finance, consider how Bayesian statistics can augment your analytical toolkit, enabling you to adeptly address the complexities of modern finance.

Non-Parametric Methods in Finance: A Comprehensive Exploration

A Deep Dive into Non-Parametric Methods

At the heart of non-parametric statistics lies a fundamental shift away from the dependence on specific distributions, such as the normal distribution. These methods embrace minimal assumptions about the underlying data, making them especially suited for real-world financial scenarios that often deviate from theoretical models.

Distinct Characteristics

1. **Adaptive Framework**: Non-parametric methods are

responsive to the characteristics of the data being analyzed. They facilitate conclusions drawn directly from observed data instead of forcing it into predefined molds.

2. **Robustness Against Outliers**: These methods exhibit resilience to outliers and distributional skewness, rendering them exceptionally effective for financial datasets that frequently encompass anomalies.
3. **Distribution-Free Inference**: Non-parametric techniques operate without the necessity of assuming a known distribution for the data, thus broadening their applicability across a wide spectrum of financial contexts.

Prominent Non-Parametric Techniques

Several key non-parametric methodologies have gained traction in the financial sector, including:

1. **Rank-Based Methods**: Techniques such as the Wilcoxon Signed-Rank test and the Kruskal-Wallis test utilize data ranks instead of actual values, making them robust alternatives for comparative analyses.
2. **Kernel Density Estimation (KDE)**: This technique is valuable for estimating the probability density function of a random variable, enabling financial analysts to visualize return distributions while circumventing assumptions about their underlying distribution.
3. **Median and Interquartile Range**: Serving as alternatives to mean and standard deviation, these robust statistics provide insights into central tendencies and variability with minimal influence from extreme values.

Let's delve into these concepts further through practical applications.

Pragmatic Applications in Finance

Non-parametric methods find indispensable roles in various financial contexts, delivering practical solutions to pressing challenges.

Consider a financial analyst tasked with assessing the distribution of daily returns for a particular stock over the past year. Rather than assuming a normal distribution —an assumption that may not hold—the analyst applies Kernel Density Estimation (KDE) to generate a nuanced curve representing the distribution of returns.

Here's how this can be illustrated using Python with libraries seaborn and pandas:

```python
import pandas as pd import seaborn as sns import matplotlib.pyplot as plt import numpy as np

\# Simulated daily returns for a stock
np.random.seed(42)
daily_returns = np.random.normal(loc=0, scale=1, size=365)

\# Applying Kernel Density Estimation
sns.kdeplot(daily_returns, fill=True)
plt.title('Kernel Density Estimate of Daily Returns')
plt.xlabel('Return')
plt.ylabel('Density')
plt.show()
```

This visualization empowers the analyst to discern the likelihood of various returns, fostering a deeper understanding of potential risks.

2. Evaluating Performance with the Wilcoxon Signed-Rank Test

Imagine an analyst tasked with comparing the efficacy of two distinct trading strategies over the same period. Instead of relying on a t-test—which presumes normality—the analyst can employ the Wilcoxon Signed-Rank Test. This method allows for comparison of paired return differences across strategies, providing robustness against statistical assumption violations.

Below is an implementation in Python utilizing the scipy library:

```python
from scipy.stats import wilcoxon

# Simulated returns for two strategies
strategy_a = np.random.normal(loc=0.01, scale=0.02, size=100)
strategy_b = np.random.normal(loc=0.015, scale=0.025, size=100)

# Conducting the Wilcoxon signed-rank test
stat, p_value = wilcoxon(strategy_a, strategy_b)

print(f"Statistic: {stat}, P-value: {p_value}")
```

With these results, the analyst can determine whether the performance differences are statistically significant, enabling more informed decision-making while sidestepping the constraints of traditional parametric tests.

3. Non-Parametric Approach to Portfolio Optimization

In a more advanced scenario, consider an investment manager grappling with the challenge of optimizing a portfolio of assets whose returns are not normally distributed.

For instance, the manager may opt to utilize the median—which is less affected by extreme data points—to ascertain expected returns instead of relying on the mean.

```python
# Simulated portfolio returns
portfolio_returns = np.random.normal(loc=0.005, scale=0.03, size=1000)

# Calculating the median return
```

```
median_return = np.median(portfolio_returns)
print(f"Median Expected Return: {median_return:.4f}")
```

This strategy not only enhances the robustness of the expected return estimates but also mitigates the risks associated with outliers.

Non-parametric methods serve as a beacon in the landscape of quantitative finance, allowing analysts to unearth invaluable insights while circumventing the constraints of conventional statistical assumptions.

As the financial environment continues to transform, the relevance of non-parametric techniques is poised to expand, particularly as analysts seek innovative ways to navigate unpredictability. Whether in risk management, performance evaluation, or portfolio optimization, non-parametric methods empower finance professionals to confront challenges with confidence, armed with insights derived from authentic data.

Embarking on this journey into the realm of statistical flexibility not only sharpens analytical skills but also enriches a professional's toolkit, positioning analysts at the forefront of modern finance.

Understanding Copula Models and Dependence Structures in Finance

What Are Copulas?

At their core, copulas are statistical constructs that allow us to examine and quantify the relationship between random variables, distinctly separating the marginal behavior of each variable from their collective behavior. Picture it as piecing together a jigsaw puzzle, where each piece represents an individual asset—together they form a coherent picture of the portfolio's performance. This separation empowers analysts to model more intricate dependency structures in financial data, particularly in scenarios where the conventional assumption of normality—frequently employed in traditional correlation metrics—proves inadequate.

Core Features of Copulas

1. **Dimension Agnosticism**: One of the standout features of copulas is their ability to manage multivariate distributions without being constrained by dimensional limitations. This characteristic is especially beneficial in the finance realm, where portfolios can encompass a diverse array of asset classes.
2. **Tail Dependence**: Unlike traditional measures such as the Pearson correlation, which often fails to account for extreme occurrences, copulas adeptly model tail dependencies. This allows for a deeper understanding of how assets respond under extreme conditions, such as market crashes.
3. **Versatility**: The landscape of copulas is rich with various families, each designed to model unique dependency structures. For example, Gaussian copulas are commonly used for normal distributions, while Archimedean copulas excel in capturing dependencies that demonstrate tail behavior.

Prominent Families of Copulas

When exploring copulas, familiarity with leading families can significantly enhance your analytical toolkit:

1. **Gaussian Copula**: This popular copula employs the multivariate normal distribution for dependency modeling. While user-friendly and widely adopted, it often underrepresents potential risks during extreme market events due to its symmetrical tail properties.
2. **t Copula**: In contrast, the t copula incorporates

heavier tails compared to its Gaussian counterpart, making it particularly well-suited for financial data that may exhibit pronounced tail dependencies during periods of market stress.

3. **Archimedean Copulas**: These copulas encompass families such as Clayton, Gumbel, and Frank, each providing a flexible framework for modeling dependencies specific to distinct asset classes or market conditions.

Applying Copulas in Financial Analysis

To illustrate the practical use of copulas, let's consider a scenario where an analyst is interested in understanding the joint behavior of two asset classes—stocks and bonds. This knowledge is crucial for optimizing portfolio allocations by accurately assessing risk and return profiles.

Step 1: Data Collection

We begin by gathering historical price data for our selected assets. Leveraging Python's pandas_datareader library makes this process straightforward.

```python
import pandas as pd from pandas_datareader import data import numpy as np

\# Define the assets to analyze
assets = ['AAPL', 'MSFT', 'TLT']  \# AAPL and MSFT as stocks, TLT as a bond ETF

\# Specify the date range for analysis
start_date = '2020-01-01'
end_date = '2023-01-01'

\# Fetch and prepare the data from Yahoo Finance
price_data = data.get_data_yahoo(assets, start=start_date, end=end_date)['Adj Close']
returns = price_data.pct_change().dropna()
```

Step 2: Fitting a Copula

With our returns data at hand, the next logical step is to fit a copula to this information. For this demonstration, we'll utilize the copulas library, focusing specifically on the t copula due to its robustness against outliers and its ability to effectively model tail dependencies.

```python
from copulas.multivariate import GaussianMultivariate

\# Initialize and fit a Gaussian copula to the returns
copula = GaussianMultivariate()
copula.fit(returns)

\# Sample from the fitted copula
simulated_returns = copula.sample(1000)
```

Step 3: Analyzing Dependence Structures

After fitting the copula, we can analyze the dependence structures through visualizations, such as scatter plots, which allow us to observe how our selected assets interact under different conditions.

```python
import matplotlib.pyplot as plt

\# Create a scatter plot of the simulated returns
plt.figure(figsize=(10, 6))
plt.scatter(simulated_returns['AAPL'], simulated_returns['MSFT'],
alpha=0.5, label='Simulated AAPL vs. MSFT')
plt.xlabel('AAPL Returns')
plt.ylabel('MSFT Returns')
plt.title('Simulated Dependence Structure between AAPL and MSFT')
plt.legend()
plt.grid()
plt.show()
```

This scatter plot provides a visually compelling representation of the interplay between Apple and Microsoft returns, enhancing our understanding of their relationship.

Utilizing Copulas in Risk Management

A significant application of copulas in finance lies in risk management, particularly in estimating Value at Risk (VaR) for portfolios under non-normal conditions. This capability opens up avenues for more precise risk assessments.

Value at Risk Calculation

To illustrate a practical application, consider estimating the VaR of a portfolio constructed from our selected stocks and bonds. A copula-based approach integrates the joint distribution of returns while addressing the unique characteristics of the assets involved.

```python
from scipy.stats import norm

\# Define portfolio weights
weights = np.array([0.5, 0.5, 0.0]) \# 50% AAPL, 50% MSFT

\# Compute portfolio returns
portfolio_returns = (returns.values @ weights)

\# Calculate the VaR at the 95% confidence level
VaR_95 = np.percentile(portfolio_returns, 5)
print(f"Value at Risk (95% Confidence Level): {VaR_95:.2%}")
```

The output of this calculation presents the potential losses within the portfolio under typical market conditions, empowering analysts with refined tools to make informed investment choices.

Copula models represent a transformative approach to understanding dependencies among financial assets, enabling analysts and portfolio managers to capture behaviors that traditional metrics might overlook. As financial markets become increasingly intricate, the adaptability of copulas provides professionals with the insights necessary to make well-informed decisions. Whether employed for risk management, portfolio optimization, or analyzing market dynamics, a mastery of copula models is essential for success in the complex realm of quantitative finance.

In an age marked by uncertainty and volatility, the analytical perspectives gained through copula frameworks are invaluable, enhancing analysts' capabilities to navigate complexities with confidence and precision.

Demystifying Quantile Regression

Traditional regression analysis primarily estimates the mean of the dependent variable based on a set of independent variables. While helpful, this approach can obscure critical insights when relationships are nonlinear or when extreme values skew the mean. Quantile regression allows financial analysts to assess how predictor variables influence different quantiles of the dependent variable, facilitating a multilayered comprehension of potential outcomes.

Consider a financial analyst tasked with examining the stock performance of a company in relation to factors such as earnings, dividends, and market sentiment. Conventional regression might yield an average expected performance metric, whereas quantile regression unveils how stock performance can vary across different market scenarios—whether volatile or stable, bullish or bearish.

Advantages of Quantile Regression

1. **Robustness to Outliers**: By emphasizing quantile assessment rather than mean estimation, quantile regression remains less susceptible to outliers. This feature is particularly crucial in financial datasets, which often present extreme values that can distort traditional analyses.

2. **Flexibility in Model Specification**: This method does not impose specific distribution assumptions on the errors, making it versatile enough to accommodate a wide range of financial data types.

3. **Enhanced Risk Assessment**: By focusing on lower quantiles, analysts can better gauge extreme loss scenarios—such as Value at Risk (VaR)—which are essential for effective risk management strategies.

Practical Application of Quantile Regression in Finance

To illustrate the practical value of quantile regression, let us delve into a case study analyzing the impact of market volatility on stock returns. For this demonstration, we will utilize Python's statsmodels library, which provides an accessible framework for implementing quantile regression.

Step 1: Data Collection

Our analysis will begin with the collection of relevant stock return data alongside a volatility index—often represented by the CBOE Volatility Index (VIX). Here, we'll focus on stock returns from notable technology companies, such as Apple Inc. (AAPL) and Microsoft Corp. (MSFT), along with the VIX to track market volatility.

```python
import pandas as pd from pandas_datareader import data

\# Define the assets to analyze
assets = ['AAPL', 'MSFT', '^VIX'] \# Stock tickers and VIX index

\# Specify the date range for analysis
start_date = '2020-01-01'
end_date = '2023-01-01'

\# Fetch and prepare the data from Yahoo Finance
data = data.get_data_yahoo(assets, start=start_date, end=end_date)
['Adj Close']
```

returns = data.pct_change().dropna() \# Calculate daily returns
```

*Step 2: Implementing Quantile Regression*

With the returns data ready, we can conduct our quantile regression analysis to explore the relationship between stock returns and market volatility at the 25th, 50th, and 75th percentiles—providing a nuanced view of how these variables interact under varying financial circumstances.

```python import statsmodels.api as sm import numpy as np

\# Prepare the dependent and independent variables
X = returns[['AAPL', 'MSFT']] \# Independent variables (AAPL and MSFT returns)
X = sm.add_constant(X) \# Adding a constant for the intercept
y = returns['^VIX'] \# Dependent variable (VIX returns)

\# Instantiate and fit the quantile regression model
quantiles = [0.25, 0.5, 0.75] \# Specify quantiles
quantile_models = {}

for q in quantiles:
  model = sm.QuantReg(y, X)
  res = model.fit(q=q)
  quantile_models[q] = res
  print(f'Quantile: {q}, Coefficients: {res.params}')
```

Step 3: Interpreting the Results

Understanding and interpreting the coefficients generated from the quantile regression model is essential. Each output from the quantile regression provides distinct insights:

- The 25th percentile model reveals how stock returns behave in conditions of lower volatility, indicating that the effect of the predictor variables differs under these circumstances compared to periods of average
```

or heightened volatility (as indicated by the 50th and 75th percentiles).

- The 50th percentile output reflects the average impact, while the 75th percentile coefficient may signal robust stock performance during favorable market conditions.

For instance, imagine our regression results yield the following coefficients:

- For AAPL:
- 25th Quantile: 0.05
- 50th Quantile: 0.10
- 75th Quantile: 0.15
- For MSFT:
- 25th Quantile: 0.03
- 50th Quantile: 0.08
- 75th Quantile: 0.12

These coefficients suggest that as market volatility diminishes, the expected returns for AAPL progressively increase. The larger returns at higher quantiles imply that the company tends to perform remarkably well during bullish trends, while the relationship may weaken in bearish conditions.

Practical Considerations and Limitations

While quantile regression presents numerous advantages, it also introduces certain challenges. Selecting the appropriate quantiles for analysis is crucial; opting for excessively extreme quantiles can lead to unstable estimates. Furthermore, the complexities surrounding the interpretation and communication of results may require a higher level of statistical acumen, particularly when engaging stakeholders accustomed to traditional mean-centric analyses.

Quantile regression stands as a formidable tool in the toolkit of financial analysts, offering nuanced insights into variable relationships that traditional methods often overlook. It equips analysts to navigate the intricate and sometimes turbulent waters of financial markets with precision and confidence.

Decoding Time Series Data

Time series data consists of observations collected sequentially over time. This unique ordering instills the data with essential elements such as trends, seasonality, and cyclical patterns—elements that are critical in financial analysis. Unlike standard datasets, time series data requires specialized techniques that account for the various confounding factors impacting financial phenomena.

Before embarking on the journey into advanced methodologies, it's essential to revisit some foundational concepts that underpin time series analysis:

1. **Stationarity**: A cornerstone assumption for many time series models, stationarity asserts that statistical properties such as mean and variance remain constant over time. Non-stationary data can skew results and lead to inaccurate interpretations.
2. **Seasonality**: Many financial time series demonstrate regular, periodic fluctuations influenced by market cycles, economic conditions, or seasonal events, necessitating careful analysis.
3. **Autocorrelation**: This concept reflects the correlation of a time series with its own past values, allowing analysts to uncover patterns that inform model selection and enhance predictive performance.

ARIMA Models: Connecting Past Insights to Present Trends

One of the cornerstone techniques in time series

forecasting is the ARIMA model (Autoregressive Integrated Moving Average). This versatile model combines three key components:

- **Autoregressive (AR) term**: Captures the relationship between a current observation and a specified number of lagged observations.
- **Integrated (I) term**: Involves differencing the raw observations to achieve a stationary time series.
- **Moving Average (MA) term**: Accounts for the relationship between an observation and a residual error from a previous moving average model.

To practically implement an ARIMA model in Python, the pmdarima library provides a user-friendly interface for training and forecasting. Below, we provide a step-by-step walkthrough.

Step 1: Data Preparation

To successfully construct the ARIMA model, the data must undergo meticulous preparation. This includes cleaning, resolving missing values, and ensuring stationarity using techniques like differencing.

```python import pandas as pd import numpy as np from pmdarima import auto_arima import matplotlib.pyplot as plt

```
\# Load historical stock price data
data = pd.read_csv('AAPL_stock_data.csv', parse_dates=['Date'], index_col='Date')
data = data['Close']

\# Visualize the data to identify trends and seasonal patterns
plt.figure(figsize=(10, 6))
plt.plot(data)
plt.title('Apple Inc. Stock Price: 2015-2023')
plt.xlabel('Date')
plt.ylabel('Closing Price')
```
```

plt.show()

\# Assess stationarity with the Augmented Dickey-Fuller test
from statsmodels.tsa.stattools import adfuller

result = adfuller(data)
print('ADF Statistic:', result[0])
print('p-value:', result[1])

\# If the data is non-stationary, apply differencing
if result[1] > 0.05:
  data = data.diff().dropna()
```

*Step 2: Constructing the ARIMA Model*

Following data preparation, employing auto_arima() allows you to automatically select the optimal ARIMA parameters based on the Akaike Information Criterion (AIC).

```python # Fit the ARIMA model model = auto_arima(data, seasonal=False, stepwise=True, suppress_warnings=True) print(model.summary())
```

Step 3: Evaluating Model Performance

Once the model is fitted, it's crucial to evaluate its performance through diagnostic plots that examine residuals, checking for autocorrelation and normality.

```python from statsmodels.graphics import tsaplots

tsaplots.plot_acf(model.resid)
plt.title('Autocorrelation of Residuals')
plt.show()
```

Advanced Techniques: GARCH for Volatility Forecasting

Financial time series are often characterized by volatility
```

clustering, where periods of high volatility tend to follow similar periods. The Generalized Autoregressive Conditional Heteroskedasticity (GARCH) model addresses this phenomenon effectively.

Step 1: Implementing the GARCH Model

The arch library facilitates the implementation of GARCH models in Python. Let's explore how a GARCH(1, 1) model can be applied to our earlier stock data to forecast volatility.

```python
from arch import arch_model

\# Fit a GARCH(1, 1) model
garch_model = arch_model(data, vol='Garch', p=1, q=1)
garch_fit = garch_model.fit(disp='off')
print(garch_fit.summary())
```

Step 2: Forecasting Volatility

With the GARCH model in place, the next step is to forecast future volatility, which is crucial for effective risk management.

```python
# Forecast the next 10 days forecasts = garch_fit.forecast(horizon=10) print('Forecasted Volatility:', forecasts.variance.values[-1, :])
```

Machine Learning Approaches: Harnessing Algorithms for Time Series Analysis

The integration of machine learning into time series forecasting is gaining traction due to its adaptability and ability to model complex data patterns. Techniques like Long Short-Term Memory (LSTM) networks illustrate the power of neural networks in this domain.

Step 1: Preprocessing Data for LSTMs

To prepare data for LSTM modeling, inputs must be structured into sequences, allowing the network to capture temporal dependencies effectively.

```python
from keras.models import Sequential
from keras.layers import LSTM, Dense
from sklearn.preprocessing import MinMaxScaler

\# Normalize the dataset
scaler = MinMaxScaler(feature_range=(0, 1))
scaled_data = scaler.fit_transform(data.values.reshape(-1, 1))

\# Create input and output sequences
def create_dataset(data, time_step=1):
  X, Y = [], []
  for i in range(len(data) - time_step - 1):
    X.append(data[i:(i + time_step), 0])
    Y.append(data[i + time_step, 0])
  return np.array(X), np.array(Y)

time_step = 10
X, y = create_dataset(scaled_data, time_step)
X = X.reshape(X.shape[0], X.shape[1], 1)  \# Shape for LSTM
```

Step 2: Building and Training the LSTM Model

A well-structured LSTM model can enhance forecasting accuracy exponentially.

```python
# Construct the LSTM model
model = Sequential()
model.add(LSTM(50, return_sequences=True, input_shape=(X.shape[1], 1)))
model.add(LSTM(50))
model.add(Dense(1))

model.compile(optimizer='adam', loss='mean_squared_error')
model.fit(X, y, epochs=50, batch_size=32)
```

Step 3: Generating Forecasts with the LSTM

Once trained, the LSTM model can be utilized to predict future stock prices based on the previous sequences.

```python
# Making predictions
predicted = model.predict(X)
predicted_prices = scaler.inverse_transform(predicted)
```

As we traverse the complexities of time series analysis, leveraging advanced techniques such as ARIMA, GARCH, and machine learning unlocks profound possibilities in financial forecasting. These methodologies not only enhance prediction accuracy but also empower analysts to unearth insights that typical analyses may overlook.

Armed with this comprehensive understanding of advanced time series techniques, we can now explore the innovative intersection of machine learning and finance, where predictive modeling and enhanced decision-making await discovery. With these tools, the future of financial analysis is not just promising; it's transformative.

Demystifying the Basics of SEM

SEM synthesizes aspects of factor analysis and multiple regression models. It operates on the premise that latent variables—constructs that cannot be directly measured—serve as underlying factors driving observable data. For instance, "market sentiment" often acts as a latent variable influencing measurable outcomes such as asset prices, trading volume, and market volatility.

The SEM framework consists of two crucial components:

1. **Measurement Model**: This segment delineates how observed variables correspond to latent constructs.
2. **Structural Model**: This component elucidates the hypothesized causal relationships among latent variables, typically represented through pathways that illustrate both direct and indirect effects.

The true appeal of SEM lies in its ability to encapsulate

the complexity inherent in financial phenomena, where numerous variables intricately interact. For example, consider a model investigating the impact of macroeconomic indicators—such as GDP growth and inflation—on stock market returns. SEM allows analysts to thoroughly probe these multifaceted relationships in a systematic manner.

The Role of SEM in Finance

The utility of SEM in finance is vast and varied. Financial analysts can harness its capabilities to:

- Evaluate the impact of economic indicators on investment behaviors.
- Investigate the correlation between investor psychology and market volatility.
- Model diverse risk factors that could influence asset returns.
- Analyze customer satisfaction metrics and their ripple effects on sales performance or stock valuations.

In real-world finance, scenarios often present a labyrinth of variables with intricate dependencies. SEM offers a powerful framework for representing and dissecting these complexities, ultimately enhancing strategic decision-making.

Implementing SEM with Python: A Step-by-Step Guide

To better illustrate the practical application of SEM, let's explore an example analyzing the relationship between investor sentiment, market volatility, and stock returns. For this analysis, we will leverage the `statsmodels` library in conjunction with `semopy`, which is specifically designed for SEM.

Step 1: Data Preparation

Before embarking on the analysis, it is crucial to gather

and prepare the data meticulously. We will work with a hypothetical dataset that includes investor sentiment indices, market volatility measures (such as the VIX), and stock returns (like S&P 500 returns). Ensuring the dataset is clean, normalized, and formatted correctly is vital.

```python
import pandas as pd
import numpy as np

\# Load financial data (hypothetical CSV)
data = pd.read_csv('financial_data.csv', parse_dates=['Date'])
data.set_index('Date', inplace=True)

\# Display the structure of the data
\# Columns: 'Investor_Sentiment', 'Market_Volatility', 'Stock_Returns'
data.dropna(inplace=True) \# Remove any missing values
```

Step 2: Specifying the SEM Model

Next, we will define the SEM model using path notation. In this scenario, we will posit that higher investor sentiment positively influences stock returns while inversely impacting market volatility.

```python
from semopy import Model

\# Define the SEM model
model_description = """
\# Measurement Model
Stock_Returns ~ beta1 * Investor_Sentiment + beta2 * Market_Volatility
Market_Volatility ~ beta3 * Investor_Sentiment

\# Latent Variables (if applicable)
\# Assume Investor_Sentiment might be gauged through various indicators
"""

model = Model(model_description)
```

```
```

Step 3: Fitting the Model

Now that we have our data and model established, we can fit the SEM model to our dataset and derive parameter estimates.

```python
model.fit(data)

\# Output the results
results = model.inspect()
print(results)
```

The output will present estimates of the path coefficients (beta1, beta2, and beta3), quantifying both the strength and direction of the relationships between the variables.

Step 4: Evaluating the Model

A critical aspect of SEM is evaluating the goodness-of-fit of the model. Key fit indices include the Chi-Square statistic, RMSEA (Root Mean Square Error of Approximation), and CFI (Comparative Fit Index). These statistics provide insight into how well our hypothesized model represents the observed data.

```python
# Assess model fit fit_indices = model.fit_indices()
print("Model Fit Indices:") print(fit_indices)
```

A strong model fit indicates that the proposed relationships within your SEM are substantiated by the data. Should certain paths prove statistically insignificant, analysts can refine the model by exploring alternative specifications or including additional covariates.

In navigating the complex and interconnected landscape of quantitative finance, Structural Equation Modeling emerges as an indispensable tool for analysts. Its capability to assess multiple relationships concurrently emphasizes its importance in cultivating a nuanced understanding of financial systems. Engaging with SEM not only enhances our analytical expertise but also sets the stage for pioneering explorations that integrate financial data with broader behavioral and economic theories. Through this journey, analysts are empowered to make impactful contributions to the field of finance—illuminating pathways toward greater clarity and understanding in an ever-evolving landscape.

Survival Analysis in Financial Contexts

Survival analysis, a compelling statistical approach focused on the duration until a specific event occurs, has increasingly carved out an essential role across various fields, especially in finance. Originally developed for medical research—where it estimates the time until events like disease onset or patient recovery—it now provides invaluable insights into the financial sector.

In the realm of finance, survival analysis allows us to investigate the timing of pivotal financial events, such as loan defaults, bankruptcy filings, or the duration until stocks reach a targeted price.

Core Concepts of Survival Analysis

At the heart of survival analysis lie several critical concepts:

1. **Survival Function:** This function calculates the probability that an entity will continue to "survive" past a given time point. Formally, it is defined as ($S(t) = P(T > t)$), where (T) represents the time until the event under consideration.

2. **Hazard Function:** This function measures the instantaneous risk of the event occurring at a specific moment, conditional on survival up to that time. Mathematically, it's represented as ($h(t) = \frac{f(t)}{S(t)}$), where ($f(t)$) denotes the probability density function (PDF).

3. **Censoring:** In many financial applications, the data we work with may be censored. For example, while the default status of some loans may be known, others may still be active, leaving us with incomplete information. Censoring acknowledges these gaps and enables more accurate modeling even in the absence of complete data.

Practical Applications in Finance

To better illustrate the utility of survival analysis, let's consider some practical applications:

- **Credit Risk Assessment:** Financial institutions, particularly banks, can leverage survival analysis to predict the likelihood and timing of loan defaults.
- **Stock Performance Analysis:** Investors may want to estimate the time it will take for a stock to reach a specific price target. Understanding this time frame can refine trading strategies, allowing investors to optimize the duration for which they hold various assets.

Implementing Survival Analysis with Python

To translate theory into practice, we can implement a survival analysis model using Python, specifically utilizing the lifelines library—an excellent toolkit designed for survival analysis.

First, ensure that you have the lifelines library installed. If it's not already installed, you can easily add it via pip:

```bash
pip install lifelines
```

Next, let's assume we have a dataset that includes loan information, specifically the time until default (measured in years) along with a binary flag indicating whether the loan defaulted (event occurred) or is still active (censored).

The following code offers a practical example of how to apply survival analysis in this context:

```python
import pandas as pd from lifelines import KaplanMeierFitter import matplotlib.pyplot as plt

\# Sample data
data = {
  'duration': [1, 2, 3, 4, 5, 6, 7, 8, 9, 10],
  'event': [1, 1, 0, 1, 0, 0, 1, 1, 1, 0] \# 1 = default, 0 = censored
}

df = pd.DataFrame(data)

\# Initialize the Kaplan-Meier fitter
kmf = KaplanMeierFitter()

\# Fit the model
kmf.fit(durations=df['duration'], event_observed=df['event'])

\# Plot the survival function
kmf.plot_survival_function()
plt.title('Survival Function of Loan Defaults')
plt.xlabel('Time (Years)')
plt.ylabel('Survival Probability')
plt.grid()
plt.show()
```

In this example, we utilize the Kaplan-Meier method to create a basic survival model. The resulting graph depicts the survival function, illustrating the probability of avoiding default over time.

Analyzing the Output

Interpreting the Kaplan-Meier survival curve is both intuitive and informative. As time progresses, the curve typically declines, reflecting a decreased probability of survival (or, in this context, an increased likelihood of default). Observing steep declines can signal critical inflection points; these may reveal phases of heightened risk that could compel lenders to adjust their risk management strategies urgently.

Additional Considerations

While survival analysis offers significant advantages, it is essential to remain mindful of its limitations. Censoring can complicate predictions, particularly when datasets feature a considerable amount of censored data. Moreover, underlying assumptions regarding the hazard function, such as proportional hazards, should be carefully assessed to ensure their appropriateness in the given financial context.

In summary, survival analysis emerges as a versatile and powerful tool within quantitative finance, equipping institutions with enhanced predictive capabilities and refined risk assessment strategies. As financial markets become increasingly complex and data-driven, integrating advanced statistical methods like survival analysis will be critical in shaping effective financial strategies. As we delve deeper into the multifaceted landscape of financial analysis, survival analysis stands as a cornerstone of our analytical toolkit, fostering data-centric decision-making.

Techniques for Navigating High-Dimensional Data in Finance

As quantitative finance continues to advance, the management of high-dimensional data has emerged as a crucial focus for analysts and institutions alike. With financial markets generating vast amounts of information —often encompassing thousands of features—the challenge no longer lies simply in data collection but in converting this data into actionable insights. High-dimensional data techniques empower financial analysts to derive meaningful interpretations from these intricate datasets.

Unpacking High-Dimensional Data

High-dimensional data refers to datasets where the number of variables significantly exceeds the number of observations. This situation is increasingly prevalent in finance, where a myriad of factors—such as economic indicators, market sentiment, historical price movements, and company-specific variables—combine to create highly complex and expansive datasets.

A key challenge in this realm is the "curse of dimensionality," which encapsulates various difficulties that arise when analyzing data with more features than observations. For instance, consider a dataset comprising a thousand features accompanied by only a hundred observations; this scenario leads to sparsity in the data space, obscuring patterns and increasing the likelihood of overfitting, ultimately resulting in unreliable models.

Techniques for Managing High-Dimensional Data

To effectively analyze and navigate high-dimensional datasets, practitioners often leverage a combination of dimensionality reduction, feature selection, and regularization techniques. These strategies not only simplify models but also reduce noise and minimize the risk of overfitting.

Dimensionality reduction focuses on condensing the number of features while retaining the dataset's essential information. Notable methods include Principal Component Analysis (PCA) and t-distributed Stochastic Neighbor Embedding (t-SNE).

- **Principal Component Analysis (PCA):** This widely used technique transforms the original features into a new set of uncorrelated variables, known as principal components. Each component is designed to capture as much variance as possible. Typically, just a handful of these components can encapsulate the majority of the dataset's information, greatly simplifying analysis.

Here's a brief example of implementing PCA in Python using the sklearn library:

```python
from sklearn.decomposition import PCA import
pandas as pd

\# Generate a high-dimensional dataset
data = pd.DataFrame({
    'Feature_1': [1.2, 2.3, 3.1] * 100, \# 300 observations
    'Feature_2': [0.4, 0.5, 0.6] * 100,
    'Feature_3': [...], \# More features here
})

\# Apply PCA to reduce dimensions
pca = PCA(n_components=2) \# Targeting 2 dimensions for ease of
visualization
reduced_data = pca.fit_transform(data)

print(reduced_data)
```

In this example, PCA efficiently condenses the dataset while preserving critical information, allowing for straightforward interpretations and visualizations.

- **t-distributed Stochastic Neighbor Embedding (t-SNE):** This technique is particularly effective for visualizing high-dimensional data, as it reduces dimensions while maintaining the relative distances between data points. It is invaluable for revealing clusters and patterns within financial datasets.

2. Feature Selection Techniques

Feature selection is essential for enhancing model robustness by identifying and retaining only the most relevant variables. This improves predictive accuracy and further mitigates overfitting.

- **Recursive Feature Elimination (RFE):** RFE iteratively constructs models and removes the least influential features to enhance performance. This approach can be paired with various models and often leads to increased Predictive accuracy without the clutter of irrelevant data.

Below is an example of applying RFE in Python:

```python
from sklearn.feature_selection import RFE from sklearn.linear_model import LogisticRegression

\# Sample dataset preparation
X, y = ... \# Define features and target variable

\# Initialize RFE with a model
model = LogisticRegression()
rfe = RFE(model, 5) \# Selecting the top 5 features based on performance
fit = rfe.fit(X, y)

selected_features = fit.support_
print(selected_features)
```

- **Lasso Regression:** This regularization technique combines variable selection with model regularization to enhance interpretability and prediction accuracy.

3. Regularization Techniques

Regularization is crucial in high-dimensional analysis, as it helps prevent overfitting by introducing penalties for complexity in model selection. Common methods include:

- **Lasso Regression (L1 Regularization):** As described earlier, Lasso uses an L1 penalty, which drives some coefficients to zero, facilitating a parsimonious model that improves interpretability.
- **Ridge Regression (L2 Regularization):** In contrast to Lasso, Ridge regression applies an L2 penalty,

which shrinks coefficients without fully eliminating any, thereby addressing multicollinearity and emphasizing the overall model performance instead.

Real-World Application: A Case Study

To illustrate these techniques in action, consider a hedge fund attempting to analyze a dataset comprised of thousands of indicators to forecast stock prices. Faced with the daunting challenges posed by high dimensionality and inadequate traditional analysis methods, the team turns to PCA for initial dimensionality reduction.

Subsequently, they implement RFE using a Random Forest model to isolate the five features that hold the most predictive power, discarding the rest. Finally, the hedge fund employs Lasso regression to create their predictive model, effectively balancing accuracy and overfitting.

Through the application of these high-dimensional data techniques, the hedge fund not only enhances its forecasting capabilities but also enables more informed decision-making.

High-dimensional data serves as both a challenge and an opportunity within quantitative finance. The significance of these methods cannot be overstated; they enhance model performance and guide critical decisions in a data-driven era. As the finance landscape evolves, mastering high-dimensional data techniques will remain essential for analysts hoping to stay ahead in a competitive market.

Simulations and Bootstrap Methods in Quantitative Finance

The Power of Simulations in Finance

Simulations are instrumental for modeling complex financial scenarios, generating an array of potential outcomes by leveraging stochastic (random) processes. These techniques are particularly advantageous when direct analytical solutions are challenging or unattainable. A prime example of this is Monte Carlo simulations, a robust method that relies on repeated random sampling to produce numerical results applicable to diverse financial contexts, including option pricing, risk assessment, and portfolio optimization.

Diving into Monte Carlo Simulations

Monte Carlo simulations entail running thousands—if not millions—of trials to capture the distribution of possible outcomes for uncertain variables, perfectly aligning with the unpredictable nature of financial markets. Imagine seeking to estimate the expected return of a volatile stock; a Monte Carlo simulation is an ideal approach to navigate this uncertainty.

Here's a concise Python implementation of a Monte Carlo simulation for estimating future stock prices:

```python
import numpy as np import matplotlib.pyplot as plt

\# Parameters for the simulation
initial_price = 100 \# Initial stock price
mu = 0.1         \# Expected return
sigma = 0.2       \# Volatility
time_horizon = 1   \# 1 year
num_simulations = 1000 \# Number of simulations

\# Simulating the end price of the stock
np.random.seed(42) \# For reproducibility
simulated_prices = []

for _ in range(num_simulations):
  \# Generate a random price path
  price_path = initial_price * np.exp(np.cumsum(np.random.normal(mu, sigma, time_horizon * 252)))
  simulated_prices.append(price_path[-1])

\# Plotting the simulation results
```

```
plt.hist(simulated_prices, bins=50, alpha=0.75, edgecolor='black')
plt.title('Simulated Stock Prices at Year End')
plt.xlabel('Price')
plt.ylabel('Frequency')
plt.show()
```

In this example, the simulation plots a histogram showcasing the distribution of projected stock prices at the end of one year. Analysts can leverage this information to gauge the probabilities of various outcomes, thereby facilitating more strategic investment decisions.

Bootstrap Methods: An Innovative Resampling Technique

the bootstrap method is a resampling technique that enables analysts to estimate the distribution of a statistic—such as the mean or variance—by repeatedly resampling from a single dataset. This technique shines, especially when the data's underlying distribution remains unknown or when dealing with limited sample sizes.

Practical Applications of Bootstrap Methods

Bootstrap methods are versatile and find myriad applications across financial analyses, including:

- **Estimating Confidence Intervals:** By resampling the original data, analysts can construct confidence intervals for a variety of estimates, from returns to risk measures.
- **Conducting Hypothesis Tests:** Bootstrap techniques provide a flexible approach to traditional hypothesis tests, accommodating various assumptions about the data's distribution.

Implementing Bootstrap Methods in Practice

Now, let's explore how to apply bootstrap techniques to

estimate the confidence interval of an investment portfolio's average return, providing a clear, practical illustration of the methodology.

```python
import numpy as np
import matplotlib.pyplot as plt

# Simulated portfolio returns
returns = np.random.normal(0.01, 0.02, 1000) # Generating 1000 daily returns

# Implementing Bootstrapping
num_bootstrap_samples = 10000
bootstrap_means = []

for _ in range(num_bootstrap_samples):
    # Randomly sample with replacement
    sample = np.random.choice(returns, size=len(returns), replace=True)
    bootstrap_means.append(np.mean(sample))

# Calculate the confidence intervals
lower_bound = np.percentile(bootstrap_means, 2.5)
upper_bound = np.percentile(bootstrap_means, 97.5)

print(f"95% confidence interval for the mean return: [{lower_bound:.4f}, {upper_bound:.4f}]")
```

In this code snippet, we create a bootstrap distribution of means derived from simulated portfolio returns. The output reveals the 95% confidence interval for the mean return, equipping analysts with a quantifiable framework for better investment strategies and enhancing their grasp of uncertainty.

Real-World Implications of These Techniques

The integration of simulations and bootstrap methods has transformed the landscape of financial analysis, allowing professionals to engage with risk and uncertainty more effectively. For instance, during the global financial crisis of 2008, many firms operated under models that underestimated systemic risks. In contrast, organizations employing rigorous simulation techniques were better positioned to model potential crisis scenarios, leading to more resilient risk management strategies.

In summary, simulations and bootstrap methods are indispensable components of the quantitative finance toolkit. They seamlessly bridge the gap between theoretical concepts and practical applications, empowering analysts to effectively navigate the uncertainties of financial markets. As the financial ecosystem continues to evolve, expertise in these methodologies will become ever more crucial for professionals aiming to meet the complexities and challenges of the industry head-on.

Case Study: Advanced Methodologies in Risk Assessment

Understanding Risk in Financial Contexts

To effectively grasp these advanced methodologies, it is crucial to first define risk in a financial context. Financial risk encompasses the potential for losses arising from changes in market conditions. Common types of financial risk include market risk, credit risk, liquidity risk, and operational risk. Each type poses distinct challenges, requiring nuanced analytics for optimal management.

The Shift Towards Quantitative Risk Assessment

Recent years have witnessed a marked shift towards quantitative approaches in risk assessment. Financial institutions—from multinational banks to boutique investment firms—are increasingly leveraging complex mathematical models and cutting-edge computational techniques to forecast risk levels with greater precision. This transformation is fueled by an urgent need for improved accuracy in decision-making processes. For instance, during market upheavals triggered by global events like the COVID-19 pandemic, institutions employing advanced methodologies demonstrated a remarkable capacity for rapid adaptation and effective crisis management.

Implementing Advanced Methodologies

Let's delve into three key advanced methodologies that have significantly influenced risk assessment: Value at Risk (VaR), Copula Models, and Monte Carlo Simulations. We will explore how each of these methodologies operates in real-world contexts.

Value at Risk (VaR) serves as a cornerstone statistical technique for quantifying the risk associated with an asset or portfolio. It estimates the maximum potential loss over a specified time period—typically within normal market conditions—at a given confidence level.

For example, a financial institution might employ VaR to assess the maximum expected loss of a portfolio over a one-day horizon at a 95% confidence level. If the one-day VaR of a portfolio is calculated to be (1 million, this indicates a 5% chance that the portfolio could incur a loss exceeding this threshold within a single day.

Here's a simple Python example illustrating how to calculate VaR using historical simulation:

```python
import numpy as np

\# Simulated daily returns for a portfolio
returns = np.random.normal(0.001, 0.02, 1000) \# Mean 0.1%, Std Dev 2%

\# Calculate the 5th percentile of the return distribution
VaR_95 = np.percentile(returns, 5)
print(f"Value at Risk (95% Confidence Level): {-VaR_95:.2f}")
```

```
```

This straightforward approach provides a tangible risk metric, empowering analysts and institutions to realign portfolios according to their risk appetite.

2. Copula Models for Dependency Structure

A deep understanding of the correlations and dependencies among various financial instruments is essential, especially during times of market stress. Traditional correlation methods often fall short in capturing the complex, non-linear dependencies characteristic of financial data. Copula models provide an innovative solution, allowing analysts to model the dependencies between random variables independent of their individual distributions.

Consider an investment firm managing a portfolio comprised of diverse asset classes, including equities, commodities, and fixed income.

Here is a basic Python illustration of how to utilize Copula functions:

```python
import numpy as np import copulas

\# Generate sample data for two assets
X = np.random.normal(0, 1, 1000)
Y = np.random.normal(0, 1, 1000)

\# Fit a Gaussian copula to the data
copula = copulas.multivariate.GaussianMultivariate()
copula.fit(np.column_stack((X, Y)))

\# Generate samples from the fitted copula
samples = copula.sample(100)
```

The insights derived from such analyses can empower firms to develop more effective hedging strategies and to achieve a nuanced understanding of risk distributions throughout various economic conditions.

3. Monte Carlo Simulations

Monte Carlo simulations stand out for their ability to model complex systems and accommodate uncertainty in risk assessment.

For instance, let's explore how a hedge fund might leverage Monte Carlo simulations to gauge the risk of a structured product. Given a multitude of underlying variables, the fund can generate price paths for the product over time, ultimately assessing the potential return distribution and identifying tail risks—rare scenarios with the potential for substantial losses.

Here is a Python implementation of a simple Monte Carlo simulation for a financial derivative:

````
```python import numpy as np import matplotlib.pyplot as plt

\# Parameters
S0 = 100 \# Initial stock price
T = 1    \# Time to maturity (in years)
r = 0.05 \# Risk-free interest rate
sigma = 0.2 \# Volatility
num_simulations = 10000

\# Simulating price paths
np.random.seed(42)
S = np.zeros(num_simulations)
for i in range(num_simulations):
  Z = np.random.normal(0, 1) \# Standard normal random variable
  S[i] = S0 * np.exp((r - 0.5 * sigma**2) * T + sigma * np.sqrt(T) * Z)

\# Plotting the results
plt.hist(S, bins=50, alpha=0.75, color='blue', edgecolor='black')
plt.title('Monte Carlo Simulation of Stock Prices')
plt.xlabel('Price')
plt.ylabel('Frequency')
````
````

```
plt.show()
```

This simulation visualizes the distribution of potential outcomes for the stock price at maturity, equipping the hedge fund with a framework to quantify risks and make strategic decisions.

The incorporation of advanced methodologies such as VaR, Copula models, and Monte Carlo simulations has transformed the landscape of risk assessment in quantitative finance. Each technique plays a pivotal role, enabling analysts to grasp, quantify, and manage financial risks with greater efficacy.

CHAPTER 9: BACKTESTING AND STRATEGY EVALUATION

Backtesting is the method of applying a trading strategy or financial model to historical market data to evaluate its past performance. This process enables traders and portfolio managers to analyze key performance metrics such as return on investment (ROI) and Sharpe ratios by retroactively implementing their strategies against historical price movements.

The Significance of Backtesting

The true value of backtesting lies in its capability to provide a pragmatic insight into a trading strategy, moving beyond mere theoretical expectations. Financial markets are not static entities; they react to a multitude of factors including economic changes, trader psychology, and unexpected events. A strategy that appears promising in theory may falter when confronted with the unpredictable nature of the market.

Backtesting serves several vital functions:

1. **Validation**: It substantiates the reasoning behind a trading strategy, confirming whether it is based on sound statistical principles and economic theory.
2. **Optimization**: By evaluating the strategy's performance across various timeframes and market conditions, analysts can adjust parameters to enhance profitability.
3. **Risk Assessment**: Backtesting facilitates a comprehensive examination of risk, allowing analysts to simulate adverse market scenarios and prepare for potential downswings.
4. **Confidence Building**: A strategy that demonstrates success through backtesting instills greater confidence in analysts and traders, which is crucial for maintaining discipline and careful execution of trades.

The Backtesting Process

A well-structured backtesting process is essential for achieving accurate and reliable outcomes. Below is a comprehensive guide to conducting effective backtesting:

Step 1: Define the Strategy

The initial step involves clearly outlining the rules of the trading strategy, including entry and exit criteria, risk management parameters, and the range of instruments being traded, such as stocks, bonds, or derivatives. For instance, a moving average crossover strategy might dictate that a trader buys when a short-term moving average crosses above a long-term moving average.

Step 2: Gather Historical Data

The accuracy of historical data is critical to successful backtesting. Data can be sourced from market data providers, financial APIs, or directly from exchanges. It should encompass price movements, trading volumes, and ideally, contextual information about market conditions during the specified timeframe.

Step 3: Implement the Strategy

Once the rules and historical data have been established, the next step is to code the strategy. For example, if we wish to develop a simple moving average strategy using Python, the following code snippet serves as a foundation:

```python
import pandas as pd import numpy as np import matplotlib.pyplot as plt

\# Load historical data
data = pd.read_csv('historical_stock_data.csv')
data['Date'] = pd.to_datetime(data['Date'])
data.set_index('Date', inplace=True)

\# Define short-term and long-term moving averages
short_window = 40
long_window = 100

data['Short_MA'] = data['Close'].rolling(window=short_window, min_periods=1).mean()
data['Long_MA'] = data['Close'].rolling(window=long_window, min_periods=1).mean()

\# Generate buy/sell signals
data['Signal'] = 0
data['Signal'][short_window:] = np.where(data['Short_MA'][short_window:] > data['Long_MA'][short_window:], 1, 0)
data['Position'] = data['Signal'].diff()
```

This code sets up a basic moving average crossover strategy, providing a solid framework for backtesting.

Step 4: Execute and Analyze

With the strategy coded, backtesting can proceed. The

historical data is applied to evaluate the strategy's performance over time, generating key metrics such as cumulative returns, maximum drawdown, and win-loss ratios. The following code can help visualize the results:

```python
# Plot the stock price along with the moving averages and buy/sell signals
plt.figure(figsize=(14, 7))
plt.plot(data['Close'], label='Close Price', alpha=0.5)
plt.plot(data['Short_MA'], label='40-Day Moving Average', color='red', alpha=0.75)
plt.plot(data['Long_MA'], label='100-Day Moving Average', color='green', alpha=0.75)

\# Plot buy signals
plt.plot(data[data['Position'] == 1].index,
    data['Short_MA'][data['Position'] == 1],
    '^', markersize=10, color='g', lw=0, label='Buy Signal')

\# Plot sell signals
plt.plot(data[data['Position'] == -1].index,
    data['Short_MA'][data['Position'] == -1],
    'v', markersize=10, color='r', lw=0, label='Sell Signal')

plt.title('Backtesting the Moving Average Strategy')
plt.legend(loc='best')
plt.show()
```

This visualization effectively illustrates where buy and sell signals were triggered in conjunction with the moving averages, allowing analysts to assess the strategy's efficacy at a glance.

Step 5: Adjust and Iterate

After obtaining initial results, the strategy can be refined based on performance feedback. This might involve adjusting parameters, introducing additional indicators, or revising foundational assumptions. Backtesting is an iterative process; continuous refinement is essential to adapt to evolving market conditions.

Challenges and Considerations

While backtesting is integral to quantitative finance, it presents its own set of challenges. One of the notable concerns is overfitting—when a strategy is too finely tuned to historical data, often resulting in disappointing performance in live trading. Moreover, the quality and reliability of the data used for backtesting can significantly influence outcomes.

To counteract these challenges, practitioners may employ strategies such as walk-forward analysis and cross-validation, ensuring that strategies are resilient across differing market landscapes.

In conclusion, backtesting is a vital component of quantitative finance, empowering analysts and traders with the necessary tools to validate their strategies prior to committing capital in the live market. A comprehensive understanding of backtesting—including meticulous execution and awareness of its limitations—sets the stage for developing effective trading strategies. As the financial landscape continues to evolve, adopting rigorous backtesting practices will remain essential for achieving sustained profitability in trading endeavors.

This foundational exploration of backtesting not only prepares readers for subsequent topics in this book, which will delve into strategy evaluation techniques, but also equips aspiring traders with a critical framework for navigating the complex world of quantitative finance.

Setting Up a Backtesting Framework

Understanding the Backtesting Framework

a backtesting framework creates a systematic environment that allows for the implementation and evaluation of trading strategies under controlled conditions. It comprises several critical components: the trading strategy, historical data, performance metrics, and analysis tools. A well-structured framework integrates these elements seamlessly, ensuring a comprehensive assessment of trading strategies. Key components include:

1. **Data Management**: High-quality data is vital for effective backtesting. The framework should efficiently gather, store, and retrieve historical market data to facilitate accurate simulations.
2. **Strategy Implementation**: This involves the code that defines the strategy's logic, including the criteria for entering and exiting trades based on specific conditions.
3. **Execution Engine**: This module simulates trades based on the generated signals, accounting for transaction costs and slippage to reflect real market conditions.
4. **Performance Metrics**: A set of key indicators evaluates the strategy's success, including return on investment (ROI), Sharpe ratio, maximum drawdown, and win/loss ratio, among others.
5. **Reporting Tools**: Comprehensive reporting and visualization options are essential to clearly convey the results and insights derived from the backtesting process.

Step 1: Establishing a Development Environment

Begin your journey by setting up a conducive development environment. Python has emerged as the go-to language for quantitative finance, thanks to its versatility and a rich array of libraries tailored for data analysis, machine learning, and financial applications.

Required Libraries

Here's a curated list of essential Python libraries that will streamline your backtesting process:

- **Pandas**: For robust data handling and analysis.
- **NumPy**: For efficient numerical computations.
- **matplotlib**: To create insightful visual representations of data.
- **Backtrader** or **Zipline**: Specialized libraries for developing and testing trading strategies.

Installation of these libraries is straightforward and can be executed using pip:

```bash
pip install pandas numpy matplotlib backtrader
```

Step 2: Importing Historical Data

The subsequent step is sourcing and managing the historical data crucial for testing your strategies. Data can be retrieved from numerous sources, including financial market APIs, CSV files, and dedicated data providers.

For instance, if you are using a CSV file containing a stock's closing prices, you could load the data like this:

```python
import pandas as pd

\# Load historical data
data = pd.read_csv('historical_stock_data.csv', parse_dates=['Date'], index_col='Date')

\# Display a sample of the data
print(data.head())
```

Step 3: Coding the Strategy

With your data in hand, the next essential task is implementing your trading strategy. This process involves clearly defining your entry and exit criteria. For demonstration purposes, we will create a basic moving average crossover strategy that operates on two different moving averages—one short-term and one long-term.

Example: Simple Moving Average Crossover Strategy

```python
class MovingAverageCrossover: def init(self, short_window=40, long_window=100): self.short_window = short_window self.long_window = long_window self.signals = pd.DataFrame()

    def generate_signals(self, data):
        self.signals['Short_MA'] = data['Close'].rolling(window=self.short_window, min_periods=1).mean()
        self.signals['Long_MA'] = data['Close'].rolling(window=self.long_window, min_periods=1).mean()
        self.signals['Signal'] = 0
        self.signals['Signal'][self.short_window:] = np.where(self.signals['Short_MA'][self.short_window:] >
                                                    self.signals['Long_MA'][self.short_window:], 1, 0)
        self.signals['Position'] = self.signals['Signal'].diff()
```

In the code above, we define a class called MovingAverageCrossover that accepts two parameters for the short and long moving averages, generates signals, and calculates corresponding buy and sell positions based on the interaction of these moving averages.

Step 4: Simulating Trades

After generating the buy/sell signals, it's crucial for your backtesting framework to simulate trades according to these signals. This process should incorporate transaction costs and slippage to closely mirror actual market conditions.

Implementation of the Execution Engine

```python
def simulate_trades(data, signals): initial_capital = float(100000.0) # Set initial capital positions = pd.DataFrame(index=signals.index).fillna(0.0) portfolio = pd.Series(index=signals.index)

positions['Stock'] = 100 * signals['Signal'] \# Simulating the purchase of 100 shares
portfolio['Holdings'] = (positions.multiply(data['Close'], axis=0)).sum(axis=1)
portfolio['Cash'] = initial_capital - (positions.diff().multiply(data['Close'], axis=0)).sum(axis=1).cumsum()
portfolio['Total'] = portfolio['Holdings'] + portfolio['Cash']

return portfolio
```

Step 5: Analyzing Performance Metrics

After executing the simulated trades, the next step is to analyze the strategy's performance over the testing period. A crucial metric to evaluate is the cumulative return, as illustrated below:

```python
def performance_analysis(portfolio): cumulative_return = portfolio['Total'][-1] / portfolio['Total'][0] - 1 print(f"Cumulative Return: {cumulative_return:.2%}")
```

This function computes the cumulative return from the start to the end of the backtesting phase, providing a quick yet effective means of assessing overall strategy effectiveness.

Step 6: Generating Reports

Finally, generating informative reports is essential to summarize the performance and visually depict trade dynamics:

```python
import matplotlib.pyplot as plt

def plot_results(portfolio):
    plt.figure(figsize=(14, 7))
    plt.plot(portfolio['Total'], label='Total Portfolio Value')
    plt.title('Backtesting Portfolio Performance')
    plt.xlabel('Date')
    plt.ylabel('Portfolio Value')
    plt.legend()
    plt.show()
```

By executing this function after completing the simulation, traders can visualize the fluctuations in portfolio value over time, making it easier to interpret the results.

Challenges in Setting Up a Backtesting Framework

Although laying the groundwork for backtesting is relatively straightforward, several challenges may emerge. Concerns such as data quality, overfitting, and insufficient risk assessment can hinder a strategy's success. To mitigate these issues, it is essential to implement rigorous checks and balances during data management and analysis stages, ensuring the reliability of the backtesting framework.

Performance Metrics for Trading Strategies

The Importance of Performance Metrics

Before diving into specific metrics, it's vital to appreciate their significance. Performance metrics allow traders and analysts to quantify the performance of their strategies over time, facilitating comparisons between different approaches and helping assess potential risks. For instance, a strategy may showcase striking returns; however, without the correct performance metrics, one might misinterpret its risk profile, leading to precarious investment choices. Thus, these metrics not only illuminate the path to profitable trading but also safeguard against risk mismanagement.

Key Performance Metrics

Return on Investment (ROI) is one of the simplest yet most powerful performance metrics. This measure calculates the gain or loss generated relative to the amount invested, providing a direct insight into profitability. The formula is:

[\text{ROI} = \frac{\text{Net Profit}}{\text{Cost of Investment}} \times 100]

For example, if a trader invests)10,000 in a strategy and later withdraws (12,000, the ROI would be:

[\text{ROI} = \frac{12000 - 10000}{10000} \times 100 = 20\%]

A higher ROI indicates a more lucrative investment, showcasing the effectiveness of the trading strategy in terms of generating returns.

2. Sharpe Ratio

Widely recognized in the finance community, the Sharpe Ratio measures the return of an investment compared to its inherent risk. Named after William F. Sharpe, it is expressed as:

[\text{Sharpe Ratio} = \frac{\text{Average Return} - \text{Risk-Free Rate}}{\text{Standard Deviation of Returns}}]

Utilizing this metric allows traders to discern whether their returns stem from astute investing or unwarranted risk-taking. For instance, if a strategy yields an average annual return of 15%, while the risk-free rate is 2% and the standard deviation of returns is 10%, the Sharpe Ratio would be computed as follows:

$$ \text{Sharpe Ratio} = \frac{15\% - 2\%}{10\%} = 1.3 $$

A Sharpe Ratio above 1 generally signifies a good risk-adjusted return, indicating that the strategy compensates well for the risks involved.

3. Maximum Drawdown

Maximum Drawdown (MDD) is a crucial metric that quantifies the largest peak-to-trough decline in the value of a portfolio over a specific period. Understanding MDD is essential for preparing for potential losses during market downturns. The formula to calculate MDD is:

$$ \text{MDD} = \frac{\text{Trough Value} - \text{Peak Value}}{\text{Peak Value}} $$

For instance, if a portfolio peaks at)50,000 and subsequently falls to a trough of (30,000, the Maximum Drawdown would be:

$$ \text{MDD} = \frac{30000 - 50000}{50000} = -0.4 \text{ or } 40\% $$

This 40% drawdown serves as a critical reminder of the potential risks involved, necessitating a thorough re-evaluation of the strategy based on individual risk tolerance.

4. Win/Loss Ratio

The Win/Loss Ratio assesses the effectiveness of a trading strategy by comparing the number of winning trades to losing trades. This ratio is vital not just for gauging profitability but also for understanding the stability and consistency of the strategy.

The Win/Loss Ratio is calculated using the formula:

$$ \text{Win/Loss Ratio} = \frac{\text{Number of Winning Trades}}{\text{Number of Losing Trades}} $$

For example, if a strategy results in 70 winning trades and 30 losing trades, the calculation would be:

$$\text{Win/Loss Ratio} = \frac{70}{30} \approx 2.33$$

This suggests the strategy is winning more than twice as often as it loses, a promising indicator of its overall performance.

5. Sortino Ratio

While similar to the Sharpe Ratio, the Sortino Ratio specifically focuses on downside volatility, penalizing only negative deviations rather than all volatility. This nuanced approach provides a more refined understanding of risk, allowing traders to concentrate on adverse movements.

The formula for the Sortino Ratio is:

$$\text{Sortino Ratio} = \frac{\text{Expected Portfolio Return} - \text{Target Rate}}{\text{Downside Deviation}}$$

In this framework, the target rate may represent the risk-free rate or a minimum acceptable return. For instance, if a strategy anticipates a return of 12%, with a minimum acceptable return of 4%, and a downside deviation of 8%, the Sortino Ratio would be:

$$\text{Sortino Ratio} = \frac{12\%-4\%}{8\%} = 1$$

A Sortino Ratio above 1 indicates that the returns are satisfactory relative to the risks taken, while a ratio below 1 signals undesirable performance.

Implementing Performance Metrics in Backtesting

In practice, integrating these performance metrics into a backtesting framework can enhance your trading strategies significantly.

The following code snippet illustrates how to calculate the Sharpe Ratio for a portfolio's returns during backtesting, employing Python:

```python
import numpy as np
```

```
def sharpe_ratio(returns, risk_free_rate=0.02):
    excess_returns = returns.mean() - risk_free_rate
    return excess_returns / returns.std()

\# Simulated portfolio returns
portfolio_returns = np.random.normal(0.001, 0.02, 1000) \# Simulated daily returns

\# Calculate the Sharpe Ratio
sr = sharpe_ratio(portfolio_returns)
print(f"Sharpe Ratio: {sr:.2f}")
```

This basic function provides invaluable insights into a trading strategy's risk-adjusted performance, empowering traders to make well-informed decisions regarding portfolio management.

Conclusion

A Comprehensive Guide to Overfitting and Its Implications

Overfitting is a pivotal concept in statistics, machine learning, and quantitative finance—one that poses significant challenges for traders and data scientists alike as they strive to create effective predictive models. In essence, overfitting occurs when a model becomes overly complex, capturing not just the underlying data patterns but also the random noise present within the dataset. This can lead to models that are remarkably accurate on their training data but fail dramatically when confronted with previously unseen data.

The Inner Workings of Overfitting

To better understand overfitting, imagine the model training process as assembling a jigsaw puzzle. A well-constructed model resembles a completed puzzle that accurately depicts the image on its box—reflective of genuine trends within the data. Conversely, an overfitted model might look flawless at first glance, as it strives to account for every minute detail, leading to a finished puzzle that doesn't truly mirror the original image.

Consider this scenario: A trader develops a predictive model to forecast stock prices based on historical data. The model fits the training dataset exceptionally well, exhibiting low error rates and seemingly precise predictions. However, once applied to new market data, its performance plummets. This drastic shift occurs because the model has "memorized" the idiosyncrasies of the training dataset instead of identifying generalizable trends, resulting in a flawed predictive capability.

How to Spot Overfitting

Identifying overfitting early is essential to safeguard against detrimental impacts on trading strategies. Here are some key indicators to watch for:

1. **Significant Performance Discrepancy:** One of the clearest signs of overfitting is a stark difference between training and test performance. For example, a model that achieves a training error of 5% but exhibits a testing error of 25% is often signaling an overfitting issue.

2. **Intricate Model Complexity:** Models that exhibit excessive complexity, such as deep neural networks with numerous parameters, are often at risk of overfitting. While these models can yield high accuracy, they necessitate careful regularization to prevent excessive memorization of the dataset.

3. **Susceptibility to Variance:** If minor changes in input result in substantial shifts in the model's output, your model may be too sensitive—an additional red

flag for overfitting.

The Fallout from Overfitting

In the high-stakes environment of quantitative finance, the consequences of overfitting can be particularly severe. Here are a few potential repercussions traders may face:

Traders utilizing overfitted models risk making decisions based on misleading predictions, potentially incurring substantial financial losses. For instance, if a model erroneously forecasts a stock's upward trajectory based on noise rather than authentic market behavior, an investor could make ill-fated purchases, later discovering that the prediction was nothing more than a statistical anomaly.

2. Resource Misallocation

The lure of complex models can lead traders into the trap of investing excessive time and resources in refining their models, often overlooking simpler approaches that may deliver better performance and generalizability. This misallocation not only squanders valuable time but can also divert financial resources away from more productive initiatives.

3. Loss of Confidence in Predictive Models

When overfitting manifests in subpar performance during real-time trading, it can erode trust in quantitative strategies. Over time, stakeholders may begin to lose faith in the reliability of automated systems, casting doubt on data-driven decision-making processes.

Strategies to Prevent Overfitting

Mitigating the risk of overfitting is crucial for developing robust predictive models. Here are several best practices to consider:

Dividing your data into training, validation, and testing sets is paramount. This splitting approach allows you to test your model on unseen data, providing a clearer understanding of its ability to generalize. A common partitioning ratio is 70% for training, 15% for validation, and 15% for testing.

Example Implementation:

To easily split your dataset using Python, leverage the train_test_split() function from sklearn:

```python
from sklearn.model_selection import train_test_split

\# Assuming "data" is your DataFrame and "target" contains the labels
X_train, X_test, y_train, y_test = train_test_split(data, target, test_size=0.15, random_state=42)
```

2. Regularization Methods

Integrating regularization techniques, such as Lasso (L1 regularization) and Ridge (L2 regularization), can bolster your model's resilience against overfitting. These methods introduce a penalty into the loss function based on model complexity, thus discouraging overly intricate structures.

3. Favoring Simplicity

When selecting models, prioritize simplicity. Start with less complex frameworks, like linear regression, to establish baseline performance before gradually exploring more complex models, all while maintaining vigilance for signs of overfitting.

4. Employing K-Fold Cross-Validation

Implementing k-fold cross-validation provides a comprehensive assessment of model performance across various data subsets. This technique helps to mitigate overfitting risk by training and validating the model on different folds of the dataset.

Example Implementation:

Here's a method to implement k-fold cross-validation in Python:

```python
from sklearn.model_selection import cross_val_score
from sklearn.linear_model import LinearRegression

model = LinearRegression()
scores = cross_val_score(model, data, target, cv=5) \# 5-fold cross-validation

print(f"Mean cross-validation score: {scores.mean():.2f}")
```

For anyone engaged in quantitative finance, understanding overfitting and its far-reaching consequences is essential. This discussion underscores the importance of vigilance in combating overfitting, which protects financial resources and reinforces confidence in predictive models.

Equipped with this knowledge, you can navigate the intricate landscape of predictive modeling with greater confidence, fostering a robust and effective trading strategy. As we delve deeper into advanced statistical methods, maintaining awareness of overfitting will continue to be a guiding principle —ensuring that our focus remains on uncovering genuine market dynamics rather than getting lost in the noise.

Walk-Forward Analysis: Navigating the Complexities of Quantitative Trading

In the intricate realm of quantitative finance, the pursuit of robust trading strategies is often fraught with challenges. Among the most significant pitfalls is overfitting, where a model achieves exceptional returns on historical data but falters in real-world applications. To mitigate this risk, walk-forward analysis emerges as a dynamic and versatile solution, providing analysts with a systematic approach to evaluate the resilience of trading strategies through iterative testing and validation.

Understanding Walk-Forward Analysis

Picture a savvy trader navigating a vibrant marketplace, cleverly adjusting their approach with each new encounter. Just as the trader adapts to real-time observations, walk-forward analysis allows analysts to break historical data into consecutive segments of in-sample (training) and out-of-sample (testing) periods. This methodology enables continuous strategy reassessment, ensuring that trading models evolve with incoming data rather than becoming stagnant relics of past market conditions.

Consider the journey of Thomas, a quant trader based in the competitive foreign exchange market of London. Initially reliant on traditional backtesting, he found himself confident that his algorithm—finely tuned to past data—would excel in the fast-paced trading arena. However, the reality proved harsher; his strategy struggled to deliver consistent returns when applied in real-time. It wasn't until he embraced walk-forward analysis that he began to unlock substantive improvements, transforming his trading outcomes.

The Walk-Forward Process

The walk-forward analysis consists of several crucial steps that guide traders through the iterative journey of model validation and refinement:

1. **Data Preparation:** Begin by collecting and preprocessing historical data to ensure accuracy and reliability. This foundation is vital—cleaning missing values, removing outliers, and formatting timestamps appropriately all contribute to the integrity of the analysis.
2. **Segmenting Data:** Define the lengths of the in-sample and out-of-sample periods. For example, one

might employ a one-year in-sample period for model development, followed by a three-month out-of-sample period to validate performance.

3. **Model Training and Testing:**
4. **Training Phase:** Utilize the in-sample data to fit your model. Imagine using a linear regression model to predict stock prices; this is where you align the model with historical patterns.
5. **Testing Phase:** After training, evaluate the model against the out-of-sample data. With walk-forward analysis, once this testing period concludes, the process rolls forward—incrementally shifting the window and repeating the training and testing until the entire dataset has been assessed.
6. **Performance Evaluation:** Analyze the model's performance during each out-of-sample period. Key performance metrics—like the Sharpe ratio, maximum drawdown, and percentage of profitable trades—offer vital insights into the strategy's effectiveness across various market conditions.
7. **Refinement:** Based on the insights gleaned from performance metrics, refine your strategy. If consistent underperformance emerges during certain market climates, traders can pivot and adapt their methods to better align with prevailing conditions.

Example Implementation in Python

To illustrate the principles of walk-forward analysis practically, let's delve into a simple implementation using Python. We'll employ a classic moving average crossover strategy, a favorite among algorithmic traders.

```python import pandas as pd import numpy as np
```

```
\# Load historical stock price data
data = pd.read_csv('historical_stock_data.csv', parse_dates=['Date'])
data.set_index('Date', inplace=True)

\# Function to calculate profit and loss
def calculate_performance(data, short_window, long_window):
  signals = pd.DataFrame(index=data.index)
  signals['price'] = data['Close']
                                         signals['short_mavg']          =
data['Close'].rolling(window=short_window).mean()
                                         signals['long_mavg']           =
data['Close'].rolling(window=long_window).mean()
  signals['signal'] = 0.0
  signals['signal'][short_window:] = np.where(
       signals['short_mavg'][short_window:] > signals['long_mavg']
[short_window:], 1.0, 0.0)
  signals['positions'] = signals['signal'].diff()

    \# Evaluate performance
  returns = data['Close'].pct_change()
  strategy_returns = returns * signals['positions'].shift(1)
  return strategy_returns.sum()

\# Parameters for walk-forward analysis
window_size = 252  \# Approximate trading days in a year
step_size = 21    \# Monthly rolling step

results = []
for start in range(0, len(data) - window_size, step_size):
  in_sample = data.iloc[start:start + window_size]
        out_of_sample  =  data.iloc[start  +  window_size:start  +
window_size + step_size]

    \# Calculate performance using different moving averages
              performance    =    calculate_performance(in_sample,
short_window=50, long_window=200)
  results.append(performance)

\# Summarize results
```

```
total_performance = sum(results)
print(f'Total Performance from Walk-Forward Analysis: {total_performance}')
```

Assessing the Results

The above implementation showcases a rolling application of a moving average strategy across different segments of historical data, systematically accumulating results from each walk-forward period. In practice, traders like Thomas discovered that their cumulative returns intensified through this iterative approach. The improved performance not only bolstered his confidence in deploying his algorithm but also highlighted the value of adaptability in a fast-changing market environment.

Walk-forward analysis stands out as an essential tool in the toolkit of quantitative finance methodologies. It serves as a crucial buffer against the perils of overfitting, equipping traders with the agility to adjust their strategies as market conditions shift. As professionals like Thomas tap into the potential of this analytical approach, the landscape of quantitative finance continues to thrive, driven by data-driven insights and informed decision-making.

Transaction Costs and Slippage in Backtesting

In the high-stakes arena of quantitative trading, where strategies are often dictated by algorithms and data-driven models, the precision of performance evaluations is paramount. Yet, beneath the surface of these meticulously formulated strategies lies a frequently underestimated challenge: transaction costs and slippage. These two factors are crucial in determining the true profitability of a trading strategy during backtesting, profoundly influencing how its performance is perceived. Join us as we delve into these vital components, examining their ramifications and discovering effective methods for their incorporation into a robust quantitative framework.

The Role of Transaction Costs

Picture yourself on a trading journey—constantly entering and exiting positions with the goal of seizing fleeting market opportunities. With each trade you make, regardless of its outcome, transaction costs arise. These costs can vary significantly across brokers, asset classes, and market conditions, comprising several elements that influence the overall trading experience.

Types of Transaction Costs:

1. **Commissions:** These are fees that brokers charge per trade, which may be fixed or based on a percentage of the trade's value. Even with discount brokers, these charges accumulate over time and can considerably diminish overall profits.

2. **Bid-Ask Spread:** The bid-ask spread represents the difference between the buying (ask) and selling (bid) prices of a security. When executing a trade, you often accept a market price that may diverge from historical data, resulting in an immediate loss proportionate to the spread.

3. **Market Impact:** Executing sizable orders can potentially shift a security's price due to variations in demand and supply. Thus, executing a large trade could unintentionally exacerbate costs, making the position entry or exit more expensive than anticipated.

4. **Financing Costs:** For strategies that involve leveraged positions—particularly in derivatives or margin accounts—the cost of borrowing capital can significantly affect profitability. These financing costs can add another layer of complexity to trading

strategies.

Understanding Slippage

Often considered the unwelcome companion to transaction costs, slippage is the discrepancy between the expected price of a trade and the price at which the trade is actually executed. This phenomenon can be especially pronounced during periods of high market volatility or when executing large orders, and it can drastically alter expected returns, undermining profits during backtesting.

Factors Influencing Slippage in Backtesting:

1. **Market Conditions:** Price movements can be volatile, particularly during significant news events or economic announcements. This volatility can lead to rapid price changes, delaying trade execution and resulting in slippage.
2. **Order Types:** The type of order placed also plays a critical role. For example, while market orders ensure execution, they are most susceptible to slippage. Conversely, limit orders provide price certainty but carry the risk of not being executed at all.
3. **Liquidity Constraints:** In markets with limited liquidity, executing trades may cause adverse price movements, exacerbating slippage issues. High-frequency trading strategies, in particular, might face challenges when executing trades in less liquid instruments.

Incorporating Transaction Costs and Slippage in Backtesting

To foster a realistic backtesting environment, it is essential to integrate transaction costs and slippage into your trading simulations. Below is a streamlined Python implementation that illustrates how to effectively account for these elements.

```python import pandas as pd import numpy as np
```

```
\# Load sample historical stock price data
data = pd.read_csv('historical_stock_data.csv', parse_dates=['Date'])
data.set_index('Date', inplace=True)

def simulate_trading_with_costs(data, entry_threshold,
exit_threshold, commission=0.001, slippage=0.02):
 position = 0
 total_profit = 0

  for i in range(1, len(data)):
  if data['Signal'][i-1] == 1 and position == 0: \# Buy signal
      trade_price = data['Close'][i] * (1 + slippage) \# Adjust for
slippage
    position = data['Close'][i] \# Open position at trade price
    total_profit -= commission * position \# Deduct commission

     elif data['Signal'][i-1] == -1 and position > 0: \# Sell signal
       trade_price = data['Close'][i] * (1 - slippage) \# Adjust for
slippage
     total_profit += trade_price - position \# Close position and
calculate profit
    total_profit -= commission * trade_price \# Deduct commission
    position = 0 \# Reset position

  return total_profit

\# Generate trading signals (e.g., simple moving average crossover)
data['Signal'] = np.where(data['Close'].diff() > 0, 1, -1) \# Basic buy/
sell signal generation

\# Run simulation
final_profit = simulate_trading_with_costs(data,
entry_threshold=0, exit_threshold=0)
print(f'Total Profit After Accounting for Transaction Costs and
Slippage: \){final_profit:.2f}')
```

Evaluating the Results

The implementation above creates a framework where trading

signals inform decisions while adjusting for transaction costs and slippage. Following the simulation, the actual profit or loss emerges, offering a clearer perspective on trading performance.

Consider this scenario: a strategy initially displays a backtested profit of (10,000. However, once transaction costs and slippage are accurately considered, the effective net profit reduces to)7,500—demonstrating the substantial impact that these factors can have on real-world performance.

As the landscape of quantitative finance evolves, recognizing the significance of transaction costs and slippage is crucial for evaluating the effectiveness of trading strategies.

As we move forward, the next phase of our exploration will delve deeper into key performance metrics used to assess trading strategies, equipping you with the knowledge to interpret and communicate your results with confidence and clarity.

Robustness Testing of Trading Strategies: A Comprehensive Guide

The Significance of Robustness Testing

Consider this scenario: you've developed a trading strategy designed to exploit the momentum of a particular security. At first glance, it seems to yield impressive returns based on historical data. However, as we know, markets are dynamic entities—they evolve with changing economic indicators, unexpected events, and novel market trends. Without a comprehensive robustness testing phase, your once-promising strategy could face significant drawdowns or, worse, catastrophic losses in live trading situations.

Robustness testing assesses a trading strategy's resilience against shifts in market conditions, variations in model parameters, and other assumptions. A model that seems successful during historical backtests may falter when faced with minor adjustments or new data inputs. Therefore, attaining robustness involves more than simple backtesting; it requires a well-thought-out approach to avoid overfitting and ensure that your models can adapt to various market scenarios.

Key Techniques for Robustness Testing

To effectively enhance the reliability of your trading strategies, several techniques can be employed. Here, we will outline three essential methods: parameter sensitivity analysis, walk-forward testing, and Monte Carlo simulations.

1. **Parameter Sensitivity Analysis**

This analysis technique measures how sensitive a trading strategy is to changes in its critical parameters. This analytical process helps identify parameters at risk of resulting in overfitting or instability.

Let's look at a simple Python implementation for parameter sensitivity analysis utilizing a moving average crossover strategy:

```python
import pandas as pd
import numpy as np

\# Load historical price data
data = pd.read_csv('historical_stock_data.csv', parse_dates=['Date'])
data.set_index('Date', inplace=True)

def moving_average_crossover(data, short_window, long_window):
    data['Short_MA'] = data['Close'].rolling(window=short_window).mean()
    data['Long_MA'] = data['Close'].rolling(window=long_window).mean()
    data['Signal'] = 0
    data['Signal'][short_window:] = np.where(data['Short_MA'][short_window:] > data['Long_MA'][short_window:], 1, 0)
    data['Position'] = data['Signal'].diff()
    return data
```

```
results = {}
for short_window in range(5, 20): \# Testing various short moving average lengths
    for long_window in range(20, 50): \# Testing various long moving average lengths
        trade_data = moving_average_crossover(data.copy(), short_window, long_window)
        total_returns = (trade_data['Position'].shift(1) * data['Close'].pct_change()).cumsum()[-1]
    results[(short_window, long_window)] = total_returns

\# Identify the optimal parameter pair
optimal_parameters = max(results, key=results.get)
print(f'Optimal Short/Long Moving Average Parameters: {optimal_parameters}, Return: {results[optimal_parameters]:.2f}')
```

1. **Walk-Forward Testing**

Walk-forward testing is a robust methodology that allows traders to assess their strategies incrementally, using an ever-evolving dataset. This technique divides the historical data into segments, first training the model on a historical dataset (the training period), followed by validating it on subsequent, unseen data (the testing period). This approach helps emulate a real-world trading experience.

Below is a conceptual implementation of walk-forward testing:

```python
def walk_forward(data, train_size, test_size):
total_test_periods = len(data) // test_size
strategy_performance = []

    for i in range(total_test_periods):
    train_data = data[i * test_size: (i * test_size) + train_size]
    test_data = data[(i * test_size) + train_size: (i + 1) * test_size]

        \# Train the strategy on the training data
        signals_train = moving_average_crossover(train_data,
```

short_window=10, long_window=30)

\# Test the strategy on the testing data
signals_test = test_data.copy()
signals_test['Signal'] = signals_train['Signal'].iloc[-1]
returns = (signals_test['Signal'].shift(1) * test_data['Close'].pct_change()).cumsum()
strategy_performance.append(returns[-1]) \# Record performance

return strategy_performance

performance_results = walk_forward(data, train_size=100, test_size=20)
print(f'Walk-forward Testing Performance over Segments: {performance_results}')
```

1. **Monte Carlo Simulations**

Monte Carlo simulations take a different approach, generating multiple potential outcomes based on random sampling. This technique allows traders to understand the distribution of returns across various market conditions, which simplifies evaluating potential risk exposure.

Here's a basic example of how to run a Monte Carlo simulation on a hypothetical trading strategy:

```python import random
def monte_carlo_simulation(initial_investment, num_simulations, profit_factor, loss_factor):
results = []

for _ in range(num_simulations):
portfolio_value = initial_investment
for trade in range(100): \# Simulating 100 trades
if random.random() < 0.5: \# 50% chance of a win or loss
portfolio_value *= (1 + profit_factor) \# Simulating a winning trade

```
        else:
            portfolio_value *= (1 - loss_factor)  \# Simulating a losing trade
        results.append(portfolio_value)
    return results

simulation_results = monte_carlo_simulation(10000, 1000, 0.05, 0.03)
print(f'Monte Carlo Simulation Results: {simulation_results}')
```

Interpreting Robustness Testing Results

Utilizing these methodologies allows you to assess your trading strategies' robustness comprehensively. Should your strategy's performance metrics fluctuate significantly in response to varying parameters, it suggests that your model may not hold up well under real-world conditions. Moreover, neglecting to implement walk-forward testing could mislead you into a false sense of security regarding a strategy that appears effective solely based on historical calibration.

The implications are significant: Robust strategies, validated through rigorous testing methods, not only instill greater confidence but also equip you to navigate the complexities and unpredictability inherent in financial markets.

Simulating Market Conditions: Enhancing Strategic Resilience in Quantitative Finance

The Importance of Simulating Market Conditions

Consider this scenario: you've crafted a trading algorithm that thrives in a bull market, consistently delivering attractive returns. However, when the tides turn and the market enters a bear phase, your algorithm could experience severe drawdowns or even catastrophic losses. This is where market condition simulations become essential. They allow traders to spot weaknesses in their strategies before they encounter real-life challenges.

Through thoughtful simulation, you can assess:

- **Sensitivity Analysis:** How responsive is your trading strategy to fluctuations in market conditions?
- **Risk Assessment:** What specific market situations could lead to amplified losses?
- **Parameter Optimization:** How do modifications to certain parameters influence strategy performance in varying environments?

Approaches to Simulating Market Conditions

There are several methodologies to effectively simulate market conditions, each offering distinct insights into potential trading performance. Here are three commonly used approaches:

1. **Historical Data Simulation**
2. **Random Walk Models**
3. **Geometric Brownian Motion (GBM)**

Let's examine each of these methods in detail, highlighting their practical applications and providing Python code illustrations for clarity.

Historical data simulation involves analyzing historical price movements to predict how a strategy might react in today's environment. This method operates on the premise that future market behavior often mirrors past patterns, allowing traders to evaluate potential outcomes based on real-world data.

Here's an example of how to conduct historical data simulation using Python:

```python
import numpy as np
import pandas as pd
import matplotlib.pyplot as plt

\# Load the historical price data
data = pd.read_csv('historical_stock_data.csv', parse_dates=['Date'])
```

```
data.set_index('Date', inplace=True)

\# Simulating market conditions using historical returns
returns = data['Close'].pct_change().dropna()
simulated_returns = np.random.choice(returns, size=(1000, len(returns)), replace=True)

\# Calculate cumulative returns from simulations
cumulative_returns = (1 + simulated_returns).cumprod(axis=1)

\# Plot the simulations
plt.figure(figsize=(14, 7))
plt.plot(cumulative_returns.T, color='blue', alpha=0.01)
plt.title('Simulated Market Conditions Using Historical Returns')
plt.xlabel('Days')
plt.ylabel('Cumulative Returns')
plt.show()
```

In this example, we draw on historical return data to generate various price paths. This approach provides valuable insights into how a particular strategy may cope with different levels of market volatility and trends.

2. Random Walk Models

Random walk models serve as mathematical representations of volatile price movements, where each step is independent of the previous one. This approach successfully captures the inherent randomness seen in many financial assets.

Here's a simple implementation of a random walk model:

```python def random_walk(start_price, num_steps, volatility): price_series = [start_price] for _ in range(num_steps): change = np.random.normal(loc=0, scale=volatility) # Random price change price_series.append(price_series[-1] * (1 + change)) return np.array(price_series)

\# Simulating a random walk
```

```
start_price = 100
num_steps = 252 \# Simulating for one year
volatility = 0.01 \# Daily volatility

simulated_prices = random_walk(start_price, num_steps, volatility)

plt.figure(figsize=(14, 7))
plt.plot(simulated_prices, color='orange')
plt.title('Simulated Random Walk of Stock Prices')
plt.xlabel('Days')
plt.ylabel('Price')
plt.show()
```

By utilizing a random walk simulation, traders can analyze how their strategies respond to synthetic price movements that mimic the sudden shifts characteristic of actual market behavior.

3. Geometric Brownian Motion (GBM)

For a more advanced simulation approach, Geometric Brownian Motion (GBM) is widely used in finance to model stock prices. GBM effectively captures both the deterministic drift of prices over time and the stochastic volatility that influences market movements.

Here's how you can implement GBM in Python:

```python
def geometric_brownian_motion(S0, mu, sigma, T, dt): N = int(T / dt) # Total number of steps t = np.linspace(0, T, N) # Time vector W = np.random.normal(0, 1, N) # Generate random normal variables for Brownian motion W = np.cumsum(W) * np.sqrt(dt) # Create the Brownian path X = (mu - 0.5 * sigma**2) * t + sigma * W # GBM formula S = S0 * np.exp(X) # Calculate the price path return S

\# Simulating GBM
S0 = 100 \# Initial price
mu = 0.1 \# Expected return
```

```
sigma = 0.2 \# Volatility
T = 1 \# One year
dt = 1/252 \# Daily time steps

gbm_prices = geometric_brownian_motion(S0, mu, sigma, T, dt)

plt.figure(figsize=(14, 7))
plt.plot(gbm_prices, color='green')
plt.title('Simulated Stock Prices using Geometric Brownian Motion')
plt.xlabel('Days')
plt.ylabel('Stock Price')
plt.show()
```

This simulation depicts a more nuanced view of price behavior, incorporating both trends and randomness, thus offering a more realistic modeling framework for traders.

Simulating market conditions is crucial for gaining insight into how different trading strategies may perform in various scenarios.

Reporting Backtesting Results: Communicating Insights and Performance

The Importance of Backtesting Result Reporting

Consider this scenario: you've developed an innovative trading strategy that yielded remarkable returns during the backtest period. Yet, when it comes time to share your findings with stakeholders or to assess the strategy's deployment potential, the effectiveness of your presentation can make all the difference. A thoughtfully crafted report not only highlights performance metrics but also contextualizes the strategy's applicability, risks, and scalability.

The significance of comprehensive reporting can be

summarized into several essential functions:

- **Transparency:** It ensures all stakeholders are aligned with the underlying assumptions, methodologies, and outcomes of the backtest.
- **Decision-Making Support:** It empowers informed decisions regarding strategy refinement, acceptance, or rejection.
- **Compliance and Audit Trails:** It provides a traceable record for compliance with regulatory requirements and internal audits.

Key Components of an Effective Backtesting Report

1. **Methodology**
2. Detail the entire backtesting process, including:
    - Data sources utilized and the specific time periods analyzed.
    - Key assumptions made (e.g., slippage, transaction costs).
    - Metrics employed for evaluating performance.
3. **Performance Metrics**
4. Present key performance indicators, such as:
    - Total Return
    - Sharpe Ratio
    - Maximum Drawdown
    - Win Rate
    - Volatility
5. Utilize visualizations to enhance comprehension and presentation of these metrics.
6. **Comparative Analysis**
7. Benchmark the strategy against relevant indices or alternative strategies to provide context. This comparison can illuminate relative performance and

robustness under various market conditions.

8. **Detailed Analysis**
9. Investigate the performance of the strategy across different market environments, including:
   - Bull vs. bear markets
   - Volatile vs. stable periods
10. Use graphs and charts to effectively convey these insights visually.
11. **Risk Assessment**
12. Address risk metrics like Value at Risk (VaR) and conduct scenario analysis to highlight the potential worst-case outcomes and the strategy's resiliency.
13. **Conclusions and Recommendations**
14. Summarize the crucial findings and propose actionable steps moving forward, which could include further optimization, considerations for live trading, or even discontinuation.

Building Your Backtesting Report with Python: A Practical Example

To illustrate effective reporting, let's assume we've implemented a simple moving average crossover strategy. The following Python script simulates the backtesting process and computes essential performance metrics.

```python
import pandas as pd import numpy as np import matplotlib.pyplot as plt

\# Load historical price data
data = pd.read_csv('historical_stock_data.csv', parse_dates=['Date'])
data.set_index('Date', inplace=True)

\# Calculate moving averages
data['SMA_20'] = data['Close'].rolling(window=20).mean()
data['SMA_50'] = data['Close'].rolling(window=50).mean()
```

```
\# Generate trading signals
data['Signal'] = 0
data.loc[20:, 'Signal'] = np.where(data['SMA_20'][20:] > data['SMA_50'][20:], 1, 0)
data['Position'] = data['Signal'].diff()

\# Calculate returns
data['Market_Return'] = data['Close'].pct_change()
data['Strategy_Return'] = data['Market_Return'] * data['Signal'].shift(1)

\# Performance metrics
total_return = (data['Strategy_Return'] + 1).prod() - 1
sharpe_ratio = np.sqrt(252) * (data['Strategy_Return'].mean() / data['Strategy_Return'].std())
max_drawdown = (data['Strategy_Return'].cumsum() - data['Strategy_Return'].cumsum().cummax()).min()

\# Print summary of results
print(f"Total Return: {total_return:.2%}")
print(f"Sharpe Ratio: {sharpe_ratio:.2f}")
print(f"Maximum Drawdown: {max_drawdown:.2%}")

\# Plot equity curve
data['Equity_Curve'] = (data['Strategy_Return'] + 1).cumprod()
plt.figure(figsize=(14, 7))
plt.plot(data['Equity_Curve'], label='Strategy Equity Curve', color='blue')
plt.title('Equity Curve of Moving Average Crossover Strategy')
plt.xlabel('Date')
plt.ylabel('Equity Value')
plt.legend()
plt.show()
```

This code outlines a backtesting framework for a simple moving average strategy, calculating total return, Sharpe ratio, and maximum drawdown. Visualizing the equity curve provides a clear depiction of the strategy's performance evolution over the analyzed period.

Best Practices for Reporting Backtesting Results

To resonate effectively with your audience, keep these best practices in mind:

- **Clarity is Key:** Strive to use straightforward language, minimizing technical jargon where possible.
- **Visualize Data:** Incorporate graphs and tables to convey information in an engaging manner.
- **Tailor to Audience Needs:** Adjust both the depth of detail and focus based on the specific interests and expertise of your audience, whether they are academics, professional traders, or investors.

Accurately and effectively reporting backtesting results is crucial for the success of any trading strategy.

In the subsequent section, we will explore the reliability of backtesting outcomes, addressing critical concepts such as overfitting and strategies to mitigate this risk. This understanding will help ensure the robustness of your trading strategies, even amid unpredictable market conditions.

Case Study: Evaluating a Quantitative Trading Strategy

In the fascinating realm of quantitative finance, the evaluation of a trading strategy transcends mere computation; it combines statistical precision, market insight, and effective communication to create a holistic approach to decision-making. This case study will present a momentum-based quantitative trading strategy, dissect its performance through rigorous backtesting, and share the valuable insights we discover along the way. Utilizing Python as our analytical partner, we will illustrate how coding can deepen our understanding and application of financial concepts.

The Strategy: Momentum Trading Using Moving Averages

For our analysis, we will explore a momentum trading strategy grounded in the principles of moving averages. This strategy operates on the belief that assets that have performed well in the recent past are likely to continue their upward trajectory, while those that have underperformed may continue to decline. Our methodology involves leveraging a short-term moving average (SMA) and a long-term moving average (LMA) to trigger buy and sell decisions.

Here's the core mechanics of our approach:

- **Buy Signal:** This signal is generated when the short-term moving average crosses above the long-term moving average—a phenomenon often referred to as a "golden cross."
- **Sell Signal:** Conversely, a sell signal occurs when the short-term moving average crosses below the long-term moving average, marking a "death cross."

Historical Context: A Case Study with Apple Inc. (AAPL)

To contextualize our strategy, we will focus on a highly liquid stock—Apple Inc. (AAPL). We will examine a particularly volatile six-month period characterized by significant market fluctuations. Historical data will be sourced from a reputable financial API, such as Alpha Vantage or Yahoo Finance, to ensure accuracy in our analysis.

Setting Up the Python Environment

Before we embark on our backtesting journey, it's essential to establish our Python environment with key libraries that will aid our analysis:

- **pandas** for efficient data manipulation,
- **numpy** for robust numerical computations,
- **matplotlib** for compelling data visualizations,
- **yfinance** to pull historical stock data effortlessly.

Here's a code snippet to kickstart our setup:

```python
# Import necessary libraries import pandas as pd import numpy as np import matplotlib.pyplot as plt import yfinance as yf

\# Set parameters for the moving averages
short_window = 20
long_window = 50

\# Fetch historical price data for Apple
data = yf.download('AAPL', start='2022-01-01', end='2022-06-30')
data['Date'] = data.index
data.reset_index(drop=True, inplace=True)
```

Implementation of the Trading Strategy

With our data in hand, we proceed to calculate the short-term and long-term moving averages, generate trading signals, and compute corresponding returns.

```python
# Calculate moving averages data['SMA_20'] = data['Close'].rolling(window=short_window).mean()
data['SMA_50'] = data['Close'].rolling(window=long_window).mean()

\# Generate trading signals
data['Signal'] = 0
data['Signal'][short_window:] = np.where(data['SMA_20'][short_window:] > data['SMA_50'][short_window:], 1, 0)
data['Position'] = data['Signal'].diff()
```

Backtesting the Strategy

Backtesting allows us to retrospectively evaluate the effectiveness of our strategy. Using the generated signals, we will calculate our returns.

```python
# Calculate daily returns data['Market_Return']
```

= data['Close'].pct_change() data['Strategy_Return'] = data['Market_Return'] * data['Signal'].shift(1)

\# Performance metrics
data['Cumulative_Market_Return'] = (data['Market_Return'] + 1).cumprod()
data['Cumulative_Strategy_Return'] = (data['Strategy_Return'] + 1).cumprod()

\# Print summary of results
total_return = data['Cumulative_Strategy_Return'][-1] - 1
sharpe_ratio = np.sqrt(252) * (data['Strategy_Return'].mean() / data['Strategy_Return'].std())

print(f"Total Strategy Return: {total_return:.2%}")
print(f"Sharpe Ratio: {sharpe_ratio:.2f}")
```

*Visualizing the Results*

To succinctly interpret our findings, we will plot the cumulative returns of our strategy alongside the market's performance.

```python # Plot the performance plt.figure(figsize=(14, 7)) plt.plot(data['Cumulative_Market_Return'], label='Market Return', color='green') plt.plot(data['Cumulative_Strategy_Return'], label='Strategy Return', color='blue') plt.title('Comparison of Strategy Returns vs Market Returns') plt.xlabel('Date') plt.ylabel('Cumulative Returns') plt.legend() plt.grid() plt.show()
```

Interpretation of Results

Upon analyzing the results, let's imagine we derive these key findings:

- **Total Strategy Return:** An impressive 35.67%
- **Sharpe Ratio:** A robust 1.85
- **Cumulative Returns Comparison:** The strategy
```

notably outperformed the market during the evaluation period, underscoring the efficacy of momentum-based trading decisions.

Areas for Improvement

While our findings are promising, they highlight several avenues for further exploration:

- **Parameter Sensitivity:** Investigating the impact of slight modifications to the moving average periods on performance.
- **Market Phases:** Identifying specific market conditions under which this strategy thrived or faltered.
- **Transaction Costs:** Integrating assumptions about transaction costs and slippage to refine our strategy evaluation.

The task of evaluating a quantitative trading strategy involves meticulous assessment and a nuanced understanding of both its strengths and limitations. This case study has illustrated the application of a momentum-based trading strategy via Python, emphasizing the critical role of backtesting in verifying trading hypotheses.

CHAPTER 10: FUTURE TRENDS IN QUANTITATIVE FINANCE AND PYTHON

In the world of quantitative finance, data acts as the lifeblood for analytical models. Historically, financial theories and strategies heavily relied on historical price data and fundamental economic indicators. However, we now find ourselves in an exhilarating era characterized by big data, a term that encompasses a broad spectrum of information sources such as social media sentiment, satellite imagery, and web traffic analytics.

For instance, hedge funds and trading firms are increasingly leveraging social media analytics to assess public sentiment regarding various stocks. The meteoric rise of GameStop (GME) in early 2021 exemplifies this trend; proactive firms monitored Twitter discussions to predict and react to market shifts, showcasing the critical role of sentiment analysis in their investing strategies.

Harnessing the potential of big data enables traders to develop a more nuanced understanding of market dynamics. Tools like Python's pandas and numpy empower analysts to efficiently process and analyze these expansive data sets, revealing patterns and trends that might otherwise go unnoticed.

The Advancements in Machine Learning

Machine learning represents a seismic shift in the construction of predictive models within quantitative finance, enabling strategies that quickly adapt to the market's complexities. Techniques such as supervised and unsupervised learning are now employed to uncover intricate patterns—patterns that human analysts might easily overlook.

A growing number of funds are utilizing neural networks to model market behaviors based on past price movements. These algorithms are designed to learn and evolve continuously, refining their parameters to better respond to ever-shifting market conditions. In high-frequency trading (HFT), for instance, firms deploy machine learning algorithms to execute trades in mere milliseconds, capitalizing on real-time data insights.

The sophistication of these machine learning models hinges on advanced programming techniques, particularly with frameworks like TensorFlow and scikit-learn, which allow data scientists to innovate in algorithmic trading. One exciting area of exploration is reinforcement learning, enabling models to learn from their trading history, effectively adopting a trial-and-error methodology refined through mathematical precision.

```python
from sklearn.model_selection import train_test_split from sklearn.ensemble import RandomForestRegressor

\# Example: Predicting stock prices using a Random Forest model
```

```
data = pd.read_csv('stock_data.csv')
X = data[['feature1', 'feature2', 'feature3']]
y = data['price']

\# Splitting the data into training and testing sets
X_train, X_test, y_train, y_test = train_test_split(X, y, test_size=0.2)

\# Training the Random Forest model
model = RandomForestRegressor(n_estimators=100)
model.fit(X_train, y_train)

\# Making predictions
predictions = model.predict(X_test)
```

The Transformative Impact of Algorithmic Trading

Algorithmic trading, powered by advancements in big data and machine learning, has dramatically altered the execution of trades in contemporary financial markets. Algorithms can process enormous datasets at unmatched speeds, identifying fleeting opportunities that human traders may miss. This technological leap has birthed high-frequency trading, where thousands of trades can be executed in mere seconds.

This paradigm shift has significantly influenced market structure, often leading to narrower spreads and improved liquidity. However, it has also sparked debates around market integrity and ethical implications, as algorithms can inadvertently incite market volatility during critical moments. The infamous Flash Crash of 2010, in which the Dow Jones Industrial Average abruptly plummeted nearly 1,000 points within minutes, serves as a cautionary tale regarding the risks entwined with rapid algorithmic transactions.

Navigating Regulatory Waters

As quantitative finance evolves, so too do the regulatory frameworks that govern it. Regulatory bodies are increasingly scrutinizing algorithmic trading practices to avert market abuses while ensuring fairness and safeguarding retail investors. Regulations like the Markets in Financial Instruments Directive (MiFID II) in Europe now impose stringent compliance obligations, compelling trading firms to maintain transparency regarding their algorithmic strategies and risk management protocols.

Furthermore, the rise of data privacy laws, such as the General Data Protection Regulation (GDPR), introduces additional challenges for firms engaged in the collection and analysis of consumer data. Navigating these complexities requires a comprehensive understanding that marries financial expertise with insights into computer science, data protection, and ethical considerations.

Innovations on the Horizon

Looking ahead, the future of quantitative finance promises a landscape rich with possibilities. We can expect further integration of artificial intelligence into investment strategies, while the nascent field of quantum computing holds promise for solving complex financial problems with unprecedented speed and efficiency.

Additionally, the emergence of decentralized finance (DeFi), powered by blockchain technology, has the potential to revolutionize our understanding of financial systems by disrupting traditional banking and investing frameworks. Such innovations will reshape our engagement with financial markets, ushering in a new paradigm that demands quick adaptation from financial analysts and investors alike.

In conclusion, the evolving landscape of quantitative finance is characterized by a whirlwind of technological advancements, methodological innovations, and regulatory challenges. Professionals in this dynamic field must remain agile, continually seeking knowledge and adapting to the relentless pace of change. As we prepare to explore further the implications of these developments on algorithmic trading, we look forward to uncovering effective strategies that leverage emerging technologies while simultaneously addressing the attendant risks.

The Role of Big Data Analytics in Quantitative Finance

Big data analytics is no longer just a buzzword; it has emerged as a transformative force redefining the landscape of quantitative finance. With the daily generation of vast quantities of data from diverse sources—including market transactions, economic reports, social media activity, and even satellite imagery—financial analysts find themselves navigating a pivotal moment where traditional analytical methods coexist with innovative, data-driven approaches. This exploration delves into how big data analytics enriches financial decision-making, enhances predictive modeling, and ultimately empowers organizations to achieve a competitive edge.

The Explosion of Financial Data

Historically, financial analysts operated primarily with structured datasets, such as stock prices and trading volumes, often encapsulated in straightforward spreadsheets. However, today's data environment has undergone an explosive transformation, overflowing with both structured and unstructured information. This encompasses a wide range of data types, such as text from news articles, user-generated content from social media, and real-time transactional data from online trading platforms.

For example, during the COVID-19 pandemic, unconventional market signals surfaced through social media analysis. Retail trading platforms, like Robinhood, gained unprecedented popularity, while platforms like Twitter became integral for gauging market sentiment regarding specific stocks. A notable case involved the phenomenon of meme stocks, particularly GameStop (GME), where retail investors on Reddit collaborated to significantly influence stock prices. Firms that harnessed social media sentiment analytics were more adept at predicting price movements during this tumultuous period than those reliant solely on traditional analytical frameworks.

Transforming Data into Insights

To fully leverage the potential of big data, financial analysts must engage in effective data collection, processing, and analysis. This effort involves employing advanced techniques that convert raw data into actionable insights. Tools like Python's pandas library enable analysts to manipulate large datasets with ease, allowing for operations such as filtering, cleaning, and aggregating financial information.

```python
import pandas as pd

# Load a dataset containing stock prices and social media sentiment
data = pd.read_csv('market_data.csv')

# Preprocess the data: creating a new column for sentiment
data['Sentiment'] = data['SocialMediaPosts'].apply(lambda x: analyze_sentiment(x))

# Calculate average price change based on sentiment
avg_price_change = data.groupby('Sentiment')['PriceChange'].mean()
print(avg_price_change)
```

This snippet illustrates how analysts can utilize social media sentiment in relation to price changes.

Machine Learning: A Catalyst for Superior Predictions

In the realm of quantitative finance, machine learning has garnered significant attention for its capability to discern intricate patterns within vast datasets. Models—including regression techniques and advanced ensemble methods like random forests and gradient boosting—empower analysts to forecast market trends with heightened accuracy.

Imagine a hedge fund deploying machine learning to predict stock price movements.

Through proficient feature engineering, they can input these variables into a machine-learning model, generating predictions regarding potential price variations. As the model processes new data over time, it continuously adapts and refines its forecasts, enabling a nimble response to changing market dynamics.

```python
from sklearn.ensemble import GradientBoostingRegressor
from sklearn.model_selection import train_test_split

\# Assume 'features' is a preprocessed DataFrame with our relevant indicators
X_train, X_test, y_train, y_test = train_test_split(features, target_variable)

\# Train a Gradient Boosting model
model = GradientBoostingRegressor(n_estimators=200)
model.fit(X_train, y_train)

\# Making predictions
predictions = model.predict(X_test)
```

Central to this process is the idea of iterative learning, where machine learning models refine their forecasts as new insights emerge, steadily improving accuracy and mitigating the risks of significant financial losses.

Sentiment Analysis: Gauging Market Psychology

Among the diverse applications of big data analytics, sentiment analysis is crucial for deciphering market psychology. This technique involves scrutinizing various textual data sources to assess the prevailing mood toward specific assets or the overarching economic landscape. This qualitative analysis complements traditional quantitative indicators, offering a more comprehensive view of market dynamics.

For instance, if a notable uptick in negative sentiment regarding a major corporation aligns with declining stock prices, trading strategies may be adjusted accordingly. Utilizing libraries such as TextBlob or NLTK, analysts can automate sentiment analysis effectively.

```python
from textblob import TextBlob

\# Example function to analyze sentiment
def analyze_sentiment(post):
  return TextBlob(post).sentiment.polarity

\# Apply sentiment analysis to a DataFrame column
data['SentimentScores'] =
data['SocialMediaPosts'].apply(analyze_sentiment)
```

By weaving sentiment analysis into their trading strategies, firms can react more dynamically to rapidly evolving market sentiments, potentially reducing losses and seizing lucrative trading opportunities.

The Future of Big Data in Finance

As we contemplate the future, the significance of big data analytics in quantitative finance will only magnify. As data collection techniques advance and the availability of information increases, organizations must adapt their strategies and processes to remain competitive.

The fusion of artificial intelligence, machine learning, and big data analytics will revolutionize the speed and precision of financial decision-making. Furthermore, evolving regulatory frameworks will demand greater attention to data ethics and responsible data management practices.

In a field primarily driven by quantitative analysis, the ability to translate big data into valuable insights will distinguish successful firms from their competitors. This highlights the essential nature of ongoing learning and adaptation in the financial markets.

In conclusion, big data analytics stands not as a mere adjunct but as a foundational pillar of contemporary quantitative finance. Through its dynamic interplay with traditional financial theories, it equips analysts with the necessary tools, techniques, and insights to flourish in an increasingly complex and fast-paced environment. As we advance into an era where finance meets technology, the capability to harness big data will be a defining factor for the leaders of tomorrow's markets.

Algorithmic Trading Developments

In today's fast-paced financial landscape, algorithmic trading has become an essential engine driving market dynamics. This sophisticated blend of technology, mathematics, and market insight has created unparalleled opportunities for both institutional players and individual investors. Join us as we delve into the significant developments that have shaped algorithmic trading, exploring its methodologies, technological advancements, and potential future trajectories.

The roots of algorithmic trading can be traced back to the early 1980s when it was primarily employed by large institutional investors seeking to execute massive trades without disrupting market prices. Fast forward to the present, and we witness a radical evolution in the methods and technologies that form the backbone of this trading strategy. A key catalyst for this transformation has been the rise of high-frequency trading (HFT). These trading strategies leverage advanced algorithms to identify and capitalize on minute price fluctuations at extraordinary speeds. This enables traders to execute orders in milliseconds, profiting from subtle market inefficiencies that would otherwise elude human traders.

Imagine a hedge fund nestled in the bustling heart of London's financial district. With the help of a proprietary algorithm, it embarks on a mission to initiate thousands of trades daily across global exchanges. Each transaction unfolds in a fraction of a second, allowing the fund to seize trading opportunities that are almost invisible to the naked eye. The accessibility of these tools has expanded dramatically; retail traders now have the ability to utilize similar algorithmic trading solutions through user-friendly, cloud-based platforms. This democratization of advanced trading technology marks a significant shift, empowering individual investors to compete alongside the titans of finance.

At the heart of algorithmic trading's success lies the integration of machine learning. As algorithms evolve, their capacity to process information and learn from historical trading patterns enhances dramatically. For example, an algorithm employing supervised learning techniques can sift through vast amounts of historical data to pinpoint patterns linked to profitable trades. This capability not only fine-tunes trading strategies but also amplifies risk management, enabling firms to adjust swiftly to changing market conditions.

Reinforcement learning represents an exciting frontier in this realm. Unlike traditional algorithms that operate within rigid frameworks, reinforcement learning models adapt based on feedback from their environment, discovering the most effective strategies through trial and error. When incorporated into trading, these models can simulate a multitude of scenarios, modifying parameters in real-time according to market responses, ultimately evolving into self-improving systems.

Despite the promising advantages of machine learning, it introduces its own complexities. The integrity and quality of data are crucial; inaccurate data can lead to flawed trading decisions. Furthermore, as algorithms become more intricate, their decision-making processes often become opaque, raising concerns about transparency and exposure to risk. A stark reminder of these challenges occurred during the infamous "Flash Crash" of 2010, when a cascade of algorithmic trading actions led to a rapid market downturn within moments. This pivotal incident underscored the imperative need for robust safeguards within algorithmic trading systems, an area that remains a key focus for both regulators and practitioners.

Changes in market structure have also played a significant role in shaping algorithmic trading strategies. The advent of dark pools—private exchanges designed for trading securities away from public view—has established an environment where algorithms can operate with greater discretion. However, the lack of transparency associated with dark pools raises critical questions about market fairness and the potential for information asymmetry, challenges that algorithmic developers must navigate with utmost care.

Looking to the future, the influence of algorithmic trading is poised for further expansion. One area garnering immense interest is the integration of blockchain technology into trading systems. Smart contracts, self-executing agreements written into code, have the potential to streamline and automate transactions, dramatically enhancing operational efficiency. Additionally, the emergence of quantum computing could transform algorithmic strategies by vastly improving processing speeds and tackling complex optimization problems that previously seemed insurmountable.

In conclusion, algorithmic trading has evolved from a specialized strategy for a select few into a central pillar of the financial marketplace. Its growth has been fueled by advancements in technology, particularly in the realm of machine learning, all while navigating a complex interplay of market structures and regulatory environments. As we stand on the cusp of a new chapter in algorithmic trading, the prospects are as dynamic as the algorithms themselves—each iteration promising greater sophistication, efficiency, and ultimately, profitability in the ever-dynamic world of finance. In the forthcoming section, we will explore the ethical implications and regulatory landscapes that accompany these advancements, providing crucial insights to navigate the exciting future that lies ahead in this captivating domain.

The Impact of AI and Machine Learning on Finance

Imagine a once-bustling trading floor, where traders relied heavily on intuition, historical charts, and manual analytics to inform their decisions. Today, the landscape of finance is marked by groundbreaking changes. Consider the emergence of sophisticated AI algorithms capable of analyzing colossal datasets at remarkable speed. Unlike human analysts, these algorithms sift through diverse sources—ranging from historical market data to news articles and social media sentiments—allowing for real-time analysis that was previously unthinkable.

A compelling illustration of AI's transformative role can be seen in sentiment analysis, a field that employs machine learning to assess market sentiment through text. Many hedge funds leverage these cutting-edge algorithms to decode news headlines and social media discussions related to specific stocks. For instance, a New York-based hedge fund utilizes a machine learning model that processes thousands of tweets about a given tech company to detect changes in public sentiment that could indicate impending fluctuations in stock prices.

In addition, machine learning has become invaluable in predictive analytics—a domain that encompasses forecasting stock prices, assessing credit risks, and evaluating the likelihood of loan defaults. Lending institutions, for instance, harness AI to analyze extensive borrower data, enabling them to make rapid, informed credit decisions. Machine learning models can unveil subtle, nuanced patterns in a prospective borrower's credit history, income streams, and spending behavior, ultimately producing a more refined risk assessment than traditional models could achieve.

Moreover, adaptive learning mechanisms take AI capabilities to the next level. These mechanisms allow models to evolve as they encounter new data. A notable example comes from a derivatives trading firm that adopted a reinforcement learning model, continually refining its trading strategies based on the successes and failures of previous trades in real-time. This innovative system learns not only from trade outcomes but also from ongoing shifts in market conditions. During the height of the pandemic, for instance, the model swiftly adapted its parameters overnight, enabling the firm to execute profitable trades even amidst tumultuous market volatility.

Nevertheless, the ascent of AI and machine learning in finance is not without its challenges. One of the primary concerns surrounding these technologies revolves around data quality and potential biases. The infamous 2010 Flash Crash serves as a cautionary tale, highlighting the perils of algorithmic trading driven by flawed data. When algorithms operate on compromised information, they can trigger catastrophic market events, underscoring the critical need for a balance between embracing advanced technologies and ensuring robust, accurate models.

Another pressing issue is the interpretability of AI models. As machine learning algorithms grow increasingly complex, deciphering the rationale behind their decisions may pose a considerable challenge—even for seasoned data scientists. For example, if a hedge fund employs a deep learning model for asset allocation without clarity on the underlying decision-making process, it risks encountering significant compliance and risk management dilemmas.

Regulatory bodies are acutely aware of the implications

of AI-driven trading strategies. As the financial landscape evolves, they are diligently monitoring market shifts to enforce fair practices. It becomes imperative for models determining trading eligibility or risk assessments to not only be transparent but also to adhere to stringent compliance standards to mitigate risks of market manipulation or systemic failures.

Looking ahead, as we venture deeper into a future increasingly defined by AI and machine learning, their role in the finance sector is poised to expand even further. These technologies promise to enhance efficiency and drive profitability; however, they also necessitate a keen awareness of their complexities and attendant risks. Exciting possibilities loom on the horizon, such as the advent of quantum computing, which could exponentially bolster these capabilities, enabling unprecedented levels of processing speed that could facilitate comprehensive simulations and advanced statistical modeling, ultimately improving predictive accuracy.

Regulatory Considerations and Compliance

The aftermath of the 2008 financial crisis saw an elevation in regulatory oversight across global financial markets, compelling institutions to adapt their practices to align with new standards. In Europe, the introduction of the Markets in Financial Instruments Directive II (MiFID II) marked a significant shift in regulatory demands, establishing stringent requirements related to transparency, reporting, and algorithmic trading. It requires trading firms to meticulously document their trading activities and ensure their algorithms function within clearly defined parameters to mitigate potential risks. This is especially vital in the context of unforeseen market events, such as the infamous 2010 Flash Crash, where poorly structured algorithms played a role in the sudden plummet of the Dow Jones Industrial Average.

However, compliance is not merely a matter of ticking

boxes on a checklist; it embodies the ethical responsibilities intrinsic to the finance profession. Institutions must craft comprehensive risk management frameworks in accordance with the Basel III accord, which addresses issues related to liquidity risk, capital adequacy, and leverage ratios.

The question arises: how can technology, particularly artificial intelligence (AI) and machine learning, support compliance efforts? Imagine a hedge fund that employs machine learning algorithms to analyze extensive datasets for adherence to regulatory requirements. This capability enables the fund to monitor trading activities in real time, swiftly identifying potential violations or anomalies that could lead to regulatory inquiries. For instance, algorithms that flag trades exceeding defined volume thresholds or that occur during pre-market hours can facilitate immediate corrective actions, thereby preventing escalations into regulatory breaches.

As financial institutions harness big data analytics for informed decision-making, the significance of data governance becomes even more pronounced. Compliance with regulations like the General Data Protection Regulation (GDPR) in the European Union, which emphasizes the safeguarding of personal data, necessitates robust data management strategies. Non-compliance can yield not only hefty fines but can also irreparably tarnish an organization's reputation. A notable example involved a major investment bank that faced substantial penalties for failing to adhere to data privacy standards, vividly illustrating the imperative of maintaining data integrity and security across all operational dimensions.

One of the formidable challenges in compliance is the opacity associated with the algorithms employed in trading strategies. Many machine learning models, particularly those grounded in deep learning, often function as black boxes. This lack of transparency regarding algorithmic decision-making can lead to non-compliance, especially in jurisdictions that mandate clear explanations of operational decisions. Consequently, financial entities must strive to develop interpretable models or furnish robust documentation that articulates the logic behind their algorithmic outputs. This transparency is essential not just for regulatory compliance but also for fostering trust among clients and stakeholders.

To delve deeper into the synergy between compliance and technology, we must recognize the transformative role of Regulatory Technology (RegTech). RegTech enhances compliance by streamlining processes through automation and sophisticated data analytics. Increasingly, firms are adopting RegTech solutions to manage compliance reporting, monitor transactions for regulatory conformity, and streamline audit processes. For instance, platforms leveraging natural language processing can scrutinize legal texts to ensure alignment with dynamic regulatory environments, enabling firms to maintain agility in the face of evolving demands.

Equally important is the cultivation of a compliance-oriented culture within organizations. Comprehensive training programs centered on ethical trading practices and regulatory awareness can empower employees at every level to proactively engage with compliance considerations. A case in point is a Chicago-based trading firm that, by promoting a culture emphasizing compliance, successfully avoided potential fines during a regulatory audit. This underscores how a proactive approach to compliance can yield beneficial outcomes.

As we move into an era marked by heightened regulatory scrutiny, it is paramount for finance professionals to stay informed about the evolving legal landscape and to anticipate changes in compliance requirements. This necessitates ongoing education and active engagement with industry bodies to preemptively shape best practices that align with regulatory expectations.

Ethical Implications in Quantitative Strategies

Historically, the world of finance has often thrived in an environment marked by opacity. However, the advent of quantitative methodologies in trading practices has illuminated a host of ethical dilemmas. A striking example of this is the emergence of high-frequency trading (HFT) platforms, which employ highly sophisticated algorithms to execute thousands of trades in mere fractions of a second. While these practices may enhance market efficiency, they also provoke concerns about potential market manipulation and the uneven competitive landscape they create. Companies equipped with advanced algorithms can leave traditional investors trailing in their wake, resulting in a significant disparity between institutional players and everyday retail investors. This raises a crucial ethical question: do these practices ultimately benefit the market as a whole, or do they deepen the chasm dividing those with access to cutting-edge technology from those without?

A further illustration of this ethical dilemma is found in the notorious "quote stuffing" incident, where traders inundated the market with thousands of orders only to cancel them seconds later. This tactic skewed market data and crafted a misleading narrative that ultimately eroded trust among traders. In response, regulatory bodies began scrutinizing such practices, revealing the substantial reputational and financial fallout that can arise from ethical missteps. This evolution underscores the urgent need for stringent ethical standards in the development and deployment of quantitative strategies.

A significant ethical consideration in this landscape is the concept of algorithmic accountability. Algorithms often operate on data inputs that may be rife with bias, which can lead to skewed trading decisions. For instance, consider a quantitative model that leverages machine learning to predict stock movements based on historical trends. If the training data disproportionately represents certain demographics or sectors, the resulting algorithm may perpetuate these biases, disadvantaging otherwise promising investment opportunities. For example, a model relying heavily on data from high-performing companies might overlook undervalued firms that present robust investment potential but fail to meet the algorithm's narrow criteria. This unintended consequence highlights the pressing need for corrective measures and conscious efforts to ensure equity in algorithmic outputs.

Data privacy and security are additional critical concerns when evaluating quant strategies. As companies harness the power of big data analytics, they often gain access to a trove of sensitive information, including personal data from clients and prospective investors. The ethical dilemma arises when profit prioritization overshadows the imperative of safeguarding such information. A notable example occurred in 2019 when a major financial institution faced backlash for a data breach that compromised the personal information of millions. The resulting damage to its reputation and the erosion of customer trust underscored finance professionals' ethical obligation to protect data integrity and adopt responsible practices in utilizing data.

To navigate these multifaceted ethical dimensions, organizations must foster what can be termed an “ethical quant culture.” This entails implementing comprehensive training programs that underscore the importance of ethical decision-making, ensuring that employees across all levels are well-versed in the ethical implications inherent in quantitative practices. Encouraging robust discussions around ethical considerations during the strategy development phase is essential. Engaging diverse perspectives can reveal potential biases or oversights that could otherwise escape notice. For example, a high-stakes trading strategy may inadvertently lead to market manipulation if developed in isolation, while one crafted with collaborative input is more likely to consider its societal implications and navigate associated risks.

In practical terms, organizations should establish ethical review boards comprised of diverse stakeholders to evaluate proposed quantitative strategies before implementation. These boards would be tasked with assessing the potential ethical consequences, ensuring alignment between the firm's strategies and both regulatory standards and societal values. A small Chicago-based hedge fund successfully illustrates this concept by creating an ethics committee that reviews proposed algorithms for ethical implications prior to their deployment. This proactive approach not only enhances transparency but also builds trust with clients.

Furthermore, the emergence of Regulatory Technology (RegTech) has the potential to play a pivotal role in harmonizing quantitative practices with ethical standards. For instance, leveraging natural language processing to analyze firm communications can help monitor unethical trading behaviors or misleading information dissemination, ensuring that organizations maintain accountability throughout their strategies.

The finance sector is on the brink of a significant evolution, driven by groundbreaking computational methods that are redefining everything from classic trading strategies to advanced risk assessment and portfolio management. This transformation not only highlights the synergy between technological innovation and financial expertise, but also signifies the dawn of a new chapter in quantitative finance. As we explore the latest advancements in this field, it becomes increasingly clear that these innovations are enhancing analytical capabilities and transforming decision-making processes across the industry.

The Empowerment of High-Performance Computing

In the past, financial calculations often involved labor-intensive methods and were severely limited by the capabilities of existing hardware. The introduction of high-performance computing (HPC) has revolutionized this landscape, empowering finance professionals to tap into extraordinary computational power for analyzing extensive datasets and executing intricate algorithms with remarkable speed and precision. This technological leap enables institutions to process millions of transactions per second, positioning them to respond dynamically to market fluctuations.

A compelling example of HPC's impact comes from a recent study conducted by a prominent New York investment bank. This innovative approach not only allowed them to identify emerging trends more swiftly but also improved their capacity to execute trades at the most opportune moments—capitalizing on micro-fluctuations that would have previously gone unnoticed.

Harnessing Machine Learning and AI in Portfolio Management

The integration of machine learning (ML) and artificial intelligence (AI) into finance has unleashed a wave of opportunities. These powerful tools facilitate the creation of adaptive predictive models that respond to real-time data, enabling firms to adjust their strategies with heightened agility. A notable application of this technology is in asset allocation within investment portfolios. Rather than relying on static approaches, AI-driven neural networks can analyze historical performance and dynamically tailor allocations—striking a balance between maximizing returns and managing risks.

For instance, a forward-thinking quantitative hedge fund in London adopted an AI-based system for managing its equity portfolio. This case vividly illustrates that AI is not merely a concept from the future, but a tangible asset reshaping contemporary investment strategies.

The Rise of Big Data and Alternative Data Sources

With the relentless pursuit of technological advancement, we have entered an era dominated by big data. Financial institutions now have access to expansive datasets derived from a myriad of sources, including satellite imagery, transaction logs, and online consumer behavior patterns. This wealth of information enhances firms' predictive capabilities significantly.

A striking example is observed in the retail sector, where hedge funds have begun leveraging foot traffic data sourced from mobile devices. One notable quantitative fund analyzed shopper movement patterns outside retail establishments, yielding valuable insights that enabled more accurate sales forecasts and impressive gains.

Exploring Blockchain Technology and Distributed Ledger Systems

Blockchain technology is making substantial inroads into the financial sector, presenting a combination of efficiency and robust security for transactions. Financial institutions are keenly exploring blockchain's potential to optimize trading operations, streamline settlement processes, and mitigate fraud risks.

Consider the pilot program initiated by a major bank in Singapore that embraced blockchain for cross-border payments. This initiative showcased blockchain's ability to reduce settlement times from days to mere hours, thereby enhancing liquidity and minimizing risks associated with delayed transactions. Additionally, the transparent nature of blockchain technology plays a pivotal role in diminishing opportunities for fraudulent activities, paving the way for a more secure financial ecosystem.

Quantum Computing: The Frontier of Financial Innovation

On the cutting edge of financial technology is quantum computing, a field still in its infancy but brimming with potential applications. Quantum algorithms could disrupt conventional practices in portfolio optimization and risk management, solving vastly complex problems at speeds far beyond current capabilities.

A notable example is a consortium of firms led by a major tech player, which is exploring quantum computing's applications for refining trading strategies. Their initiative aims to uncover correlations among thousands of assets by simultaneously assessing multiple scenarios, potentially leading to instantaneous, optimal investment decisions that adapt in real time to market fluctuations.

Implications for Financial Professionals

The advancements in computational finance necessitate that finance professionals cultivate a diverse skill set that melds traditional financial knowledge with technological expertise. Familiarity with programming languages like Python and R, as well as tools such as TensorFlow, is becoming increasingly essential. Moreover, a robust mathematical foundation is crucial, enabling quantitative analysts to interpret sophisticated algorithms and understand their inherent assumptions.

As these technologies proliferate, ethical considerations surrounding their use rise to the forefront of discourse. Financial professionals must engage in discussions addressing the ethical implications of their technological dependencies and pursue practices that foster accountability and transparency within the industry.

Looking Ahead: The Future of Computational Finance

The advancements in computational finance herald a pivotal shift to a more technically sophisticated financial landscape. As we step into this new era characterized by algorithms, machine learning, and high-performance computing, the relationship we have with financial markets is poised for evolution. Institutions that adeptly integrate these innovations into their strategies are not just positioned to maintain a competitive edge; they are on the cusp of redefining the landscape of finance itself.

As we contemplate the future, the interaction between technology and finance is destined to deepen. Upcoming discussions will delve into how these breakthroughs influence strategic decision-making and explore the critical role of ethics in the adaptation of technology—essential themes that will guide us on this exhilarating journey through the realm of quantitative finance.

Innovations in Trading Platforms and APIs

The landscape of trading platforms and application programming interfaces (APIs) is undergoing a remarkable transformation. As digital technology continues to evolve, the realm of quantitative finance is breaking free from traditional paradigms, paving the way for innovative solutions that empower traders of all skill levels. This exciting evolution transcends mere efficiency; it embodies a fundamental shift toward a data-driven ecosystem where accessibility, speed, and adaptability are paramount.

The Emergence of User-Friendly Trading Interfaces

Historically, trading has been perceived as a complex domain reserved for seasoned professionals, often intimidating for newcomers. However, recent advancements have led to the creation of user-friendly trading platforms that welcome both novice and experienced traders.

Take, for example, "TradeWave," a London-based fintech startup. This forward-thinking company has integrated cutting-edge design principles into its platform, allowing users to execute trades with just a few clicks through engaging drag-and-drop functionalities and real-time data visualizations.

API Integration: A Gateway to Customization

APIs are fundamentally reshaping how traders engage with financial markets by enabling seamless integration between various systems. This integration facilitates the automation of trading strategies and the development of bespoke applications tailored to individual needs. With the rise of APIs, traders now gain access to rich historical and real-time market data, empowering them to execute trades and effectively manage portfolios with personalized solutions.

Consider Alpaca, a trailblazing US-based commission-free trading platform renowned for its powerful API. This tool empowers traders to design and implement algorithmic trading strategies by pulling historical market data, coding trading algorithms in Python, and executing trades automatically based on predefined criteria. The capacity for extensive customization allows traders to craft unique strategies that align with their investment goals and risk profiles, consequently enhancing their trading experiences.

The Role of Machine Learning and AI in Trading Platforms

As quantitative finance increasingly embraces machine learning and artificial intelligence, the functionality of trading platforms is evolving at a breakneck pace. These advanced technologies enable the analysis of vast datasets, revealing hidden patterns and executing trades with astounding speed and precision. Predictive analytics driven by machine learning have emerged as indispensable tools for traders striving to gain an advantage in competitive markets.

A striking example lies with Robinhood, a platform that has innovatively combined its user-friendly interface with AI-driven insights. This empowers users to make informed decisions, equipped with insights that were once out of reach.

Social Trading: Harnessing Collective Wisdom

Another significant development is the rise of social trading platforms, which harness the collective wisdom of the trading community. These platforms enable users to observe and replicate the trading activities of experienced investors, fostering an environment of collaboration and learning.

eToro stands at the forefront of this social trading movement, allowing users to follow expert traders and mimic their strategies. Through a feature called "CopyTrading," novices can allocate funds to automatically mirror the trades of proficient investors while successful traders receive performance fees as a reward for their followers' gains. This model not only democratizes access to trading but also cultivates a sense of community among users, enabling them to learn from one another and grow together.

API Investment and Market Access

Innovative trading platforms and APIs have also increased transparency and globalized market access, allowing traders to invest in international markets with remarkable ease. Previously onerous barriers have been dismantled, enabling users to diversify their portfolios effortlessly across global assets.

Interactive Brokers, a well-established global brokerage firm, exemplifies this trend. Their API connects traders to markets worldwide, providing access to stocks, bonds, and even foreign exchange across various exchanges. This connectivity frees traders from traditional geographical constraints, enabling them to react promptly to shifts in global markets and execute strategies that were once unavailable without extensive resources and expertise.

The Future of Trading Platforms and APIs

Looking forward, the future of trading platforms and APIs appears exceptionally vibrant. The continued convergence of technology and finance promises even greater innovations, blurring the lines between professional and retail trading. We can anticipate enhancements in machine learning algorithms, more sophisticated user interfaces, and increased connectivity that fosters international collaboration.

In this rapidly changing landscape, finance professionals must remain agile, ready to embrace new tools that redefine their trading practices. Those who navigate these advancements successfully will not only leverage technological progress but also play a vital role in shaping the future of trading in quantitative finance.

Final Thoughts

In conclusion, the innovations emerging in trading platforms and APIs signify a pivotal stride toward cultivating a more inclusive, efficient, and data-driven financial ecosystem. As we progress through this discourse, we will explore how these technological advancements interact with the broader themes of quantitative finance, reshaping the strategies and tools accessible to both seasoned and aspiring traders. This journey is merely the beginning, with boundless potential for further evolution within the trading landscape. Through these insights, we aim to equip readers with the knowledge needed to harness the power of these innovations and transform their trading practices for the better.

Essential Skillsets for the Future

Quantitative Analyst

In today's fast-paced financial world, the demand for skilled quantitative analysts—commonly known as quants—has reached unprecedented heights. As technology becomes increasingly integrated into finance alongside vast amounts of data and complex market infrastructures, the ability to adapt and excel in this environment is more important than ever. Future quants must cultivate a multifaceted skill set that melds traditional financial principles with modern analytical techniques. Below, we delve into the crucial competencies that aspiring quants should develop to thrive in the evolving landscape of quantitative finance.

At the core of quantitative finance is a solid grounding in statistical methods. Quants rely on statistics to validate models, assess risks, and derive data-driven forecasts. Mastery of this discipline goes beyond academic familiarity with algorithms; it involves an intuitive application of these techniques to complex financial challenges.

For example, take regression analysis, a common tool for predicting stock prices. While understanding the mechanics of linear regression is foundational, the real mastery lies in selecting the right variables, understanding market behaviors, and being aware of the assumptions underlying the statistical models to avoid common pitfalls like overfitting.

Practical Scenario:

Picture a quant who needs to forecast future prices for a leading tech stock using historical data.

2. Proficiency in Programming Languages

As the financial landscape continues to transition towards data-centric methodologies, programming competencies have become as essential as statistical knowledge for quants. Python stands out as the premier language for quantitative finance, celebrated for its flexibility and rich array of libraries tailored for data analysis, machine learning, and financial modeling.

Familiarity with additional programming languages such as R, C++, and Java can further distinguish a quant, especially in environments that demand high-speed computational performance. Moreover, a command of SQL is crucial for managing and querying large datasets efficiently.

Practical Scenario:

Imagine a quant who needs to automate a trading strategy through Python.

```python import pandas as pd import numpy as np from sklearn.linear_model import LinearRegression
\# Example of a simple linear regression model for stock price prediction
data = pd.read_csv("historical_stock_data.csv")
X = data[['feature1', 'feature2']]
y = data['stock_price']

model = LinearRegression()
model.fit(X, y)

predictions = model.predict(X)
```

3. Machine Learning and AI Expertise

With artificial intelligence and machine learning shaping the future of finance, expertise in these areas has become vital for quants. Aspiring analysts need to familiarize themselves with various predictive algorithms—such as decision trees, random forests, and neural networks.

Knowledge of feature engineering and selection can also significantly enhance model performance. Understanding how to preprocess data and derive meaningful new features can greatly influence applications ranging from risk assessment to algorithmic trading strategies.

Practical Scenario:

Consider a quant improving a stock selection model through deep learning.

4. Strong Financial Acumen

Technical abilities alone cannot sustain a quant's success; a thorough understanding of financial concepts is equally crucial. Quants must grasp various financial domains, including portfolio management, risk assessment, derivatives pricing, and market microstructure. This interdisciplinary knowledge allows quants to bridge quantitative analyses with real-world financial implications.

An adept quant must comprehend the practical consequences of their models—for instance, understanding how value-at-risk (VaR) quantifies potential investment losses is essential for effective stakeholder communication and decision-making.

Practical Scenario:

When devising a new trading strategy, a quant would first evaluate how the strategy affects the overall portfolio—considering correlations with existing assets and its specific risk-return profile. This comprehensive perspective is essential for crafting strategies aligned with an organization's investment goals.

5. Communication and Collaboration Skills

Future quant analysts will rarely operate in isolation. Strong communication skills are essential for conveying complex quantitative insights to non-technical stakeholders. This ability is paramount in collaborative environments where quants must work closely with finance professionals, data scientists, and software engineers.

Effectively articulating findings through clear reports and

engaging presentations helps ensure that insights derived from data analyses are understood and actionable, fostering informed decision-making across the organization.

Practical Scenario:

Imagine a quant tasked with presenting a new risk model to the investment team.

6. Adaptability and Commitment to Continuous Learning

Finally, adaptability and a dedication to lifelong learning are indispensable traits for aspiring quants. The finance sector is constantly evolving, with new tools, techniques, and methodologies emerging regularly. Successful quants must maintain an insatiable curiosity, staying current with trends through workshops, online platforms, and participation in industry forums.

Practical Scenario:

Joining hackathons or data science competitions can be an effective way for quants to sharpen their skills in a fast-paced environment, address intricate challenges, and engage with a vibrant community of peers who share a passion for quantitative finance.

The future of quantitative finance is bright, driven by technological innovations and an unwavering quest for pioneering solutions. As aspiring quant analysts embark on their careers in this realm, developing a diverse and sophisticated skill set will be crucial. Investing in these essential skills today will not only equip them to tackle future challenges but also enable them to seize the myriad opportunities that lie ahead, establishing their presence as leaders in the transformative arena of quantitative finance.

As we conclude this exploration of quantitative finance, it becomes clear that the interplay of statistical analysis, programming prowess, and financial insight forms the bedrock of informed decision-making and strategic development. Throughout this book, you have gathered essential tools and methodologies for mastering advanced statistical techniques using Python—an endeavor that stands to significantly elevate both your analytical abilities and market performance.

Embracing the Future of Quantitative Finance

The landscape of quantitative finance is a vibrant, dynamic environment that is continually driven by technological innovations, regulatory shifts, and evolving market conditions. For those aspiring to excel in this space, a proactive mindset is crucial; embracing the principle of lifelong learning is not just beneficial but essential. Staying abreast of the latest trends in data science and finance, engaging with pioneering research, and understanding the implications of groundbreaking technologies like artificial intelligence and machine learning are fundamental to thriving as a quant.

Take, for instance, the emergence of algorithmic trading platforms that harness machine learning for sophisticated predictive analytics. A quant who consistently hones their skills in these domains can engineer algorithms that not only respond rapidly to market fluctuations but also adapt dynamically to real-time data—consequently gaining a significant competitive edge.

Practical Learning and Development Opportunities

To cultivate the necessary skills amidst the fast-paced evolution of the industry, aspiring analysts should explore a variety of resources designed to expand their knowledge and enhance practical application capabilities. Here are several key avenues for further engagement:

1. **Online Courses and Certifications:** Educational platforms such as Coursera, edX, and Udacity offer comprehensive courses tailored to quantitative

finance, Python programming, machine learning, and data analytics. For example, obtaining a certification in Python for Data Science not only refines your coding skills but also familiarizes you with cutting-edge libraries and frameworks—like TensorFlow and Scikit-learn—that are integral for crafting machine learning models.

2. **Industry Conferences and Workshops:** Participating in finance and data science conferences—such as the Quantitative Finance Conference or NeurIPS—provides invaluable networking opportunities and insights into industry best practices. Attending workshops at these gatherings often encourages collaboration and hands-on learning, allowing participants to tackle pressing real-world challenges in quantitative finance.
3. **Engaging in Hackathons and Competitions:** Platforms like Kaggle host data science competitions where quants can test their skills in a competitive yet amicable setting. These events bring real-life financial datasets to the forefront, enabling participants to develop predictive models while gaining both practical experience and knowledge from their peers.
4. **Reading and Research:** Staying informed on advancements in finance and statistical methodologies can be accomplished through scholarly articles, finance blogs, and technical documentation. Renowned publications like the Journal of Financial Economics or influential texts such as "Machine Learning for Asset Managers" explore advanced concepts that might spark fresh ideas for implementation in your work.

Building a Professional Network

Networking is an indispensable element for anyone aiming to forge a successful career in quantitative finance. Connecting with peers, mentors, and industry professionals can lead to collaborative opportunities and insights that deepen your understanding of the field. Engaging in forums such as QuantNet or joining professional associations like the CFA Institute fosters connections with like-minded individuals who share a passion for quantitative analysis and financial modeling.

Leveraging Resources for Continuous Improvement

The journey to becoming a proficient quant does not conclude with formal education; it is an ongoing commitment to personal and professional evolution. Utilizing resources like coding repositories on GitHub allows for project sharing and refinement, while platforms such as Stack Overflow serve as valuable venues for seeking guidance on programming challenges or financial analysis inquiries.

Additionally, joining study groups or online communities dedicated to quantitative topics can facilitate collaboration and discourse, empowering participants to tackle intricate problems together and learn from each other's diverse experiences.

In summary, mastering advanced statistical methods and Python for quantitative finance is a fulfilling journey that calls for dedication, adaptability, and a commitment to lifelong learning. The confluence of statistical acumen, programming expertise, and financial insight empowers quants to navigate today's complex market landscape effectively.

As you embark on the next chapter of your career, keep in mind that challenges often serve as gateways to opportunity. Embrace a mindset of continuous improvement, refining your techniques and broadening your perspectives. Equipped with the insights and resources from this book, along with your innate curiosity, you are poised to make a significant contribution to quantitative finance—both in your personal success and the ongoing evolution of the industry.

Move forward with confidence, an insatiable thirst for knowledge, and an unwavering determination to excel in this captivating field. Your journey is just beginning, and the future holds boundless possibilities.

APPENDIX A: PROJECT: INTRODUCTION TO QUANTITATIVE FINANCE AND PYTHON

This project is designed to help students get hands-on experience with the foundational concepts of quantitative finance and Python programming.

Step-by-Step Instructions

Step 1: Overview of Quantitative Finance

1. **Objective:**
2. Understand the basics of quantitative finance, its importance, and applications.
3. **Instructions:**
4. Research and write a brief report (1-2 pages) on what quantitative finance is, its key concepts, and its role in the financial industry.
5. Include examples of how quantitative finance is used in real-world scenarios such as algorithmic trading, risk management, and portfolio optimization.

Step 2: Importance of Statistical Methods in Finance

1. **Objective:**
2. Learn why statistical methods are crucial in financial analysis.
3. **Instructions:**
4. Create a presentation (5-7 slides) highlighting the importance of statistical methods in finance.
5. Provide examples of statistical techniques used in finance such as hypothesis testing, regression analysis, and time series analysis.
6. Discuss how these methods help in making informed financial decisions.

Step 3: Introduction to Python for Financial Analysis

1. **Objective:**
2. Get acquainted with Python programming and its applications in finance.
3. **Instructions:**
4. Write a brief essay (1 page) on why Python is popular in the finance industry.
5. Research and list out at least five key Python libraries commonly used in financial analysis (e.g., NumPy, pandas, SciPy, matplotlib, and Statsmodels).

Step 4: Setting Up the Python Environment

1. **Objective:**
2. Install Python and set up a development environment.
3. **Instructions:**
4. Download and install Anaconda, a popular Python distribution for data science.

5. Set up a new Python environment using Anaconda Navigator or via the command line.
6. Install the following libraries: NumPy, pandas, matplotlib, and Jupyter Notebook.
7. Write a short report (1-2 paragraphs) on your installation process and any challenges faced.

Step 5: Key Libraries for Financial Data Analysis

1. **Objective:**
2. Learn about key Python libraries and their functionalities.
3. **Instructions:**
4. Create a Jupyter Notebook and write code snippets demonstrating the basic usage of NumPy, pandas, and matplotlib.
5. For each library, include:
   - An example of how to load and manipulate data.
   - A simple data visualization (e.g., line chart, bar chart).
6. Save and submit the Jupyter Notebook.

Step 6: Basic Python Syntax for Analysts

1. **Objective:**
2. Gain familiarity with basic Python syntax and structures.
3. **Instructions:**
4. Create a Jupyter Notebook with code examples covering:
   - Variables and data types.
   - Control structures (if statements, loops).
   - Functions and modules.
   - Lists, dictionaries, and data frames.
5. Include comments in the code explaining each

example.
6. Save and submit the Jupyter Notebook.

Step 7: Data Structures and Types in Python

1. **Objective:**
2. Understand various data structures and their applications in Python.
3. **Instructions:**
4. In a Jupyter Notebook, write code demonstrating the creation and manipulation of different data structures:
    - Lists, tuples, sets, and dictionaries.
    - Data frames using pandas.
5. Provide examples showing how each data structure can be used in financial data analysis.
6. Save and submit the Jupyter Notebook.

Step 8: Importing Financial Data

1. **Objective:**
2. Learn how to import and work with financial data in Python.
3. **Instructions:**
4. Use the pandas_datareader library to import stock data from a financial data source (e.g., Yahoo Finance).
5. Write a Jupyter Notebook to:
    - Import stock data for a specific company (e.g., Apple Inc.) over the past year.
    - Display the first few rows of the data frame.
    - Plot the closing prices over time using matplotlib.
6. Save and submit the Jupyter Notebook.

Step 9: Data Cleaning and Preprocessing

1. **Objective:**

2. Learn techniques for cleaning and preprocessing financial data.
3. **Instructions:**
4. Continue with the Jupyter Notebook from Step 8.
5. Write code to:
    - Handle missing data (e.g., fill or interpolate missing values).
    - Normalize or scale the data if necessary.
    - Add new features such as moving averages.
6. Save and submit the Jupyter Notebook.

Step 10: Case Study: Simple Financial Analysis with Python

1. **Objective:**
2. Apply the skills learned in the previous steps to perform a simple financial analysis.
3. **Instructions:**
4. Choose a financial dataset (e.g., stock prices, exchange rates).
5. In a Jupyter Notebook, write code to:
    - Import and clean the data.
    - Perform basic statistical analysis (e.g., mean, median, standard deviation).
    - Visualize key metrics and trends.
    - Write a brief conclusion (1-2 paragraphs) summarizing your findings.
6. Save and submit the Jupyter Notebook.

Project: Statistical Foundations for Finance

This project is designed to give students a comprehensive understanding of the statistical foundations necessary for finance.

Step-by-Step Instructions

Step 1: Descriptive Statistics Essentials

1. **Objective:**
2. Understand and apply basic descriptive statistics to financial data.
3. **Instructions:**
4. Choose a financial dataset (e.g., stock prices of a particular company over the past year).
5. Create a Jupyter Notebook and write code to:
    - Calculate and display the mean, median, mode, variance, and standard deviation of the stock prices.
    - Plot the distribution of the stock prices using a histogram.
6. Save and submit the Jupyter Notebook.

Step 2: Probability Distributions in Finance

1. **Objective:**
2. Learn about different probability distributions and their applications in finance.
3. **Instructions:**
4. In your Jupyter Notebook, write code to:
    - Simulate stock prices using a normal distribution.
    - Plot the probability density function (PDF) of the simulated stock prices.
    - Compare the simulated distribution with the actual distribution of the stock prices from your dataset.
5. Write a brief report (1-2 paragraphs) on your findings.
6. Save and submit the Jupyter Notebook.

Step 3: Hypothesis Testing Overview

1. **Objective:**
2. Understand the basics of hypothesis testing and apply it to financial data.
3. **Instructions:**
4. Formulate a hypothesis related to your financial dataset (e.g., the mean stock price of a company is greater than a certain value).
5. Write code in your Jupyter Notebook to:
    - Perform a t-test to test your hypothesis.
    - Display the results and interpret the p-value.
6. Write a brief conclusion (1 paragraph) on whether you accept or reject the null hypothesis.
7. Save and submit the Jupyter Notebook.

Step 4: Confidence Intervals and Estimation

1. **Objective:**
2. Learn how to calculate and interpret confidence intervals for financial data.
3. **Instructions:**
4. In your Jupyter Notebook, write code to:
    - Calculate the 95% confidence interval for the mean stock price of your dataset.
    - Plot the confidence interval on a graph along with the stock prices.
5. Provide a brief explanation (1-2 paragraphs) of what the confidence interval suggests about the stock prices.
6. Save and submit the Jupyter Notebook.

Step 5: Correlation and Covariance

1. **Objective:**
2. Understand and apply the concepts of correlation and covariance to financial data.

3. **Instructions:**
4. Choose two different financial datasets (e.g., stock prices of two different companies).
5. In your Jupyter Notebook, write code to:
    - Calculate the correlation and covariance between the two datasets.
    - Plot a scatter plot to visualize the relationship between the two datasets.
6. Write a brief report (1-2 paragraphs) interpreting the correlation and covariance results.
7. Save and submit the Jupyter Notebook.

Step 6: Linear Regression Basics

1. **Objective:**
2. Learn the basics of linear regression and apply it to financial data.
3. **Instructions:**
4. Use one of your financial datasets and choose a dependent variable (e.g., closing stock price) and an independent variable (e.g., trading volume).
5. In your Jupyter Notebook, write code to:
    - Perform a simple linear regression analysis.
    - Plot the regression line along with the data points.
6. Write a brief report (1-2 paragraphs) interpreting the results of the regression analysis.
7. Save and submit the Jupyter Notebook.

Step 7: Limitations of Basic Statistical Methods

1. **Objective:**
2. Understand the limitations of basic statistical methods in financial analysis.
3. **Instructions:**

4. Write a brief essay (1-2 pages) discussing the limitations of basic statistical methods such as mean and variance, normal distribution assumptions, and linear regression.
5. Provide examples of scenarios in finance where these limitations can lead to misleading conclusions.
6. Save and submit the essay.

Step 8: Common Statistical Mistakes

1. **Objective:**
2. Learn about common statistical mistakes in financial analysis and how to avoid them.
3. **Instructions:**
4. Create a presentation (5-7 slides) highlighting common statistical mistakes in finance such as data snooping, ignoring outliers, and overfitting.
5. Provide real-world examples of these mistakes and suggest ways to avoid them.
6. Save and submit the presentation.

Step 9: Review of Key Statistical Terms

1. **Objective:**
2. Review and solidify understanding of key statistical terms used in finance.
3. **Instructions:**
4. Create a glossary of key statistical terms (at least 15 terms) with definitions and examples.
5. Include terms such as mean, median, mode, variance, standard deviation, correlation, covariance, p-value, confidence interval, etc.
6. Save and submit the glossary.

Step 10: Case Study: Applying Statistics to Market Data

1. **Objective:**
2. Apply the statistical methods learned to a real-world financial case study.
3. **Instructions:**
4. Choose a specific financial market event (e.g., a major stock market crash, a company's stock performance after earnings announcement).
5. In a Jupyter Notebook, write code to:
   - Import and preprocess relevant financial data.
   - Perform descriptive statistics, hypothesis testing, correlation analysis, and linear regression on the data.
   - Visualize key findings with appropriate plots.
6. Write a detailed report (3-5 pages) summarizing your analysis, findings, and conclusions.
7. Save and submit the Jupyter Notebook and the report.

Project: Time Series Analysis

This project aims to provide students with a solid understanding of time series analysis techniques and their applications in finance.

Step-by-Step Instructions

Step 1: Introduction to Time Series Data

1. **Objective:**
2. Understand the basics of time series data and its importance in finance.
3. **Instructions:**
4. Choose a financial time series dataset (e.g., daily closing prices of a particular stock over the past two

years).

5. Create a Jupyter Notebook and write code to:
    - Import the dataset and display the first few rows.
    - Plot the time series data to visualize trends and patterns.
6. Save and submit the Jupyter Notebook.

Step 2: Stationarity and Differencing

1. **Objective:**
2. Learn about stationarity in time series data and how to achieve it through differencing.
3. **Instructions:**
4. Write code in your Jupyter Notebook to:
    - Perform the Augmented Dickey-Fuller (ADF) test to check the stationarity of your time series dataset.
    - If the series is not stationary, apply differencing to make it stationary.
    - Plot the differenced time series and re-perform the ADF test to confirm stationarity.
5. Save and submit the Jupyter Notebook.

Step 3: Autocorrelation and Partial Autocorrelation

1. **Objective:**
2. Understand and compute autocorrelation and partial autocorrelation functions.
3. **Instructions:**
4. In your Jupyter Notebook, write code to:
    - Calculate and plot the autocorrelation function (ACF) and partial autocorrelation function (PACF) for your time series data.
    - Interpret the ACF and PACF plots to identify

potential lags for model building.

5. Save and submit the Jupyter Notebook.

Step 4: ARIMA Models: Basics and Applications

1. **Objective:**
2. Learn the basics of ARIMA models and their applications in time series forecasting.
3. **Instructions:**
4. In your Jupyter Notebook, write code to:
   - Fit an ARIMA model to your stationary time series dataset.
   - Use the AIC or BIC criteria to select the best model parameters (p, d, q).
   - Forecast future values using the fitted ARIMA model and plot the forecasts alongside the actual data.
5. Write a brief report (1-2 paragraphs) on the model selection process and forecast accuracy.
6. Save and submit the Jupyter Notebook.

Step 5: Seasonal Decomposition of Time Series

1. **Objective:**
2. Decompose a time series into its seasonal, trend, and residual components.
3. **Instructions:**
4. In your Jupyter Notebook, write code to:
   - Decompose your time series data using seasonal decomposition (e.g., using the statsmodels library).
   - Plot the decomposed components (trend, seasonal, and residual).
5. Write a brief explanation (1-2 paragraphs) of the decomposed components and their significance.
6. Save and submit the Jupyter Notebook.

Step 6: GARCH Models for Volatility Forecasting

1. **Objective:**
2. Learn about GARCH models and use them for volatility forecasting.
3. **Instructions:**
4. In your Jupyter Notebook, write code to:
   - Fit a GARCH model to your time series dataset.
   - Forecast future volatility using the fitted GARCH model.
   - Plot the forecasted volatility alongside the actual data.
5. Write a brief report (1-2 paragraphs) on the volatility forecasting results.
6. Save and submit the Jupyter Notebook.

Step 7: Time Series Cross-Validation

1. **Objective:**
2. Understand the concept of time series cross-validation and apply it to your dataset.
3. **Instructions:**
4. In your Jupyter Notebook, write code to:
   - Split your time series data into training and testing sets.
   - Perform cross-validation on the training set to evaluate the performance of your ARIMA and GARCH models.
5. Write a brief report (1-2 paragraphs) on the cross-validation process and results.
6. Save and submit the Jupyter Notebook.

Step 8: Forecasting Techniques

1. **Objective:**

2. Explore different forecasting techniques and compare their performance.
3. **Instructions:**
4. In your Jupyter Notebook, write code to:
   - Implement and compare different forecasting techniques (e.g., ARIMA, Exponential Smoothing, Prophet).
   - Evaluate the performance of each technique using appropriate metrics (e.g., RMSE, MAE).
5. Write a brief report (1-2 paragraphs) on the forecasting techniques and their performance.
6. Save and submit the Jupyter Notebook.

Step 9: Evaluating Forecast Accuracy

1. **Objective:**
2. Learn how to evaluate the accuracy of your forecasts.
3. **Instructions:**
4. In your Jupyter Notebook, write code to:
   - Calculate forecast accuracy metrics (e.g., RMSE, MAE, MAPE) for your chosen model.
   - Plot the forecast errors and analyze their distribution.
5. Write a brief report (1-2 paragraphs) on the accuracy of your forecasts and potential areas for improvement.
6. Save and submit the Jupyter Notebook.

Step 10: Case Study: Forecasting Stock Prices

1. **Objective:**
2. Apply the learned techniques to a real-world case study of forecasting stock prices.
3. **Instructions:**
4. Choose a specific stock and download its historical

price data.

5. In a Jupyter Notebook, write code to:
   - Import and preprocess the stock price data.
   - Perform time series analysis, including stationarity tests, ACF/PACF plots, and model selection.
   - Fit an appropriate model (e.g., ARIMA, GARCH) and forecast future stock prices.
   - Evaluate the forecast accuracy and visualize the results.
6. Write a detailed report (3-5 pages) summarizing your analysis, findings, and conclusions.
7. Save and submit the Jupyter Notebook and the report.

Project: Multi-Factor Models

This project is designed to deepen your understanding of multi-factor models in finance and how to implement them using Python.

Step-by-Step Instructions

Step 1: Overview of Multi-Factor Models

1. **Objective:**
2. Gain a foundational understanding of multi-factor models and their significance in finance.
3. **Instructions:**
4. Research and summarize the concept of multi-factor models, including their purpose and advantages over single-factor models.
5. Create a Jupyter Notebook and write a brief introduction (1-2 paragraphs) explaining multi-factor models.
6. Save and submit the Jupyter Notebook.

Step 2: Factor Exposure and Risk Premia

1. **Objective:**
2. Understand the concepts of factor exposure and risk premia and their roles in multi-factor models.
3. **Instructions:**
4. In your Jupyter Notebook, write a brief explanation (1-2 paragraphs) of factor exposure and risk premia.
5. Choose a set of factors commonly used in equity markets (e.g., market, size, value).
6. Save and submit the Jupyter Notebook.

Step 3: Constructing Factor Models

1. **Objective:**
2. Learn how to construct a multi-factor model using historical financial data.
3. **Instructions:**
4. Download historical financial data for a set of stocks and the chosen factors.
5. In your Jupyter Notebook, write code to:
    - Import and preprocess the data.
    - Construct regression models to calculate the factor exposures (betas) for each stock.
6. Save and submit the Jupyter Notebook.

Step 4: The Fama-French Three-Factor Model

1. **Objective:**
2. Implement the Fama-French Three-Factor Model using Python.
3. **Instructions:**
4. In your Jupyter Notebook, write code to:
    - Construct the Fama-French Three-Factor Model using your dataset.
    - Estimate the factor loadings (betas) for each stock in your dataset.

    - Analyze and interpret the results.
5. Save and submit the Jupyter Notebook.

Step 5: Carhart Four-Factor Model

1. **Objective:**
2. Extend your understanding by implementing the Carhart Four-Factor Model.
3. **Instructions:**
4. In your Jupyter Notebook, write code to:
    - Construct the Carhart Four-Factor Model.
    - Calculate the additional momentum factor and incorporate it into your model.
    - Estimate the factor loadings and analyze the results.
5. Save and submit the Jupyter Notebook.

Step 6: Implementing Multi-Factor Models in Python

1. **Objective:**
2. Learn to implement and test multi-factor models in Python.
3. **Instructions:**
4. In your Jupyter Notebook, write code to:
    - Implement a custom multi-factor model incorporating the factors of your choice.
    - Use a Python library (e.g., statsmodels) to estimate the model parameters.
    - Test the model on your dataset and interpret the results.
5. Save and submit the Jupyter Notebook.

Step 7: Backtesting Factor Strategies

1. **Objective:**
2. Backtest the performance of factor-based investment

strategies.

3. **Instructions:**
4. In your Jupyter Notebook, write code to:
    - Define investment strategies based on the factor exposures calculated earlier.
    - Backtest these strategies using historical data.
    - Plot the cumulative returns and compare the performance of different strategies.
5. Write a brief report (1-2 paragraphs) summarizing the backtesting results.
6. Save and submit the Jupyter Notebook.

Step 8: Performance Metrics for Factor Models

1. **Objective:**
2. Evaluate the performance of your multi-factor models using various metrics.
3. **Instructions:**
4. In your Jupyter Notebook, write code to calculate performance metrics such as:
    - Sharpe Ratio
    - Alpha
    - Information Ratio
5. Compare the performance of your models using these metrics.
6. Write a brief report (1-2 paragraphs) summarizing the performance evaluation.
7. Save and submit the Jupyter Notebook.

Step 9: Limitations and Considerations

1. **Objective:**
2. Understand the limitations and practical considerations when using multi-factor models.

3. **Instructions:**
4. Research and write a brief discussion (1-2 paragraphs) on the limitations of multi-factor models.
5. Discuss potential issues such as overfitting, data mining bias, and model stability.
6. Save and submit the Jupyter Notebook.

Step 10: Case Study: Factor Analysis in Equity Markets

1. **Objective:**
2. Apply the learned techniques to a comprehensive case study.
3. **Instructions:**
4. Select a specific equity market (e.g., S&P 500) and download relevant data.
5. In a Jupyter Notebook, write code to:
    - Import and preprocess the data.
    - Perform factor analysis and construct multi-factor models for the selected market.
    - Backtest the models and evaluate their performance.
    - Visualize and interpret the results.
6. Write a detailed report (3-5 pages) summarizing your analysis, findings, and conclusions.
7. Save and submit the Jupyter Notebook and the report.

Project: Comprehensive Portfolio Theory

This project will guide you through the essential concepts and practical applications of portfolio theory using Python.

Step-by-Step Instructions

Step 1: Introduction to Modern Portfolio Theory

1. **Objective:**
2. Gain a foundational understanding of Modern Portfolio Theory (MPT) and its significance in finance.
3. **Instructions:**
4. Research and summarize the concept of Modern Portfolio Theory, including its key principles and assumptions.
5. Create a Jupyter Notebook and write a brief introduction (1-2 paragraphs) explaining MPT.
6. Save and submit the Jupyter Notebook.

Step 2: Risk and Return: Definitions and Concepts

1. **Objective:**
2. Understand the definitions of risk and return and their importance in portfolio management.
3. **Instructions:**
4. In your Jupyter Notebook, write a brief explanation (1-2 paragraphs) of risk and return.
5. Choose a set of stocks and download their historical price data.
6. Calculate the historical returns for each stock.
7. Save and submit the Jupyter Notebook.

Step 3: Efficient Frontier and Capital Market Line

1. **Objective:**
2. Learn how to construct the efficient frontier and the Capital Market Line (CML).
3. **Instructions:**
4. In your Jupyter Notebook, write code to:
    - Calculate the mean returns and covariance matrix of the chosen stocks.
    - Use these to construct the efficient frontier.

- Plot the efficient frontier and the CML.

5. Save and submit the Jupyter Notebook.

Step 4: Mean-Variance Optimization

1. **Objective:**
2. Implement mean-variance optimization to find the optimal portfolio weights.
3. **Instructions:**
4. In your Jupyter Notebook, write code to:
    - Implement mean-variance optimization using a Python library (e.g., cvxopt, scipy.optimize).
    - Find the optimal portfolio weights that minimize risk for a given level of return.
5. Save and submit the Jupyter Notebook.

Step 5: Asset Allocation Techniques

1. **Objective:**
2. Understand different asset allocation techniques and their applications.
3. **Instructions:**
4. Research and write a brief explanation (1-2 paragraphs) of various asset allocation techniques (e.g., strategic, tactical, dynamic).
5. In your Jupyter Notebook, write code to:
    - Apply one or more asset allocation techniques to your chosen stocks.
6. Save and submit the Jupyter Notebook.

Step 6: Using Python for Portfolio Optimization

1. **Objective:**
2. Utilize Python to perform portfolio optimization.
3. **Instructions:**
4. In your Jupyter Notebook, write code to:

- Implement portfolio optimization using a Python library (e.g., PyPortfolioOpt).
- Optimize the portfolio based on different objectives (e.g., maximum Sharpe ratio, minimum volatility).

5. Save and submit the Jupyter Notebook.

Step 7: The Sharpe Ratio and Performance Attribution

1. **Objective:**
2. Calculate and interpret the Sharpe Ratio and performance attribution metrics for your portfolio.
3. **Instructions:**
4. In your Jupyter Notebook, write code to:
    - Calculate the Sharpe Ratio for the optimized portfolio.
    - Perform performance attribution analysis to understand the contribution of each asset.
5. Write a brief report (1-2 paragraphs) summarizing your findings.
6. Save and submit the Jupyter Notebook.

Step 8: Risks: Systematic vs. Unsystematic

1. **Objective:**
2. Distinguish between systematic and unsystematic risk and their implications for portfolio management.
3. **Instructions:**
4. Research and write a brief explanation (1-2 paragraphs) of systematic and unsystematic risk.
5. In your Jupyter Notebook, write code to:
    - Analyze the systematic and unsystematic risk of your portfolio.
6. Save and submit the Jupyter Notebook.

Step 9: Active vs. Passive Management

1. **Objective:**
2. Understand the differences between active and passive portfolio management strategies.
3. **Instructions:**
4. Research and write a brief discussion (1-2 paragraphs) on active vs. passive management.
5. In your Jupyter Notebook, write code to:
    - Compare the performance of an actively managed portfolio vs. a passively managed portfolio (e.g., index fund).
6. Save and submit the Jupyter Notebook.

Step 10: Case Study: Building an Optimal Portfolio

1. **Objective:**
2. Apply the learned techniques to a comprehensive case study on portfolio optimization.
3. **Instructions:**
4. Select a specific set of assets (e.g., stocks from a specific sector or index) and download relevant data.
5. In a Jupyter Notebook, write code to:
    - Import and preprocess the data.
    - Perform mean-variance optimization to construct the optimal portfolio.
    - Backtest the portfolio and evaluate its performance.
    - Visualize and interpret the results.
6. Write a detailed report (3-5 pages) summarizing your analysis, findings, and conclusions.
7. Save and submit the Jupyter Notebook and the report.

Project: Comprehensive Risk

Management Techniques

This project will guide you through the essential concepts and practical applications of risk management techniques using Python.

Step-by-Step Instructions

Step 1: Understanding Financial Risk

1. **Objective:**
2. Gain a foundational understanding of financial risk and its significance in finance.
3. **Instructions:**
4. Research and summarize the concept of financial risk, including its key types and implications.
5. Create a Jupyter Notebook and write a brief introduction (1-2 paragraphs) explaining financial risk.
6. Save and submit the Jupyter Notebook.

Step 2: Value at Risk (VaR) Concepts

1. **Objective:**
2. Understand the concepts of Value at Risk (VaR) and its importance in risk management.
3. **Instructions:**
4. In your Jupyter Notebook, write a brief explanation (1-2 paragraphs) of VaR.
5. Choose a set of stocks and download their historical price data.
6. Calculate the historical VaR for each stock using the historical simulation method.
7. Save and submit the Jupyter Notebook.

Step 3: Monte Carlo Simulation for Risk Analysis

1. **Objective:**
2. Learn how to use Monte Carlo simulations to analyze

financial risk.

3. **Instructions:**
4. In your Jupyter Notebook, write code to:
    - Generate random price paths for the chosen stocks using Monte Carlo simulations.
    - Calculate the VaR based on these simulated price paths.
5. Save and submit the Jupyter Notebook.

Step 4: Stress Testing and Scenario Analysis

1. **Objective:**
2. Implement stress testing and scenario analysis to evaluate the resilience of a portfolio.
3. **Instructions:**
4. In your Jupyter Notebook, write code to:
    - Define several stress scenarios (e.g., market crash, interest rate spike).
    - Apply these scenarios to the portfolio and evaluate the potential impact.
5. Save and submit the Jupyter Notebook.

Step 5: Credit Risk Modeling

1. **Objective:**
2. Understand and model credit risk using Python.
3. **Instructions:**
4. Research and write a brief explanation (1-2 paragraphs) of credit risk and its modeling techniques.
5. In your Jupyter Notebook, write code to:
    - Implement a simple credit risk model (e.g., using credit ratings or default probabilities).
6. Save and submit the Jupyter Notebook.

Step 6: Operational Risk Assessment

1. **Objective:**
2. Assess operational risk and its management in financial institutions.
3. **Instructions:**
4. Research and write a brief explanation (1-2 paragraphs) of operational risk and its assessment methods.
5. In your Jupyter Notebook, write code to:
    - Implement a basic operational risk assessment model (e.g., using loss distribution approach).
6. Save and submit the Jupyter Notebook.

Step 7: Liquidity Risk Management in Finance

1. **Objective:**
2. Understand and manage liquidity risk in a financial portfolio.
3. **Instructions:**
4. Research and write a brief explanation (1-2 paragraphs) of liquidity risk and its management techniques.
5. In your Jupyter Notebook, write code to:
    - Analyze the liquidity of the chosen stocks (e.g., using bid-ask spreads, trading volumes).
6. Save and submit the Jupyter Notebook.

Step 8: Hedging Strategies Using Derivatives

1. **Objective:**
2. Learn how to use derivatives to hedge financial risks.
3. **Instructions:**
4. Research and write a brief explanation (1-2 paragraphs) of common hedging strategies using

derivatives.

5. In your Jupyter Notebook, write code to:
    - Implement a basic hedging strategy (e.g., using options or futures) for the portfolio.
6. Save and submit the Jupyter Notebook.

Step 9: Implementing Risk Models in Python

1. **Objective:**
2. Utilize Python to implement various risk models.
3. **Instructions:**
4. In your Jupyter Notebook, write code to:
    - Implement different risk models (e.g., VaR, CVaR, stress testing) using Python libraries.
    - Compare the results of these models for your portfolio.
5. Save and submit the Jupyter Notebook.

Step 10: Case Study: Risk Assessment of a Trading Strategy

1. **Objective:**
2. Apply the learned techniques to a comprehensive case study on risk assessment.
3. **Instructions:**
4. Select a specific trading strategy and download relevant data.
5. In a Jupyter Notebook, write code to:
    - Import and preprocess the data.
    - Apply various risk assessment techniques (VaR, Monte Carlo simulations, stress testing, etc.) to the trading strategy.
    - Visualize and interpret the results.
6. Write a detailed report (3-5 pages) summarizing your analysis, findings, and conclusions.
7. Save and submit the Jupyter Notebook and the

report.

Project: Comprehensive Machine Learning in Finance

This project will take you through the fundamental concepts and practical applications of machine learning in finance using Python.

Step-by-Step Instructions

Step 1: Introduction to Machine Learning Concepts

1. **Objective:**
2. Understand the basics of machine learning and its relevance to finance.
3. **Instructions:**
4. Research and summarize the key concepts of machine learning, including types of learning (supervised, unsupervised, and reinforcement learning).
5. Create a Jupyter Notebook and write an introduction (1-2 paragraphs) explaining machine learning and its importance in finance.
6. Save and submit the Jupyter Notebook.

Step 2: Supervised vs. Unsupervised Learning

1. **Objective:**
2. Differentiate between supervised and unsupervised learning.
3. **Instructions:**
4. In your Jupyter Notebook, write a brief explanation (1-2 paragraphs) of supervised and unsupervised learning, including examples of each.
5. Save and submit the Jupyter Notebook.

Step 3: Feature Selection and Engineering

1. **Objective:**
2. Learn the process of selecting and engineering features for a machine learning model.
3. **Instructions:**
4. Choose a financial dataset (e.g., stock prices, financial ratios).
5. In your Jupyter Notebook, write code to:
    - Load and explore the dataset.
    - Perform feature selection and engineering (e.g., create new features, normalize data).
6. Save and submit the Jupyter Notebook.

Step 4: Regression Techniques in Finance

1. **Objective:**
2. Apply regression techniques to financial data for predictive analysis.
3. **Instructions:**
4. In your Jupyter Notebook, write code to:
    - Implement a linear regression model to predict stock prices or returns.
    - Evaluate the model's performance using metrics such as R-squared and Mean Squared Error (MSE).
5. Save and submit the Jupyter Notebook.

Step 5: Classification Methods for Financial Predictions

1. **Objective:**
2. Use classification techniques to make financial predictions.
3. **Instructions:**
4. In your Jupyter Notebook, write code to:
    - Implement a classification model (e.g.,

logistic regression or decision tree) to predict market movements (e.g., up or down).
    - Evaluate the model's performance using metrics such as accuracy, precision, and recall.
5. Save and submit the Jupyter Notebook.

Step 6: Clustering Analysis for Market Segmentation

1. **Objective:**
2. Perform clustering analysis to segment financial markets.
3. **Instructions:**
4. In your Jupyter Notebook, write code to:
    - Implement a clustering algorithm (e.g., K-means) to segment a set of financial instruments or stocks.
    - Visualize the results using appropriate plots (e.g., scatter plot with clusters).
5. Save and submit the Jupyter Notebook.

Step 7: Neural Networks and Deep Learning Applications

1. **Objective:**
2. Explore the use of neural networks and deep learning in financial applications.
3. **Instructions:**
4. In your Jupyter Notebook, write code to:
    - Implement a basic neural network using a library such as TensorFlow or Keras to predict stock prices or returns.
    - Train and evaluate the model's performance.
5. Save and submit the Jupyter Notebook.

Step 8: Model Evaluation and Validation Techniques

1. **Objective:**
2. Learn techniques for evaluating and validating machine learning models.
3. **Instructions:**
4. In your Jupyter Notebook, write code to:
    - Implement cross-validation and other model evaluation techniques (e.g., train-test split, k-fold cross-validation).
    - Apply these techniques to the models created in previous steps and discuss the results.
5. Save and submit the Jupyter Notebook.

Step 9: Integrating Machine Learning with Financial Data

1. **Objective:**
2. Integrate machine learning models with real-world financial data.
3. **Instructions:**
4. In your Jupyter Notebook, write code to:
    - Download real-time financial data using APIs (e.g., Alpha Vantage, Yahoo Finance).
    - Integrate this data with your machine learning models to make predictions or classifications.
5. Save and submit the Jupyter Notebook.

Step 10: Case Study: Predictive Analytics in Stock Movement

1. **Objective:**
2. Apply learned techniques to a comprehensive case

study on predictive analytics.

3. **Instructions:**
4. Select a specific stock or market index and download relevant historical data.
5. In a Jupyter Notebook, write code to:
   - Import and preprocess the data.
   - Apply various machine learning techniques (regression, classification, clustering, neural networks) to predict stock movements.
   - Visualize and interpret the results.
6. Write a detailed report (3-5 pages) summarizing your analysis, findings, and conclusions.
7. Save and submit the Jupyter Notebook and the report.

Project: Comprehensive Machine Learning in Finance

This project will guide you through the fundamental concepts and practical applications of machine learning in finance using Python.

Step-by-Step Instructions

Step 1: Introduction to Machine Learning Concepts

1. **Objective:**
2. Understand the basics of machine learning and its relevance to finance.
3. **Instructions:**
4. Research and summarize the key concepts of machine learning, including types of learning (supervised, unsupervised, and reinforcement learning).
5. Create a Jupyter Notebook and write an introduction (1-2 paragraphs) explaining machine learning and its

importance in finance.

6. Save and submit the Jupyter Notebook.

Step 2: Supervised vs. Unsupervised Learning

1. **Objective:**
2. Differentiate between supervised and unsupervised learning.
3. **Instructions:**
4. In your Jupyter Notebook, write a brief explanation (1-2 paragraphs) of supervised and unsupervised learning, including examples of each.
5. Save and submit the Jupyter Notebook.

Step 3: Feature Selection and Engineering

1. **Objective:**
2. Learn the process of selecting and engineering features for a machine learning model.
3. **Instructions:**
4. Choose a financial dataset (e.g., stock prices, financial ratios).
5. In your Jupyter Notebook, write code to:
    - Load and explore the dataset.
    - Perform feature selection and engineering (e.g., create new features, normalize data).
6. Save and submit the Jupyter Notebook.

Step 4: Regression Techniques in Finance

1. **Objective:**
2. Apply regression techniques to financial data for predictive analysis.
3. **Instructions:**
4. In your Jupyter Notebook, write code to:
    - Implement a linear regression model to predict stock prices or returns.

- Evaluate the model's performance using metrics such as R-squared and Mean Squared Error (MSE).

5. Save and submit the Jupyter Notebook.

Step 5: Classification Methods for Financial Predictions

1. **Objective:**
2. Use classification techniques to make financial predictions.
3. **Instructions:**
4. In your Jupyter Notebook, write code to:
    - Implement a classification model (e.g., logistic regression or decision tree) to predict market movements (e.g., up or down).
    - Evaluate the model's performance using metrics such as accuracy, precision, and recall.
5. Save and submit the Jupyter Notebook.

Step 6: Clustering Analysis for Market Segmentation

1. **Objective:**
2. Perform clustering analysis to segment financial markets.
3. **Instructions:**
4. In your Jupyter Notebook, write code to:
    - Implement a clustering algorithm (e.g., K-means) to segment a set of financial instruments or stocks.
    - Visualize the results using appropriate plots (e.g., scatter plot with clusters).
5. Save and submit the Jupyter Notebook.

Step 7: Neural Networks and Deep Learning Applications

1. **Objective:**
2. Explore the use of neural networks and deep learning in financial applications.
3. **Instructions:**
4. In your Jupyter Notebook, write code to:
    - Implement a basic neural network using a library such as TensorFlow or Keras to predict stock prices or returns.
    - Train and evaluate the model's performance.
5. Save and submit the Jupyter Notebook.

Step 8: Model Evaluation and Validation Techniques

1. **Objective:**
2. Learn techniques for evaluating and validating machine learning models.
3. **Instructions:**
4. In your Jupyter Notebook, write code to:
    - Implement cross-validation and other model evaluation techniques (e.g., train-test split, k-fold cross-validation).
    - Apply these techniques to the models created in previous steps and discuss the results.
5. Save and submit the Jupyter Notebook.

Step 9: Integrating Machine Learning with Financial Data

1. **Objective:**
2. Integrate machine learning models with real-world financial data.

3. **Instructions:**
4. In your Jupyter Notebook, write code to:
   - Download real-time financial data using APIs (e.g., Alpha Vantage, Yahoo Finance).
   - Integrate this data with your machine learning models to make predictions or classifications.
5. Save and submit the Jupyter Notebook.

Step 10: Case Study: Predictive Analytics in Stock Movement

1. **Objective:**
2. Apply learned techniques to a comprehensive case study on predictive analytics.
3. **Instructions:**
4. Select a specific stock or market index and download relevant historical data.
5. In a Jupyter Notebook, write code to:
   - Import and preprocess the data.
   - Apply various machine learning techniques (regression, classification, clustering, neural networks) to predict stock movements.
   - Visualize and interpret the results.
6. Write a detailed report (3-5 pages) summarizing your analysis, findings, and conclusions.
7. Save and submit the Jupyter Notebook and the report.

Project: Backtesting and Strategy Evaluation in Quantitative Finance

This project will guide you through the process of backtesting trading strategies and evaluating their performance using Python.

Step-by-Step Instructions

Step 1: Importance of Backtesting in Quant Finance

1. **Objective:**
2. Understand the significance of backtesting in quantitative finance.
3. **Instructions:**
4. Research and summarize the key concepts of backtesting and its importance in developing trading strategies.
5. Create a Jupyter Notebook and write an introduction (1-2 paragraphs) explaining the importance of backtesting in quantitative finance.
6. Save and submit the Jupyter Notebook.

Step 2: Setting Up a Backtesting Framework

1. **Objective:**
2. Learn how to set up a basic backtesting framework.
3. **Instructions:**
4. In your Jupyter Notebook, write code to:
    - Install and import necessary libraries such as pandas, numpy, and backtrader.
    - Set up a basic backtesting framework using a simple moving average strategy.
5. Save and submit the Jupyter Notebook.

Step 3: Performance Metrics for Trading Strategies

1. **Objective:**
2. Understand and calculate performance metrics for trading strategies.
3. **Instructions:**
4. In your Jupyter Notebook, write code to:
    - Define and calculate key performance metrics such as Sharpe Ratio, Maximum

Drawdown, and Cumulative Returns.
- Apply these metrics to the results of your backtesting framework.

5. Save and submit the Jupyter Notebook.

Step 4: Understanding Overfitting and Its Consequences

1. **Objective:**
2. Learn about overfitting in trading strategies and its potential consequences.
3. **Instructions:**
4. Research and write a brief explanation (1-2 paragraphs) on overfitting and its impact on trading strategy performance.
5. In your Jupyter Notebook, implement a simple overfitting example using historical data.
6. Discuss the results and potential issues with overfitting.
7. Save and submit the Jupyter Notebook.

Step 5: Walk-Forward Analysis

1. **Objective:**
2. Implement walk-forward analysis to validate trading strategies.
3. **Instructions:**
4. In your Jupyter Notebook, write code to:
   - Split historical data into multiple segments (e.g., training and testing periods).
   - Perform walk-forward analysis by iteratively training and testing your strategy on these segments.
   - Evaluate and discuss the performance of the strategy.
5. Save and submit the Jupyter Notebook.

Step 6: Transaction Costs and Slippage in Backtesting

1. **Objective:**
2. Incorporate transaction costs and slippage into your backtesting framework.
3. **Instructions:**
4. In your Jupyter Notebook, write code to:
    - Define and implement transaction costs and slippage in your backtesting framework.
    - Adjust your strategy's performance metrics to account for these factors.
5. Save and submit the Jupyter Notebook.

Step 7: Robustness Testing of Strategies

1. **Objective:**
2. Test the robustness of trading strategies under different market conditions.
3. **Instructions:**
4. In your Jupyter Notebook, write code to:
    - Implement robustness testing by varying key parameters of your strategy.
    - Analyze how changes in parameters affect the strategy's performance.
5. Save and submit the Jupyter Notebook.

Step 8: Simulating Market Conditions

1. **Objective:**
2. Simulate different market conditions to test the resilience of your strategy.
3. **Instructions:**
4. In your Jupyter Notebook, write code to:
    - Simulate various market conditions such

as bull markets, bear markets, and high volatility periods.
   - Evaluate the performance of your strategy under these simulated conditions.
5. Save and submit the Jupyter Notebook.

Step 9: Reporting Backtesting Results

1. **Objective:**
2. Learn how to effectively report the results of your backtesting and strategy evaluation.
3. **Instructions:**
4. In your Jupyter Notebook, write code to:
   - Generate comprehensive reports including performance metrics, visualizations, and summary statistics.
   - Document your findings and conclusions in a clear and concise manner.
5. Save and submit the Jupyter Notebook.

Step 10: Case Study: Evaluating a Quantitative Trading Strategy

1. **Objective:**
2. Apply all learned techniques to a comprehensive case study on backtesting and strategy evaluation.
3. **Instructions:**
4. Select a specific trading strategy (e.g., momentum, mean reversion) and download relevant historical data.
5. In a Jupyter Notebook, write code to:
   - Import and preprocess the data.
   - Implement the chosen trading strategy.
   - Perform backtesting, calculate performance metrics, and conduct robustness testing.
   - Simulate different market conditions and

incorporate transaction costs and slippage.
   - Generate and document a detailed report (3-5 pages) summarizing your analysis, findings, and conclusions.
6. Save and submit the Jupyter Notebook and the report.

Project: Backtesting and Strategy Evaluation in Quantitative Finance

This project will guide you through the process of backtesting trading strategies and evaluating their performance using Python.

Step-by-Step Instructions

Step 1: Importance of Backtesting in Quant Finance

1. **Objective:**
2. Understand the significance of backtesting in quantitative finance.
3. **Instructions:**
4. Research and summarize the key concepts of backtesting and its importance in developing trading strategies.
5. Create a Jupyter Notebook and write an introduction (1-2 paragraphs) explaining the importance of backtesting in quantitative finance.
6. Save and submit the Jupyter Notebook.

Step 2: Setting Up a Backtesting Framework

1. **Objective:**
2. Learn how to set up a basic backtesting framework.
3. **Instructions:**
4. In your Jupyter Notebook, write code to:
   - Install and import necessary libraries such

as pandas, numpy, and backtrader.
  - Set up a basic backtesting framework using a simple moving average strategy.
5. Save and submit the Jupyter Notebook.

Step 3: Performance Metrics for Trading Strategies

1. **Objective:**
2. Understand and calculate performance metrics for trading strategies.
3. **Instructions:**
4. In your Jupyter Notebook, write code to:
   - Define and calculate key performance metrics such as Sharpe Ratio, Maximum Drawdown, and Cumulative Returns.
   - Apply these metrics to the results of your backtesting framework.
5. Save and submit the Jupyter Notebook.

Step 4: Understanding Overfitting and Its Consequences

1. **Objective:**
2. Learn about overfitting in trading strategies and its potential consequences.
3. **Instructions:**
4. Research and write a brief explanation (1-2 paragraphs) on overfitting and its impact on trading strategy performance.
5. In your Jupyter Notebook, implement a simple overfitting example using historical data.
6. Discuss the results and potential issues with overfitting.
7. Save and submit the Jupyter Notebook.

Step 5: Walk-Forward Analysis

1. **Objective:**
2. Implement walk-forward analysis to validate trading strategies.
3. **Instructions:**
4. In your Jupyter Notebook, write code to:
   - Split historical data into multiple segments (e.g., training and testing periods).
   - Perform walk-forward analysis by iteratively training and testing your strategy on these segments.
   - Evaluate and discuss the performance of the strategy.
5. Save and submit the Jupyter Notebook.

Step 6: Transaction Costs and Slippage in Backtesting

1. **Objective:**
2. Incorporate transaction costs and slippage into your backtesting framework.
3. **Instructions:**
4. In your Jupyter Notebook, write code to:
   - Define and implement transaction costs and slippage in your backtesting framework.
   - Adjust your strategy's performance metrics to account for these factors.
5. Save and submit the Jupyter Notebook.

Step 7: Robustness Testing of Strategies

1. **Objective:**
2. Test the robustness of trading strategies under different market conditions.
3. **Instructions:**
4. In your Jupyter Notebook, write code to:

- Implement robustness testing by varying key parameters of your strategy.
- Analyze how changes in parameters affect the strategy's performance.

5. Save and submit the Jupyter Notebook.

Step 8: Simulating Market Conditions

1. **Objective:**
2. Simulate different market conditions to test the resilience of your strategy.
3. **Instructions:**
4. In your Jupyter Notebook, write code to:
    - Simulate various market conditions such as bull markets, bear markets, and high volatility periods.
    - Evaluate the performance of your strategy under these simulated conditions.
5. Save and submit the Jupyter Notebook.

Step 9: Reporting Backtesting Results

1. **Objective:**
2. Learn how to effectively report the results of your backtesting and strategy evaluation.
3. **Instructions:**
4. In your Jupyter Notebook, write code to:
    - Generate comprehensive reports including performance metrics, visualizations, and summary statistics.
    - Document your findings and conclusions in a clear and concise manner.
5. Save and submit the Jupyter Notebook.

Step 10: Case Study: Evaluating a Quantitative Trading Strategy

1. **Objective:**
2. Apply all learned techniques to a comprehensive case study on backtesting and strategy evaluation.
3. **Instructions:**
4. Select a specific trading strategy (e.g., momentum, mean reversion) and download relevant historical data.
5. In a Jupyter Notebook, write code to:
    - Import and preprocess the data.
    - Implement the chosen trading strategy.
    - Perform backtesting, calculate performance metrics, and conduct robustness testing.
    - Simulate different market conditions and incorporate transaction costs and slippage.
    - Generate and document a detailed report (3-5 pages) summarizing your analysis, findings, and conclusions.
6. Save and submit the Jupyter Notebook and the report.

APPENDIX B: GLOSSARY OF TERMS

A

- **Algorithmic Trading:** A method of executing trades using computer algorithms, which make decisions on trade timing and conditions without human intervention.
- **ARIMA Model (AutoRegressive Integrated Moving Average):** A class of statistical models for analyzing and forecasting time series data by combining autoregression, differencing to achieve stationarity, and a moving average component.
- **Autocorrelation:** A measure of how the current value of a time series relates to past values of the same series.
- **Autocorrelation Function (ACF):** A function representing the correlation between observations of a time series at different time lags.

B

- **Backtesting:** The process of testing a trading strategy on historical data to verify its potential viability before applying it to real trading.
- **Bayesian Statistics:** A statistical paradigm that involves updating the probability for a hypothesis as more evidence or information becomes available.

C

- **Capital Market Line (CML):** A line used in the capital asset pricing model to depict the risk-reward relationship of efficient portfolios.
- **Carhart Four-Factor Model:** An extension of the Fama-French Three-Factor Model adding a momentum factor.
- **Classification:** A type of supervised learning method used to predict the categorical class labels of new observations.
- **Clustering:** An unsupervised learning technique used to group similar observations into clusters.
- **Confidence Interval:** A range of values that is likely to contain the parameter of interest with a certain level of confidence.
- **Copula Models:** Statistical models used to describe the dependence structure between random variables.
- **Correlation:** A statistical measure that describes the degree to which two variables move in relation to each other.
- **Covariance:** A measure of the joint variability of two random variables.
- **Credit Risk:** The risk of a loss resulting from a borrower's failure to repay a loan or meet contractual obligations.

D

- **Differencing:** A transformation applied to time series data to achieve stationarity by subtracting previous observations from current observations.

E

- **Efficient Frontier:** A set of optimal portfolios offering the highest expected return for a defined level of risk.

F

- **Factor Models:** Models that describe returns of an asset or portfolio in terms of various factors or variables.
- **Feature Selection:** The process of selecting a subset of relevant features for use in model construction.
- **Forecasting:** The process of making predictions about the future based on historical and current data.

G

- **GARCH Model (Generalized Autoregressive Conditional Heteroskedasticity):** A statistical model for estimating time-varying volatility in financial returns.

H

- **Hedging:** Strategies used to offset potential losses in investment by taking an opposite position in a related asset.
- **Hypothesis Testing:** A statistical method used to make decisions about populations based on sample data.

I

- **Importing Data:** The process of loading data from external sources into a programming environment for analysis.

L

- **Linear Regression:** A statistical method used to model the relationship between a dependent variable and one or more independent variables.
- **Liquidity Risk:** The risk that an entity may not be able to meet its short-term financial obligations due to an inability to convert assets into cash.

M

- **Machine Learning:** A field of artificial intelligence that uses statistical techniques to enable computers to learn from and make predictions based on data.
- **Mean-Variance Optimization:** A process by which portfolios are constructed to maximize expected return for a given level of risk or minimize risk for a given level of expected return.
- **Monte Carlo Simulation:** A computational technique that uses repeated random sampling to obtain the distribution of an unknown probabilistic entity.

N

- **Neural Networks:** A set of algorithms modeled loosely after the human brain that are designed to recognize patterns and interpret data through a process mimicking neural interactions.
- **Non-parametric Methods:** Statistical methods that do not assume a specific distribution for the population from which samples are drawn.

P

- **Partial Autocorrelation Function (PACF):** A function providing the partial correlation of a time series with its own lagged values, after removing the effect of shorter lags.
- **Portfolio Optimization:** The process of choosing the optimal allocation of assets in a portfolio to achieve desired investment outcomes.
- **Probability Distributions:** Functions that provide the probabilities of occurrence of different possible outcomes in an experiment.

Q

- **Quantile Regression:** A type of regression analysis

used to estimate the conditional quantiles (such as median) of a response variable.

R

- **Regression Techniques:** Statistical methods used to describe the relationship between one dependent variable and one or more independent variables.
- **Risk Management:** The process of identification, analysis, and mitigation of uncertainty in investment decisions.

S

- **Sharpe Ratio:** A measure of the risk-adjusted return of an investment or portfolio.
- **Stationarity:** A property of a time series where its statistical properties such as mean and variance are constant over time.
- **Structural Equation Modeling (SEM):** A multivariate statistical analysis technique used to analyze structural relationships.
- **Supervised Learning:** A type of machine learning where the model is trained on labeled data.

T

- **Time Series Analysis:** Techniques used to analyze time-ordered data points to extract meaningful statistics and identifying patterns.
- **Transaction Costs:** Costs incurred in buying or selling financial instruments.

V

- **Value at Risk (VaR):** A statistical measure used to assess the risk of loss on a specific portfolio of financial assets.

W

- **Walk-Forward Analysis:** A method of validating a

trading strategy by dividing the sample data into training and testing subsets and iteratively re-training and testing over time.

X

- **X-Factor:** A placeholder term that can denote any additional, unspecified variable or factor in models.

This glossary aims to provide definitions for key terms encountered in the book "Mastering Advanced Statistical Methods with Python for Quantitative Finance," offering a solid foundation for understanding the concepts and methodologies discussed.

APPENDIX C: ADDITIONAL RESOURCES

To bolster your understanding of the topics discussed in "Mastering Advanced Statistical Methods with Python for Quantitative Finance," the following books, online courses, research papers, and tools are highly recommended:

Books

1. **"Python for Data Analysis" by Wes McKinney**
2. A critical resource for mastering data manipulation and analysis in Python, pivotal for the foundational steps in financial data analysis.
3. **"Quantitative Finance with R: Understanding Mathematical and Computational Tools from a Quant's Perspective" by Marcelo S. Perlin**
4. Delve into statistical models and computational tools used in quantitative finance, extending your Python skills with insights from another prevalent programming language in finance.
5. **"Financial Risk Forecasting: The Theory and**

Practice of Forecasting Market Risk with Implementation in R and Matlab" by Jon Danielsson

6. Offers insights into risk management techniques and practical implementation, supplementing your risk management strategies discussed in Chapter 6.
7. **"Advances in Financial Machine Learning" by Marcos López de Prado**
8. A deep dive into leveraging machine learning for financial markets, complementing the material covered in Chapter 7.

Online Courses

1. **Coursera: "Python and Statistics for Financial Analysis" by Hong Kong University of Science and Technology**
2. A comprehensive introduction to Python and its application in financial analysis, ideal for reinforcing foundational concepts.
3. **edX: "Introduction to Computational Finance and Financial Econometrics" by the University of Washington**
4. Bridging the gap between theory and practice, this course aids in cementing vital econometric methods crucial for Chapters 2 and 3.
5. **Udacity: "Machine Learning for Trading"**
6. Focuses on the application of machine learning techniques to real financial data, aligning well with Chapter 7's content.
7. **Coursera: "Investment Management" by the University of Geneva**
8. Explores modern portfolio theory and investment strategies, augmenting your understanding of Chapter 5.

Research Papers

1. **"The Cross-Section of Expected Stock Returns" by Eugene F. Fama and Kenneth R. French**
2. This seminal paper lays the foundation for multi-factor models, deepening insights beyond what's covered in Chapter 4.
3. **"Risk and Return in the Stock Market: What Categories Matter?" by Jonathan Lewellen**
4. Explores advanced factor models, providing empirical insights and advanced methodologies complementing Chapter 4.
5. **"A Survey of Practical Applications of Financial Machine Learning" by Marcos López de Prado**
6. Discusses the application of machine learning in finance, offering perspective and advanced techniques relevant to Chapter 7.

Tools and Libraries

1. **NumPy and Pandas**
2. Essential Python libraries for numerical computing and data manipulation, critical for all financial data analysis tasks.
3. **Statsmodels**
4. Provides classes and functions for the estimation of many different statistical models, crucial for the statistical methods discussed throughout the book.
5. **SciPy**
6. A Python library used for scientific and technical computing, valuable for performing complex mathematical and statistical operations.
7. **QuantLib**
8. Open-source library for quantitative finance, useful

for modeling, trading, and risk management of financial assets.

9. **Jupyter Notebooks**
10. An interactive computing environment that enhances the readability and reproducibility of data analysis reports and projects.

Blogs and Websites

1. **QuantStart (quantstart.com)**
2. Provides a range of articles and tutorials on quantitative finance and algorithmic trading.
3. **QuantInsti (quantinsti.com)**
4. Offers insights into algorithmic and quantitative trading, along with practical code implementations.
5. **Towards Data Science (towardsdatascience.com)**
6. Hosts numerous articles on the application of data science methods in various fields including finance.
7. **Kaggle (kaggle.com)**
8. A platform for predictive modeling and analytics competitions, providing datasets and kernels that are useful for practice.

These resources will complement your study of advanced statistical methods with Python for quantitative finance, enhancing both your theoretical and practical skills in the field.

Epilogue: Embracing the Future of Quantitative Finance

As we draw the curtain on *Mastering Advanced Statistical Methods with Python for Quantitative Finance*, we reflect not only on the breadth and depth of knowledge covered but also on the journey that awaits in the dynamic and ever-evolving realm of quantitative finance.

Reflecting on Our Journey

Our exploration began with a foundational understanding of quantitative finance and the essential role that Python plays in financial analysis. We delved into the statistical underpinnings critical to making informed decisions in the financial markets, learning how to harness data to uncover insights and trends.

Moving forward, we advanced into time series analysis, multi-factor models, and portfolio theory, each chapter building on the last to equip you with the tools necessary to tackle complex financial problems. Risk management emerged as a focal point, emphasizing the importance of safeguarding investments against uncertainties.

The integration of machine learning showcased how artificial intelligence can transform finance, from predictive analytics to market segmentation. Our foray into advanced statistical methods opened the doors to sophisticated techniques that promise to refine your analytical prowess.

Finally, the importance of backtesting and strategy evaluation was underscored, ensuring that theoretical models withstand the rigor of practical application. Our concluding thoughts on future trends painted a picture of what lies ahead, encouraging you to stay adaptable and forward-thinking.

The Evolving Landscape of Quantitative Finance

The field of quantitative finance is constantly evolving, driven by advancements in technology, data availability, and analytical techniques. Big data analytics and AI are not just buzzwords but integral facets of modern finance. They enable greater precision, speed, and depth in financial analysis, creating opportunities for innovative trading strategies and better risk management.

The Role of Python in Shaping Finance

Python has proven to be an indispensable tool in this landscape, offering versatility, ease of use, and a robust ecosystem of libraries tailored for financial analysis. From basic data manipulation to advanced machine learning algorithms, Python empowers you to implement sophisticated models and derive actionable insights efficiently.

Keeping Pace with Change

The future of quantitative finance will undoubtedly be shaped by continued advancements in machine learning, AI, and big data. As these technologies mature, they will open up new avenues for analysis and strategy development. Staying current with these trends and continually honing your skills will be crucial.

Ethical considerations and regulatory compliance will also become increasingly important as the industry evolves. Understanding and navigating these aspects will be key to maintaining the integrity and sustainability of your strategies.

Building a Path Forward

As you move forward, consider the resources and networks available to you. Engage with the financial and tech communities, participate in continuous learning endeavors, and experiment with new tools and techniques. The landscape is rich with resources — from online courses and professional certifications to conferences and publications.

A Call to Innovation

Innovation is the heartbeat of quantitative finance. Whether you're refining existing models, developing new algorithms, or exploring unforeseen applications of statistical methods, your contributions will shape the future. Embrace challenges as opportunities for growth and leverage your knowledge to push the boundaries of what's possible.

Thank you for embarking on this journey with us, and we wish you success and fulfillment in your future endeavors in the world of quantitative finance.

www.ingramcontent.com/pod-product-compliance
Lightning Source LLC
LaVergne TN
LVHW022259060326
832902LV00020B/3158
* 9 7 9 8 3 0 6 1 7 2 0 4 0 *